Christian Socialism

"Turner's elegant volume casts a welcome light on the Anglican Christian Socialist tradition, from the nineteenth century to the present. While the book lays bare some of the flaws of this movement, more importantly Turner illuminates the positive challenges and promises that its proponents—people like Maurice, Tawney, Gore, or Williams and Milbank—still offer to the diseased and fractured life of contemporary liberal society. Turner's approach is theological and ethical—just as our social lives in Christian terms ought to be framed—and he brings to bear the sharply honed tools of a master thinker and teacher. Compact, accessible, and penetrating, this is a book for scholars and students alike, and one that demands the attention of the wider church."

—EPHRAIM RADNER, Wycliffe College

"Touching upon our own world's rapid social, political, and economic change, Philip Turner has produced a timely book that reclaims the insights of the Christian Socialist movement in the Church of England, tracing its roots and analyzing its present-day influence. Turner values this tradition's emphasis upon ideals, but tempers it with his own emphasis on the church's practice of the virtues. In a political climate where 'socialism' is bound for reappraisal, Turner's book is invaluable."

—JOHN BAUERSCHMIDT, Bishop of the Episcopal Diocese of Tennessee

"In a time of mounting concern over inequality in our society, the nineteenth-century Christian Socialists suddenly seem strangely relevant. Philip Turner not only provides a helpful guide to the movement, but offers a sober and unsentimental assessment of its strengths and weaknesses. His treatment of the theopolitics of Rowan Williams and John Milbank brings the story up to date in an engaging, lively way."

—JOSEPH MANGINA, University of Toronto

"By means of both historical retrieval and theological exploration, Philip Turner examines—appreciatively, though not uncritically—the continuing relevance of the Christian Socialist tradition in England. His study will be a significant vehicle for a deeper and renewed appreciation of 'the promise of an almost forgotten tradition.'"

—GILBERT MEILAENDER, Valparaiso University

"Bravo! From Maurice to Temple to Rowan Williams and John Milbank, Phil Turner tells the history not told before of the theological and moral claims and questions that form the Anglican tradition of Christian social thought that reveal the promise and challenge to live and address what is needed in the crisis of failed states."
—Timothy F. Sedgwick, Virginia Theological Seminary

"Philip Turner finds in Christian—Anglican—Socialism a still-vital tradition of critique of the depredations of capitalistic modernity in the name of catholic counter-witness. Common care for one another, and shared moral commitment, properly precede self-expression and self-interest. Life together comes first. This is, indeed, a hope for today: that the church may speak anew of duty and holiness in the form of the Servant, and model in her own life the gospel of love."
—Christopher Wells, The Living Church Foundation

"This is so much more than a readable guide to Christian Socialism, its Anglican origins, history, and contemporary advocates. Drawing on decades of teaching and ministry, Philip Turner's critical engagement with this tradition gives us a much bigger picture—a vision for Christian social ethics and the mission of the church which arises from not only the incarnation but a richer, wider, and deeper biblical and theological vision."
—Andrew Goddard, Tutor in Christian Ethics, Ridley Hall, Cambridge, United Kingdom

Christian Socialism

THE PROMISE OF AN
ALMOST FORGOTTEN TRADITION

Philip Turner

Foreword by Stanley Hauerwas

CASCADE Books • Eugene, Oregon

CHRISTIAN SOCIALISM
The Promise of an Almost Forgotten Tradition

Copyright © 2021 Philip Turner. All rights reserved. Except for brief quotations in critical publications or reviews, no part of this book may be reproduced in any manner without prior written permission from the publisher. Write: Permissions, Wipf and Stock Publishers, 199 W. 8th Ave., Suite 3, Eugene, OR 97401.

Cascade Books
An Imprint of Wipf and Stock Publishers
199 W. 8th Ave., Suite 3
Eugene, OR 97401

www.wipfandstock.com

PAPERBACK ISBN: 978-1-7252-5940-9
HARDCOVER ISBN: 978-1-7252-5941-6
EBOOK ISBN: 978-1-7252-5942-3

Cataloguing-in-Publication data:

Names: Turner, Philip, 1935–, author. | Hauerwas, Stanley, 1940–, foreword.

Title: Christian socialism : the promise of an almost forgotten tradition / Philip Turner ; foreword by Stanley Hauerwas.

Description: Eugene, OR : Cascade Books, 2021 | Includes bibliographical references and index.

Identifiers: ISBN 978-1-7252-5940-9 (paperback) | ISBN 978-1-7252-5941-6 (hardcover) | ISBN 978-1-7252-5942-3 (ebook)

Subjects: LCSH: Christian socialism. | Socialists—Biography.

Classification: HX51 .T87 2021 (print) | HX51 .T87 (ebook)

Manufactured in the U.S.A.   January 5, 2021

For my children
Philip, Cantey, Kristin, and Elisa
and
For my grandchildren
Sam, Lorenzo and Rosa

Who will live through the challenges the Christian Socialists so clearly foresaw

Contents

Foreword by Stanley Hauerwas xi
Acknowledgments xiii
Introduction xv

PART ONE: *Origins: Historical and Theological*

A. Historical Change and Establishment 3
B. Theological: The Incarnation as a Foundation for Christian Social Ethics and Ecclesiology 19

PART TWO: *The Incarnation: How Firm a Foundation?*

A. Social Ethics 39
B. The Role of the Church in Society 52

PART THREE: *Moral Ideals: Their Statement and Application*

A. Statement 71
B. Application 96
   1. The Way of Judgment 96
   2. Walk as Wise 105

PART FOUR: *Assessment, Influence, and Promise*

A. Assessment 117
B. Influence 137
C. Promise 175

Bibliography 189
Index 193

Foreword

SOME WILL WONDER IF I should be writing this foreword to commend Philip Turner's book on the English Christian Socialist tradition. I am after all a card-carrying critic of establishment Christianity, and no Christianity is more established than that church called the Church of England. As Turner makes clear, moreover, it is hard to imagine the Christian Socialist tradition, a tradition that may be quite morally impressive, without the presumption that the Church of England was and is the soul of a nation.

I have no reason to deny that there is not some tension between my understanding of church and world and that of the Christian Socialists. Yet those people Turner seeks to recover have always been for me people I deeply admire. To be sure, as Turner acknowledges, many of the Christian Socialists sought a "return to Christendom." In particular Westcott and Tawney thought they were continuing in the legacy of F. D. Maurice, who sought to renew the Christian vision of society by instilling in the English people a long-lost piety. That ambition may strike us as unrealistic, but given these men's desire to make the church an alternative to capitalism their strategies were not without reason.

Turner first and foremost has written this book hoping it will help us not forget these extraordinary Christians. While his book can serve as a good historical introduction to the major figures in the Christian Socialist movement, Turner does not mean for the book to be a history of that movement. Rather, by reminding us of these remarkable Christians and their attempt to forge an alternative to capitalism, Turner seeks to enrich our imaginations. Nothing is more important because our imaginations are now held captive by the presumption there is no alternative to the market. We are consumers, and the only thing we have not chosen is to be consumers.

One of the great attractions of Turner's portrayal of the Christian Socialists is how he puts them in conversation with contemporary thinkers such as Oliver O'Donovan, Rowan Williams, and John Milbank. In particular he calls attention to the Christian Socialist understanding of social cooperation that has influenced Milbank. Milbank and the Christian Socialists provide an account of social cooperation that makes possible the creation of social bonds through many levels of social exchange. To be sure the development of such bonds can result in hierarchies that tempt one to a top-down social strategy, but it can equally make possible a pluralism that can act as a check on nationalism.

In his magisterial *Christ and the Common Life: Political Theology and the Case for Democracy*, Luke Bretherton, in the chapter on Anglican political theory, characterizes the "method" of Anglican moral theology as entailing a "providential reading of history." Such a reading, Bretherton suggests, is always tempted to make nation or church rather than Jesus Christ the center and subject of history. The alternative is to give priority to the voice of those on the underside of history. Bretherton judges that the Christian Socialists put the incarnation at the center, but unfortunately, that did not lead them to draw on the actual experience of poor people.

No doubt Bretherton is right that the Christian Socialists sometimes failed to appreciate the actual lives of those for whom they labored. But Turner's portrayal of these men (and it was primarily a masculine movement) reminds us that they were priests who served everyday people. They were socialists, but they were also Christians. Turner makes clear that the word *Christian* makes all the difference. We are, therefore, in Turner's debt for reminding us of the difference we can make as Christians in our confusing world.

—Stanley Hauerwas

Acknowledgments

THIS PROJECT HAS TAKEN some time to come to fruition, and in this time of gestation I have had conversations with a number of people. Many of these are now forgotten and to these forgotten partners I owe a debt of gratitude that I am, because of the fragility of memory, no longer able to repay. Nevertheless, there are a number of people I do remember. Chief among them are Ephraim Radner and Stanley Hauerwas, who encouraged me when my spirits were low. They gave me invaluable advice about the content of this book and how to prepare it for publication. Stanley Hauerwas has offered, in addition, a valuable foreword that perfectly states my purpose in writing this interpretive essay on Christian Socialism. Near the top of my list of those who have been of assistance is Charlie Collier, Theology and Ethics editor for Wipf and Stock Publishers. He has both encouraged me and borne patiently with my struggles with the changing forms of footnotes and bibliography. I would like to express my profound thanks to Jacob Martin for the care and competence he showed in preparing this manuscript for publication. The blame for any errors of style appearing in these pages lies at my feet alone. Among my conversation partners I must mention five in particular: H. W. Perry, Clarence Bonnen, Nathan Jennings, Dan Joslyn-Siemiatkoski, and Timothy Sedgwick. Again, any errors of content or coherence should be charged to my account, not theirs. I also wish to thank the Very Rev. Cynthia Kittredge, Dean and President of the Seminary of the Southwest, whose hospitality gave me access to the many fine libraries in the Austin area. Finally, I must thank my wife, the Rev. Elizabeth Zarelli Turner, whose love, care, and truthfulness carry me through what often seems a crazy time.

Introduction

THIS PROJECT BEGAN AS a bit of unfinished business. When I was a student at the Virginia Theological Seminary, one of my teachers mentioned the fact that a number of Anglo-Catholic priests in the Church of England who had been influenced by what came to be called Christian Socialism were heavily involved in ministries to London's poor. Nothing more was said of them during the remainder of my time at Virginia, but I wondered who these people were and why they had given themselves to what I assumed (falsely) was an iteration of what we Americans understood to be the Social Gospel. The question remained, but I did nothing to answer it until I retired from my position as Dean of the Berkeley Divinity School at Yale. In response to this event, a friend and colleague wrote a piece on the ethics of growing old.[1] In that essay, he made many wise remarks about aging, but one that stood out for me was this: in this time of withdrawal we call retirement, it is important to attend to unfinished business. I was arrested by his comment and realized that the remark of my teacher had remained with me though the years. So I began reading about the Christian Socialists. The chapters that follow comprise the results of my attempt to attend to unfinished business. I am immensely grateful for my friend's moral advice, and I am glad that I have followed it because I have discovered the riches of what in my title I have called "an almost forgotten tradition."

As my studies progressed, I saw ever more clearly that the issues addressed by the Christian Socialists are remarkably similar to those that now confront the churches not only in England and America but also throughout the world. They were confronted with the fallout of the Industrial Revolution. We are confronted by the fallout of the digital revolution. They were confronted by what was then called "political

---

1. O'Donovan, "The Practice of Being Old."

economy," a view of economic relations that allowed no room for moral considerations. We are confronted by "neoliberalism," many of whose devotees hold very similar views. They were confronted, as are we, with vast inequalities of wealth existing alongside of grinding poverty and social disorder. Most of all, they were confronted, as are we, by the inability of the church to respond in an adequate fashion to these challenges.

This study begins not only with a sketch of the social conditions that occasioned the rise of the Christian Socialist movement, but also with an examination of the nature of their response. Increasingly, the response of the churches has focused on policies designed to remedy social conditions. The churches, through their instruments of governance and service, have become advocates of social policy. There were exceptions, of course, but the response of the Christian Socialists had as its aim not institutional reform but reform of the religious and moral foundations of the nation and of the role of the church in restoring those foundations. They were interested in foundational ideals from which they believed would spring a renewed national life. It is this sort of reform that, for them, defined the social mission of the Church of England.

Contemporary readers may be tempted to dismiss this view of the social mission of the church as utterly inadequate, but easy dismissal will prove unwise. The reasons the Christian Socialists give for reluctance to assign the governing structures of the church (though not its individual members and their voluntary societies) this focus for social mission are highly instructive. Furthermore, their criticism of a more activist stance is telling. In this case, the point is the difference! It is in confronting difference that new understandings emerge. This difference in understanding the role of the governing structures of the church provides precisely an opportunity to see the role of the church in a different way. It also provides an opportunity to see socialism in a different way. Generally speaking, socialism calls to mind public ownership of the means of production. For the Christian Socialists, socialism meant something entirely different. It meant challenging the individualistic and competitive view of human nature and social life that provided a basis for political economy and for that view substituting another that saw human nature as essentially social and human society as essentially cooperative. When the Christian Socialists spoke of socialism they did not refer to state control of the economy. They spoke of cooperative efforts to improve social relations in ways that produce human flourishing and harmony.

The question they faced was what must be done to restore the religious and moral foundations of British society, and to give an account of the role of the church in this effort. Their prescription for the disease was first to diagnose the source of the "rot" they saw in the life of the nation. In his well-known book *The Acquisitive Society*, R. H. Tawney posited greed as the chief expression of England's disease, but greed was only a symptom of the real illness. The Christian Socialists believed the ground from which greed grew was a mistaken conception of human nature and human society. To their minds, the ills of society were caused by a false individualism that exalted competition and denied the social and cooperative nature of human beings. As a result of this false account of human nature and society, people tended to place rights before duties. The result of this reversal of proper moral order, they held, was an incessant struggle to establish the rights of contending individuals and social groups.

Their diagnosis of the sickness was individualism, competition, and greed. Their prescription for a cure was reestablishment of the social and cooperative nature of human beings, the priority of duties over rights, and the inculcation of the ideals suggested by the life of Jesus and the social/cooperative nature of humankind. They believed that the health of society depends upon the guiding presence of these ideals; of primary importance to them were community, love, equality, fellowship, duty, service, personality, character, freedom, and property. Community, love, equality, fellowship, duty, and service are rather easily understood. Personality, character, freedom, and property are less so. They become clear, however, once it is understood that, according to the Christian Socialists, the very purpose of social life is the nurture of "persons" (human beings with a fully formed personality) who develop as they should and have sufficient freedom and means to undertake such a journey.

Everything the Christian Socialists struggled to accomplish depended upon establishing these ideals in the minds and hearts of their fellow countrymen. Much of what this book contains is an account of their successes and failures. Theirs was no small task. Idealism, well meant as it may be, is full of challenges. Idealists are prone to utopian visions. They can easily be blinded by the very ideals they profess and so become quite fanatical. They can proceed without providing a sound foundation for their commitments or cogent arguments for their conclusions. The Christian Socialists faced all these charges and many others, the last being the most immediately pressing. They had to provide a Christian warrant for their views and intentions. In the nineteenth century, Evangelicals were the dominant force in the Church of England. They did hold poor relief to be a primary Christian duty. Nevertheless, their focus was on the state of individual souls rather than the general state of society. In his seminal work *The Kingdom of Christ*, F. D. Maurice provided an alternative perspective. His focus switched from the atoning sacrifice of the cross to the incarnation of God in Christ. He argued that by becoming fully human God showed his concern and care for all aspects of human life. Further, by entering fully into the life of the world, God established his dominion over all people, whether they acknowledge that fact or not.

To a contemporary reader foregrounding the incarnation as a warrant for a Christian social ethic seems an obvious move. Nonetheless, serious, often unaddressed questions remain. Is a single Christian doctrine, even one as central as the incarnation, an adequate foundation upon which to build a social ethic? This question, the answer to which is certainly not self-evident, prompts several others. Is the account Christian Socialists give of the ideals they champion adequate? Even if adequate, given the limits of human sin and finitude, do these ideals, in the end, do any real work or do they simply idle in a transcendent ether, having no real contact with life as we know it? Or again, what is the role of the governing structures of the church in spreading these ideals and pointing out their practical implications? More important still, what is the role of the body of people who comprise the membership of local congregations and parishes in forming believers on the basis of these ideals? Further, how are these ideals to be lived out in the everyday and morally compromised world they inhabit?

These are a few of the questions addressed in the following pages, but there is one other of particular importance not as yet mentioned. Is the tradition of Christian Socialism, as it developed in England, still alive and still making its voice heard? The answer to this question is yes. The voice of the Christian Socialists echoes throughout the works of Rowan Williams and John Milbank. Each in his own way has immersed himself in this tradition, and each in his own way has carried it forward and developed it. They have addressed both liberals and conservatives out of this tradition and, in so doing, pressed them to take a close look at the state of their society and the character of their common life. They have also offered an alternative vision of another form of life that Milbank terms "the postmodern alternative." This book is an invitation to take a fresh look at their work and that of their predecessors in the hope that its readers can find a way to live together that leads not to further social conflict but to a postmodern form of life built upon friendship, cooperation, harmony, and human flourishing.

Philip Turner
Austin, Texas
December 17, 2019

Part One

Origins: Historical and Theological

A. Historical Change and Establishment

MOST PEOPLE ARE ONLY dimly, if at all, aware of a tradition of social, political, economic, and moral thought known as Christian Socialism. In the nineteenth century it appeared in various forms not only in England but also in America and on the continent of Europe. The focus of the following chapters will be on Christian Socialism in England, but with the purpose of showing as well the promise this tradition holds in a time of crisis for the churches in North America. In England, as an organized movement, Christian Socialism lasted for only a short time; but its influence was extensive and continues, though in a weakened form, to this day. Its supporters published several journals, started schools for working-class people, and, in a more practical vein, founded cooperatives through which artisans could share in the production and distribution of goods and services and in the profits of such enterprise. They also formed societies (the left-leaning Guild of St. Matthew and the more centrist Christian Social Union) whose purpose was both education and advocacy. Through these efforts its supporters gained a wide following. Without question the movement had an influence on the Labor Government that came to power after the end of the Second World War. Indeed, at one point, a significant number of the new bishops within the Church of England were in some way or another associated with the movement. It numbered among its advocates such clerical luminaries as F. D. Maurice and bishops Westcott, Gore, and Temple, and among its lay members people of the caliber of John Ludlow and R. H. Tawney. Though influential, followers of this tradition were not of one mind in respect to the sort of socialism they espoused. It is certainly the case that its exponents in England held views different from their American cousins. Nonetheless, its English supporters shared a set of ideas of sufficient similarity to generate a tradition. The chapters that follow do not contain a comprehensive narrative of either their life and thought or of the institutions they founded. It is rather an interpretive essay intended to identify the theological foundations and major themes of the English version of this tradition and to highlight its value as an account of the social mission of the churches. This assessment will reveal a tradition that elicits hope because it is full of promise and, at times, pathos because its failures draw from us sympathy rather than disdain.

A critical account of Christian Socialism in England recommends itself for a number of reasons. First, the similarities between the present age and the one in which this tradition had its origins are striking. The Industrial Revolution, which came to full flower in the nineteenth century, uprooted significant numbers of people and, in so doing, presented English society with social, economic, political, and moral questions for which there were no ready answers. In like manner, today people are living through what might be called a "digital revolution." As in the case of its predecessor, the digital revolution has brought with it dramatic social changes. These changes have presented populations throughout the world with social, economic, political, and moral questions of even greater complexity. Once again there are no ready answers to the questions these social changes present. Once again, social change and inequality have brought with them social and political conflicts that threaten the stability of society and its institutions. Once again, the churches find themselves divided, and once again they are being forced by circumstance to reexamine their relation to the societies of which they are a part.

A second reason, particularly for Americans, to focus on the English version of Christian Socialism is that, in contradistinction to the American version, its exponents, in responding to their circumstances, tended to be cautious in respect to policy advocacy and institutional reform. Instead of structural change they sought to convey to the British public a normative view of life in society. Their aim was to educate the public conscience through the articulation of a "Christian Sociology," a view of life together shaped by what at times they called "ideals" and at others "Christian principles." As Maurice Reckitt points out, the Christian Socialists in England believed that the church had a high calling, namely, to save their civilization by becoming disentangled from the basic assumptions of the "progressive" forces of the day.[1] In place of these assumptions the Christian Socialists sought to provide English society not with

---

1. Reckitt, *Maurice to Temple*, 11.

a political program of reform but with a view of its social conditions in light of the eternal purposes of God. It is precisely this understanding of the calling of the Church of England that poses a question to the Protestant churches of America. There is no established church in America, but its churches have nonetheless, until recently, been charged with providing a religious and moral foundation for the nation.[2] Is this still the case? Even if it is, one is forced to ask if the focus of America's churches on public policy and institutional reform is the right way to fulfill this charge. To frame the question in an even wider context, establishment or no establishment, does a focus on ideals have a necessary place in any account of Christian social thought, or does talk of ideals, Christian or otherwise, within a political and economic order do no real work? These were questions presented to the Christian Socialists in their era, and they remain questions posed to Christian citizens at the present time.

So a third and fourth reason for an examination of Christian Socialist thought lies first of all in its call to consider the relevance of ideals within an economic and political order and second of all in its assessment of what ought to be the aim of Christian witness within society. There is, finally, a fifth reason for giving attention to this tradition. In making their defense of Christian ideals, the Christian Socialists in England had important things to say about the basic moral vocabulary we use to think about and promote what ought to be the political, economic, and social goals of life in society. So, for example, they argued that duties should be given priority over rights, the common good over individual interests, and public over private responsibility for addressing social problems.

For the Christian Socialists in England, the answer to these questions and others lay in a very distinctive understanding of socialism. To understand and assess the matters of importance to them one must begin with what they understood socialism to be when viewed from a Christian perspective. In his introduction to a collection of essays by Christian Socialists entitled *The Return of Christendom*, Bishop Charles Gore made clear the difference between the views of "Christian Socialists" and those of "Socialists" who wished government to address economic inequality by nationalizing the means of production. Speaking of Christian Socialists he wrote,

> These are all Socialists in a general sense, that is to say, they are all at one in believing *that no stable or healthy industrial or social*

2. See, e.g., Heclo, *Christianity and American Democracy*.

> *fabric can be built upon the principle of Individualism, or is consistent with the assertion of an almost unrestricted Right of Private Property.* Accordingly, they hold that our present industrial society rests upon a rotten foundation; and that what is needed to remedy the manifest "sickness" of our "Acquisitive Society," is something much more than particular social reforms. There is needed the substitution of a true ideal or principle of Society—that is of Socialism in some sense—for false. What they ask for is such a peaceful and gradual revolution as can only come about if men's minds come to be so fully possessed with a certain set of ideas, which are now in the air, as that they shall gain compelling or driving power in practical affairs.[3]

The concerns that led to this quest for "ideals" or "principles of society" that might provide an alternative to the "rotten foundation" of English society arose within a set of moral, social, economic, and political conditions easily recognizable in the present age. Social and economic change had forced large numbers of people off the land and crowded them into urban slums. Social dislocation was accompanied not only by grinding poverty but also by a high incidence of social insecurity and disorder. The depressed condition of these displaced urban dwellers stood in marked contrast to the huge concentrations of wealth that resulted from inheritance and the profits generated by the age of the machine. As is now the case with the arrival of a digital economy (perhaps the ultimate expression of the machine age), so the arrival of an industrial economy brought with it social disruption and a degree of economic inequality that threatened social stability. It was also accompanied by a form of competitive individualism that stood in marked contrast to the sense of commonality that had heretofore been characteristic of English society. It was this ideal that the Church of England (as the established church) supported, and upon it rested its moral responsibilities.

As previously noted, the response of the Christian Socialists in England was, with marked exceptions, unlike that of the Fabians in England, the Marxists in Europe, or the socialist followers of Walter Rauschenbusch in America. They sought no social or political revolution. Rather, in accord with the romantic idealism common in their age, they sought a "return of Christendom." Their aim was to reestablish a society whose foundation rested in Christian belief and practice—a society of ideals

---

3. Gore, introduction to A Group of Churchmen, *Return of Christendom*, xv–xvi; emphasis added.

that could be offered as a response to the holiness of God made known to the world in and through the incarnation of God in Christ.

It is important to note that, in pursuing this goal, they were not pursuing a social end discordant with the moral temper of English society of the day. As Gertrude Himmelfarb has pointed out, there was in England at that time moral agreement among the general populace that "those who were blessed not with poverty but with riches had a sacred duty of charity, the obligation to sustain the holy poor and to relieve the misery of the unholy."[4] Also, as Himmelfarb notes, the concern of most people was not industrialism and capitalism; they were concerned that society itself had deteriorated. They were troubled by what she calls "the complex of ideas, attitudes, values, and practices epitomized by a dismal philosophy that dehumanized human beings and the dismal science that demoralized social relations."[5] She refers here to "political economy," the notion that economies work by laws internal to their operation and not in relation to moral norms. John Ruskin, whose work *Unto This Last* had, for several generations, a huge influence on Christian Socialists, described this dismal philosophy in the following manner:

> Among the delusions which at different periods have possessed themselves of the minds of large masses of the human race, perhaps the most curious—certainly the least creditable—is the modern *soi-disant* science of political economy, based on the idea that an advantageous code of social action may be determined irrespectively of the influence of social affection.
>
> Of course, as in the instances of alchemy, astrology, witchcraft, and other such popular creeds, political economy has a plausible idea at the root of it. "The social affections," says the economist, "are accidental and disturbing elements in human nature; but avarice and the desire of progress are constant elements. Let us eliminate the inconstants, and, considering the human being merely as a covetous machine, examine by what laws of labor, purchase, and sale, the greatest accumulative result in wealth is obtainable. Those laws once determined, it will be for each individual afterwards to introduce as much of the disturbing affectionate element as he chooses, and to determine for himself the result on the new conditions supposed."[6]

---

4. Himmelfarb, *Idea of Poverty*, 4.
5. Himmelfarb, *Idea of Poverty*, 528.
6. Ruskin, *Unto This Last*, loc. 30 of 534, Kindle.

Ruskin concludes, "This would be a perfectly logical and successful method of analysis, if the accidentals afterwards to be introduced were of the same nature as the powers first examined."[7]

The Christian Socialists in England were concerned first of all with the view of economic relations Ruskin here describes—a view that excluded moral considerations and allowed only for the mechanisms of the market driven by a desire for profit. Ruskin illustrates the fact that in opposing opinions such as this one, Christian Socialists were not swimming against a stream of popular opinion. Indeed, they shared a general concern within the British populace for the moral state of the nation and its class divisions. This moral concern was widespread and socially powerful. The moral earnestness of Victorians was remarkable. By 1869 there were some seven hundred philanthropic organizations, and these organizations spent seven million pounds per year on poor relief. Further, the Charity Organization Society (a society meant to coordinate charitable initiatives) urged home visiting as a means of overcoming class divisions.[8]

Despite this pervasive social concern the Christian Socialists felt a particular responsibility to address the condition of the poor and through the poor the moral state of the nation. They shared a belief that, because it was established, the Church of England had a particular responsibility to address the moral challenges before the nation. This is not to say that they were concerned only for the role and status of the Church of England. They were motivated as well by a genuine sympathy for the plight of the poor. As Edward Norman has noted, what the Christian Socialists valued in F. D. Maurice (a man generally considered to be the father of Christian Socialism in England) was not a social and political principle but sympathy for humanity.[9] For example, after beginning his work as a lawyer, and under the influence of F. D. Maurice, John Ludlow, a leading voice among Christian Socialists, undertook the practice of visiting poor people in their homes. He describes one such visit in this way:

> In a large house on the north side of the street, on the ground floor, I found a married couple, the wife dying of consumption, in a simple closet off the hall, formerly no doubt, when the house was better inhabited, a housemaid's closet, with no light but from a pane in the door, and absolutely no communication with the outer air, no ventilation except through the door

---

7. Ruskin, *Unto This Last*, loc. 30 of 534, Kindle.
8. See Himmelfarb, *Poverty and Compassion*, 186, 199.
9. Norman, *Victorian Christian Socialists*, 24.

leading into the hall. When I asked the man how he could possibly have taken such a room, his plea was that it was cheap... How the surgeon attending the poor woman could have allowed her to remain in this dark closet, where she never could get a breath of fresh air, I could not understand. But the poor creature was too far-gone to make it worthwhile or even possible to move her. She died between two of my visits. I cannot recall the place to my mind without horror.[10]

What Henry Mayhew called "the riot, the struggle and the scramble for a living" that surrounded this poor woman genuinely moved the Christian Socialists.[11] In *The Great World of London* Mayhew gave this picture of industrial London in the early morning: "As the streets grow blue with the coming light, and the church spires and roof-tops stand out against the clear sky with a sharpness of outline that is seen only in London before its million chimneys cover the town with their smoke—then come sauntering forth the unwashed poor; some with greasy wallets on their backs to hunt over each dust-heap, and eke out life by seeking refuse bones, or stray rags and pieces of old iron..."[12]

These two pictures of London's poor call immediately to mind the terrible human waste that was characteristic of the slums of London, but it in no way does justice to the extent of the threat they posed to human life. In 1849 no fewer than thirteen thousand people died of cholera within three months. On September 10 of that year there were 432 deaths in a single day.[13] These accounts of the London poor provide a graphic picture of the conditions that so troubled the Christian Socialists. Nevertheless, troubled though they were, they did not address in adequate fashion a question these graphic descriptions left in the minds of Mayhew's readers. Was the character of "the poor" fixed by birth and moral state or by social circumstance? As will become clear, this question remained without a satisfactory answer throughout the course of their history, and so it remains to this day.

10. Murray, *John Ludlow*, 105–6.

11. Quoted by Douglas-Fairhurst in his introduction to Mayhew, *London Labour and the London Poor*, xv.

12. Quoted by Douglas-Fairhurst in his introduction to Mayhew, *London Labour and the London Poor*, xiv.

13. Douglas-Fairhurst, introduction to Mayhew, *London Labour and the London Poor*, xviii–xix.

The moralistic and impractical character of the Christian Socialists' response has been frequently alleged.[14] Nevertheless, that charge, though in some ways merited, in no way nullifies the sincerity of their reaction, and I hope to show that it is in important ways unfair. What is not in doubt, however, is the pain England's social and economic conditions caused them. As the passage previously quoted from Ludlow's diary plainly illustrates, their concern for the state of the poor was profound. It was not, however, the face of human suffering or the corruption of social institutions that served as the primary motive for their response. Neither was it a program of social reform that would address this suffering. Their chief concern was to fulfill the mission of the Church of England and in so doing provide a moral vision that would prick the conscience of the English people by calling to mind a group of social ideals the Christian Socialists believed would lead the nation to a renewed and markedly Christian vision of its common life.

All agreed that provision of a set of social ideals was central to the mission of an established church. Nevertheless, the Industrial Revolution and its aftermath brought about and served to expose an inability on the part of the Church of England to fulfill this very mission. As Owen Chadwick notes, "Between 1780 and 1860 a large number of Englishmen, whose families worked upon the land since families existed, moved into towns and cities. Whether or not the father attended the country church, the son was not likely to attend the city church. So far as the churches or chapels possessed the allegiance of the working class of England and Wales, they lost that allegiance when the country laborer became a town laborer."[15] He goes on to point out that the diminished social position and growing incapacity of the Church of England did not become obvious until the third quarter of the nineteenth century. In the industrial cities, by that time, there was "no squire, no parson, no tradition, no community. Instead there was a proletariat. Ten millions were added to the population between 1801 and 1851. Most of the increase lived in large cities. In 1851 more than half the population of London aged 20 and over had not been born in London."[16]

It was simply a fact that nothing in the cities, neither municipal government nor housing, sanitation nor public services, were up to such

---

14. See, e.g., Preston, *Church and Society in the Late Twentieth Century*, 33.
15. Chadwick, *Victorian Church*, 325.
16. Chadwick, *Victorian Church*, 325.

a challenge. It is to the credit of the Christian Socialists that they recognized that the Church of England was making a thoroughly inadequate response to rapidly changing social conditions. It is especially to their credit that they woke the Church of England to the serious nature of the state of the poor and the inadequacy of the church's response. Both the state of the poor and the state of the church were in serious disrepair. As to the church, there was no longer room in its graveyards to bury the dead. Education of the young now lay beyond the resources of the parish church. Indeed, as Owen Chadwick has written, "If there was no room for the dead in the cemeteries for the dead, there was no room for the living in the churches."[17]

To be sure, both church and chapel responded with a spate of new churches that did much to lessen the shortage of adequate places to worship. Nonetheless, there remained the problem of filling them and finding competent clergy to lead these congregations. The best efforts of the Church of England in the poorer areas of England's cities proved ineffective not in the first instance because of poor facilities and incompetent clergy but because of the extent of anticlericalism among the working classes. The clergy who served in these parishes found that their neighbors did not lack faith. What they lacked was trust in their pastors and the church they served.[18]

A lack of infrastructure, competent pastoral leadership and sympathy along with antichurch, anticlerical opinion were, however, neither the only nor the most formidable obstacles facing the Christian Socialists in their efforts to promote Christian ideals. There were three other factors all too infrequently noted. First, the people of England had an inadequate understanding of the nature and causes of poverty. Second, they were confronted with changing views of who was responsible for poor relief. Third, the intellectual project of the Christian Socialists, a project that resonated in a positive way with public opinion, nonetheless faced a critical, even hostile intellectual environment associated (sometimes inaccurately) with many of the century's leading intellects.

First, in respect to the nature and causes of poverty, a case can be made that the Christian Socialists, along with the British populace in general, had available to them a notion of poor people but little notion of a social condition called poverty. As Gertrude Himmelfarb points

---

17. Chadwick, *Victorian Church*, 128.
18. Chadwick, *Victorian Church*, 333.

out, until the latter part of the nineteenth century, members of English society tended to speak not of "poverty" as an identifiable social condition but of "the poor"—a term that referred to needy individuals—a class of people who were worthy or unworthy, deserving or undeserving, but nonetheless "poor."[19] The collective representations available to the British public (and the Church of England) that referred to those in dire economic straits (the poor) focused on their moral lives rather than on general social conditions (poverty) related to, even generated by, ambient social facts. It is no wonder then that the Christian Socialists, along with the Church of England and most of their fellow citizens, addressed the state of the poor in terms of moral praise or blame rather than in terms of social conditions and social policy. Their available vocabulary and social experience pressed them to think first of moral culpability or rectitude rather than social structure and circumstance. So it was that they referred to the "deserving and undeserving" poor, a term that did not go out of general use until the 1880s.[20] So it was also that Henry Mayhew, the most perceptive chronicler of London's poor, said that members of every community could be divided into the *energetic* and the *anergetic*. Of the latter he said that they were indisposed to work. This "indolent" class he divided between those who cannot work and those who will not work.[21] Poverty was always then a possible indicator of one's moral state. This view is not a thing of the past. It lives on and is a matter of fierce debate to this day.

Second, in respect to the location of responsibility for poor relief, the Christian Socialists (along with the British public) were confronted with changes in social thought and order that rendered obsolete prior practices and posed a difficult challenge for the Church of England. In a former time, the Church of England played a primary role in addressing the misery of the poor. Poor relief centered in the parish church. Further, there was a general understanding that those blessed with riches had a sacred duty to be charitable. Poverty and charity were penetrated with religious meaning. The church was understood to be the instrument both of social amelioration and of spiritual salvation. Nevertheless, by the time of the Wesleyan revival, the conception of poverty and its remedy were becoming more secularized. In prior common usage poverty was taken

---

19. Himmelfarb, *Poverty and Compassion*, 102–22.
20. Himmelfarb, *Poverty and Compassion*, 12.
21. Mayhew, *London Labour and the London Poor*, 330–31.

to refer to the voluntary or involuntary, ignoble poverty of the "lower orders." Now, however, poverty was coming to be seen by a growing number of people as a natural but unfortunate condition to be alleviated not by the church but by society. Alleviation of this sort on the part of the state became for a growing number the moral measure of a civilization.[22] Indeed, England alone among the nations of Europe, though faced with significant public resistance, passed laws that made government funds available for poor relief. For some, measures such as these came to be seen as a measure of civilization. However, this point of view seemed novel to a significant number of the leaders of the Church of England.

In sum, the Christian Socialists addressed the question of the responsibility of the Church of England for both the poor and the conscience of the nation in a time of social flux. They lived in a time when the focus of social attention was moving from the poor as a moral indicator to poverty understood as a social condition rather than a personal state. It was also a time in which responsibility for poor relief was shifting from private or ecclesial acts of charity to government policies seeking relief of a social condition. It is little wonder then that the Christian Socialists struggled over whether the focus of the church and its clergy should be upon the moral state of the poor and the nation or upon policies of government intended to give redress to a social condition. Further, given their institutional links to the role of the church in previous ages, it is little wonder that they were reluctant to enter the fray of public policy. They were, however, faced in a stark manner with what the role of the church in these changed circumstances ought to be.

It is important for readers in the twenty-first century to take these factors into account. If they are not, it will be difficult to give the Christian Socialists a fair reading. Why are they so concerned about the deserving and undeserving poor? Why are they so skittish about the role of government and issues of public policy? If one looks, it is easy to see that there are understandable reasons they thought as they thought and did as they did—reasons that if taken into account will make it possible to learn from them rather than disparage them.

There is also a third factor that if taken into account will lead to a more sympathetic reading of their work. The Christian Socialists undertook their labors in the midst of an intellectual climate that, from their perspective, seemed to exclude the introduction of moral considerations

---

22. Mayhew, *London Labour and the London Poor*.

into discussions of what then was called "political economy." As previously indicated, political economy, as understood (often unfairly) by the Christian Socialists, was thought to operate on the basis of internal laws that govern its operation. These laws, it was thought, left no space for the deployment of moral considerations and so also no room for the calling of the church as it was then understood.

The leading social thinkers of the age contributed, more often than not unintentionally, to this understanding of economic relations. This intellectual elite included Adam Smith, Charles Darwin, Thomas Malthus, David Ricardo, Bernard Mandeville, and John Stuart Mill. Particular blame is frequently laid at the feet of Adam Smith, whose notion of an "invisible hand" had been mistakenly understood to mean that the market had its own laws of adjustment—laws not to be tampered with by the likes of fallible humans. Study of his ethical writings reveals clearly that Adam Smith did not in fact envision a marketplace devoid of moral guidance.[23] The real culprits of the amoral market were Thomas Malthus and David Ricardo, who broke the relation between the welfare of the nation and that of the lower classes. For them there was no link between individual interest and general interest.[24] Nonetheless, all the men listed above provided a set of observations and ideas that were understood to say that moral considerations in fact play little or no part in the way in which a political economy actually works. Smith wrote sparsely of "an invisible hand" that guided economies. Darwin suggested that life on Earth evolves through a process of natural selection wherein only the fittest survive. Malthus contended that population growth would outstrip the supply of food needed for its support and so, again, only the fit survive. Mandeville insisted that society is not based on friendship or the virtue of self-denial but upon natural and moral evil. Ricardo was convinced that the value and quantity of a commodity depends on the quantity of labor necessary for its production and not upon the compensation paid for that labor. Mill suggested that social policy ought to be determined by that course of action that produced the greatest happiness for the greatest number. In different ways, these ideas, often taken out of context, served to support the idea of a political economy, a system of production and consumption that operates not by moral constraint but by the law of self-interest.

23. For a very clear presentation of the many ways in which Smith has been misinterpreted, see Kidd, "Moral Sentiments," 24–25.

24. Himmelfarb, *Poverty and Compassion*, 300–301.

So it was that a view of economic and political relations was born that had no place for moral concerns or guidance. It was this exclusion that most exorcised the Christian Socialists. An economic and political order that had no place for morals had as well no place for a national church commissioned to provide a moral foundation for national life. R. H. Tawney's well-known study *The Acquisitive Society* provides the most adequate account of the matters that sparked the Christian Socialists' concern and response to these formidable challenges. England, he claimed, had become an "acquisitive society," and by this he meant several things. Social institutions, he wrote, are the visible expression of a scale of moral values. He argued that sometime in the 1700s England had deserted the moral ideals upon which its society had been built. As a result, industry no longer served its proper "function" or purpose. That purpose is to provide services that are "necessary, useful or beautiful, and thus bring life to body and spirit."[25] However, the changes of the eighteenth century brought an end to the social ideal championed by the Christian Socialists, namely, social institutions and economic activities ought to be related to common moral ends that give them their significance.

By their account, these ideals provided the keystone of the arch of English society and if they were removed, the Christian Socialists feared, social relations would devolve into a jumble of individual rights claims and conflicting private interests. These rights, protected by government, would become the ultimate social reality. As Tawney writes, "The result of such ideas . . . was a society which was ruled by law, not by the caprice of Governments, but which recognized no moral limitation on the pursuit by individuals of their economic self-interest."[26] In such a society, the purpose of social organization is to produce the greatest happiness for the greatest number. Now happiness, he noted, is individual, and to make happiness the object of society "is to resolve society itself into the ambitions of numberless individuals, each directed towards the satisfaction of some desire and the consequent attainment of some personal purpose."[27]

Societies such as these Tawney terms "acquisitive societies," because "their whole tendency and interest and preoccupation is to promote the acquisition of wealth."[28] Acquisitive societies are consequently sub-

---

25. Tawney, *Acquisitive Society*, 8.
26. Tawney, *Acquisitive Society*, 14.
27. Tawney, *Acquisitive Society*, 29.
28. Tawney, *Acquisitive Society*, 29.

ject first of all to "irrational" inequalities in wealth. They also become societies torn by "fierce antagonisms" and warlike competition. In such societies only the fit survive, and those who lose out in the competition are soon considered in some way morally reprobate. As Tawney notes in *Religion and the Rise of Capitalism*, "The most curious feature in the whole discussion . . . was the resolute refusal to admit that society had any responsibility for the causes of distress."[29]

After reading Tawney's account of the social and economic climate of his time, it is impossible to miss parallels with the climate of our present day.[30] In our day, political economy has been replaced by neoliberalism, a term first coined by Milton Friedman in his 1951 essay "Neoliberalism and Its Prospects." As presently employed, "neoliberalism" is a term that takes *laissez-faire* economics and radicalizes them. The notion of freedom as freedom from constraint is interpreted solely in economic terms. The meaning of the common good is consequently changed beyond all recognition. For neoliberals the common good simply falls out from the free exercise of rational behavior and self-interest on the part of economic agents. The free exercise of rational choice within the market is sort of an invisible hand that works for the benefit of all.

Now, when the exercise of negative liberty crashes into capital markets, humanity receives a new definition. Human being is defined as a form of capital—by whether one is able to participate in the market either as a self-interested agent or as a speck of human capital. Anyone unable to participate either as a profit-seeking entrepreneur or as a speck of human capital is simply a nonperson. Indeed, all spheres of life are economized. All relations are measured by profit or loss. In all relations we are judged as market actors. Such persons are controlled by their desires and as such are politically manageable. Government can now act on the social environment so as to meet or create desires. In response to these social facts, a friend of mine has come up with a new way to start a conversation with someone you don't know: "Hello, my name is Philip. Buy anything interesting this week?"

This account of neoliberalism is remarkably close to Tawney's description of "the acquisitive society." Both are damning and both describe a view of the world against which Christian Socialists launched their

---

29. Tawney, *Religion and the Rise of Capitalism*, loc. 4105 of 6663, Kindle.

30. The following account of neoliberalism has been provided by Susan Lucas. See, e.g., Lucas, "The Temple Legacy Today," in Spencer, *Theology Reforming Society*, locs. 2009–52 of 3130, Kindle.

attack. Nevertheless, both descriptions are extreme. They simply go too far. The fact is that English society (like American society) was in conflict over how to meet the challenges—moral, social, economic, and political—brought about by the changes all faced. Nevertheless, it is not the case that England (or present-day America) has degenerated to the extent that it has become the mechanistic and morally vacuous amalgam that was the subject of the Christian Socialist attack. If Gertrude Himmelfarb is to be believed, despite all the talk of the amoral character of political economy, English society (like that of present-day America) remained at its root "benevolent." The English enlightenment did not focus on the sufficiency of reason, as did the French. Rather, "the 'moral sense' or 'moral sentiment,' the 'social virtues' or 'social affections,' the ideas of 'benevolence,' 'sympathy,' 'compassion,' 'fellow-feeling'—these were the defining terms of the moral philosophy that was at the heart of the British Enlightenment. It was this social ethos that was the common denominator of . . . secular philosophers and religious enthusiasts, of Church of England bishops and Wesleyan preachers and missionaries. And it was this ethos that found expression in the reform movements and philanthropic enterprises that flourished during the century."[31] It was this ethos that led to an age of benevolence and a new humanitarianism. Himmelfarb goes on to show how this spirit of benevolence found expression in literature, voluntary societies, philanthropic activity, education, and attempts on the part of poor people to help one another through their own voluntary societies.[32] Many have pointed out the inadequacies of these efforts, but, inadequate or not, they were real and they sprang from genuinely benevolent motives.

Facts force one to the conclusion that to some extent the Christian Socialists boxed against imagined foes who were neither as perverse nor as powerful as they feared. Nevertheless, they were not wrong to worry about the destructive force of a portrayal of economic relations that excluded moral considerations. They were certainly right to see that the problem could not be met adequately by the virtue of benevolence. They rightly believed that a renewed vision of the moral character of common life was needed if the nation was to meet in a morally satisfactory way the challenges it faced. Thus, in searching for a "Christian Sociology" they were not running in a direction diametrically opposed to that of English

---

31. Himmelfarb, *Roads to Modernity*, 131.
32. Himmelfarb, *Roads to Modernity*, 131–46.

society. They were, however, stressing the importance of a renewed moral vision for that society. They were not wrong to worry about a view of social life that portrayed it as a struggle in which only the fittest survive, and they were not wrong to be distressed by the destructive effects of poverty. In response, they were right to put forward a set of ideals that might provide an alternative to a political economy. This alternative claimed a stellar group of thinkers as its progenitors—an alternative that might provide relief to a destitute population and moral wisdom to the people of England.

As the collection of essays entitled *The Return of Christendom* so clearly displays, the Christian Socialists often looked to the Middle Ages to find a concrete example of a society organized around "function" in service to a common good rather than a quest for private wealth. In search of a social ideal upon which to restore a Christian society, as noted above, many sought "the return of Christendom." In this search they showed themselves to be naïve, ill informed in respect to basic economics, and impractical. Nevertheless, their primary aim was moral. It was to form the conscience of a nation, and this aim, no matter how adverse the circumstances, remains a necessary one for any Christian account of social ethics.

B. Theological

The Incarnation as a Foundation for Christian Social Ethics and Ecclesiology

THE CHRISTIAN SOCIALISTS RIGHTLY believed that no account of Christian living could admit a moral "no-fly zone." The question was what theological warrant did they have for making their proposal for an alternative to the acquisitive society. In their attempt to establish Christian ideals as the basis of English society they were confronted with a formidable problem from within their own church. In the mid-eighteenth century and part of the nineteenth, Evangelicals dominated the life of the Church of England. As Owen Chadwick has written of them, "They were men of the Reformation, who preached the cross, the depravity of man, and justification by faith alone. Some of them were Calvinists and more of them were not . . . They pondered long and daily over the Bible, were decisive and orthodox Protestants." He goes on, "They exalted the prayer book, valued the establishment, resented assaults upon a state church . . . Most of them were conservative in politics and wanted the established church to control education."[1] Nevertheless, their primary interest was the state of individual souls before God. Duties to the poor to their mind were quite real—linked as they were to concern for both their physical and spiritual wellbeing. Poor relief for them was, however, not properly a matter for government policy but individual practice, linked as it was to evangelistic efforts, the moral reform of individuals, and private acts of charity.

The Christian Socialists sought a moral vision that was not focused on individual virtue and personal discipleship but upon a view of human

---

1. Chadwick, *Victorian Church*, 440–42.

life as at root social and a view of the church that stressed its corporate nature. Overly individualistic views of the moral responsibilities of Christians such as those held by Evangelicals, to their minds, bared the way to an adequate response on the part of the Church of England to the intellectual climate and the social conditions that so concerned them. The great accomplishment of Christian Socialism was to make available to the Church of England a socially conscious faith. It was F. D. Maurice who, with his focus on incarnation rather than atonement, provided such a vision. In his *Tract on Christian Socialism* (1850), he stated that Christianity is the only foundation of socialism and that socialism is the necessary result of a sound Christianity. His focus on the social nature of human beings led him to say further that the watchword of the socialist is cooperation and the watchword of an antisocial person is competition. In hindsight it is difficult to grasp the radical nature of Maurice's interpretation of the incarnation and its social and moral implications. Nevertheless, in its context it was indeed radical. Maurice's central point was simply this: In Christ, God has come to us in a fully human life. In doing so, he has sanctified not only the lives of individuals but also all dimensions of human life, including its physical base in nature and its corporate character as social. Jeremy Morris has recently argued (persuasively) that the continuing influence of Maurice on Christian Socialism has been overestimated.[2] Nonetheless, he does credit Maurice with the following concerns on the part of the Christian Socialists. Maurice's continuing influence on the movement can, he says, be summed up in four points: (1) his social vision suggests a more integrated model for social theology; (2) his social theology invites ecclesial reflection and devotional elaboration; (3) his social theology dissolves into broader categories of theological description (such as the Holy Trinity); and (4) he provides an identifiable way for Christian working in the world, that is to say, love expressed as fellowship, cooperation, collaboration, and co-working. Alison Milbank goes even further and claims that aspects of his views frequently thought to be weaknesses are not really weaknesses at all.[3] She refers, in particular, to his stress on ecclesiology, his hesitation about church support for large political and state programs, and his emphasis on education. In respect to all these points, there is good reason to believe she may well have a point.

2. Morris, "F. D. Maurice and the Myth of Christian Socialist Origins," in Spencer, *Theology Reforming Society*, loc. 165 of 3130, Kindle.

3. Milbank, "Maurice as a Resource for the Church Today," in Spencer, *Theology Reforming Society*, loc. 593 of 3130, Kindle.

Whatever the case may be, Maurice laid aside an individualistic account of life with God and in its place proposed a more social one. In his discussion of Methodism in his major work, *The Kingdom of Christ*, Maurice asks this question: "We have often been obliged to ask ourselves, whether these distinct individual acts, on which Protestantism dwells so excessively, may not, must not, depend at last upon some relation in which men stand to their fellows; whether we can take our start from individuals, and form a society out of them; whether the existence of society be not implied in their existence; and whether, consequently, if each man have a spiritual existence, and be subjected to a spiritual government, there must not be somewhere a spiritual body, of which he should account himself a member?"[4]

Maurice insists that we understand ourselves first not as individuals but as social beings. Our social being provides the soil from which our individual being grows. It is not the other way around! He insists also that God in his providential governance of creation has over the ages established families and nations as instantiations of social life. Each has its own integrity, but both individually and conjointly these smaller societies point toward the presence of a universal society. That society is the Christian church. Baptism is a sign of its existence and its universal nature. Christ in his incarnation has established this society. The incarnate Christ, who has lived, died and risen, is its ruler. It is a society therefore that includes all people as the objects of God's love expressed in the life of his Son. All people exist under the dominion of Christ and the providence of God, whether they know it or not. All people are recipients of God's love and all are subject to his governance, whether they know it or not.

In a rather stirring passage he summarizes his position as follows:

> It is distinctly admitted that Christ came to establish a universal dispensation, which did not exist previously; that this dispensation is grounded upon a manifestation of God as absolute, universal love; upon the fact that he has entered into relations in the person of his Son with man as he is, and that to men so united to his Son, He gives his Spirit, that they may be endowed with that same universal love which is his own essential nature, and which has been displayed in the acts and sufferings of a real man. This revelation and this command lie at the foundation of the Christian Church; this is expressed in our Baptism "into the

---

4. Maurice, *Kingdom of Christ*, 139.

name of the Father, and of the Son, and of the Holy Ghost." They who enter into this state are bound to love their enemies, are bound to love all men, because they see that God loves all; they love those who hate and persecute them, because for these enemies and persecutors Christ died. They love even the enemies of God, because they regard them as creatures still bearing the flesh which Christ bore—not yet finally separated from Him, not deserted by his Spirit. They keep the command given in his Sermon on the Mount strictly, fully, spiritually, for the reason the Lawgiver himself lays down, because they "are the children of their father in heaven."[5]

On this account of the incarnation of Christ, all people are children of God, whether they know it or not. In this way Maurice opposes individualism. All people exist under the umbrella of divine love and so God establishes a fellowship that includes all people. Further, on this account, the institutions of common life exist under the providence of God and are intended to serve this fellowship. As aspects of divine providence, the common life of family and nation are, out of love for God and neighbor, to be tended and cared for. In this account of the Christian doctrine of the incarnation, Christian Socialists found a charter for promoting ideals that might lead to changes of heart and so also to a change in the conditions under which their fellow citizens lived. It is the doctrine of the incarnation that provided the Christian Socialists a theological foundation for the Christian Sociology many of them sought to develop and disseminate.

Nevertheless, the vision of Christian Socialism proposed by F. D. Maurice, despite its concern for the poor and its warnings of moral danger to the rich, was remarkably conservative in respect to the reform of social institutions. Maurice believed that God, in his providence, has provided all peoples with the political and familial institutions that order their common life. Because they are from God, social institutions are to be minded and tended rather than reformed. Maurice wanted to "dig down" below these social arrangements to the moral status and qualities of the people whose lives they ordered. Consequently, he opposed all attempts at social change that were not focused on the moral lives of the citizenry. The way to address the evils of society was not to change its institutions but to change the moral lives of its individual members by drawing them into the fellowship God's universal love engenders and

---

5. Maurice, *Kingdom of Christ*, 461–62.

supports. Maurice's vision was the harmonious cooperation of each person and each social estate in a way that produces peace, prosperity, and fellowship for all. He believed it was the calling of the Church of England to develop among the English citizenry the moral rectitude upon which this sort of vibrant and healthy social life rests. It was not the job of the church to get behind the reform of social institutions. Social life was to be changed from the bottom up through the regeneration of a citizenry rather than from the top down by the creation of new or improved social institutions.

At this point it is necessary to note that most people know the work of F. D. Maurice through that of H. R. Niebuhr, who, in his vastly influential work *Christ and Culture*, presented Maurice as defender of the view that Christ is best understood as a "transformer of culture." It is certainly true that Maurice presented Christ as the transformer of both individual Christian lives and their common life. According to Maurice, all people are in Christ, whether they know it or not. Those who do know it are subject to the transformation of their lives by the indwelling Spirit of Christ who transforms lives rooted in self-love into lives rooted in love for God and neighbor. No doubt this personal transformation has transformative consequences in all the dimensions of life. One must ask, however, if these changes lead in some direct and identifiable way to transformations of culture in the broad and inclusive sense Niebuhr assigned it.

At best this claim is one whose truth is quite limited. Niebuhr defines culture as "the sum of all that has *spontaneously* arisen for the advancement of material life and as an expression of spiritual and moral life—all social intercourse, technologies, arts, literature and science."[6] Culture, he says, is a "human achievement." As such it includes "speech, education, tradition, myth, science, art, philosophy, government, law, rite, beliefs, inventions, technologies."[7] He goes on to insist that culture is a realm of values that include ideas about what is "good for man."[8] He also notes that pluralism is characteristic of all cultures.

Culture, for Niebuhr, is an expansive notion, and the question is this: Let us grant that Christ transforms the lives of individuals. Let us grant that Christ through the Spirit brings into being a culture in which people learn to love God and neighbor. Let us grant that this transformation

---

6. Niebuhr, *Christ and Culture*, 31.
7. Niebuhr, *Christ and Culture*, 33.
8. Niebuhr, *Christ and Culture*, 35.

of life can lead to changes on the part of believers in patterns of understanding and behavior in various dimension of the life of society. But do these personal transformations lead directly to transformations in all dimensions of culture? Maurice does not think so. Indeed he consistently opposed efforts on the part of his colleagues to develop programs that might transform the familial, political, and economic structures of English society. Indeed, he was an ardent critic of democracy as a form of government. As previously noted, he believed that the structures of society were the work of divine providence and so were to be honored rather than transformed. For example, the class structure of English society was not to be changed. Rather, members of each class were to learn to love and serve one another so that all members both contributed to and received from others cooperation and so fellowship. In this case the Spirit of Christ in the lives of believers serves to transform a noncooperative and competitive social life into one that is built upon fellowship and mutual service.

This is certainly a significant transformation, but it is not the sort of broad transformation most of Niebuhr's readers took him to have in mind when he spoke of Maurice's presentation of Christ as a transformer of culture. They took him to imply that Maurice sought to promote the transformative effect of Christian belief and practice across the board, upon the familial, social, economic, and political arrangements that define a society. Maurice was most certainly not an advocate of such changes. Rather, he sought to "dig down" to the base level of human values and there identify the work of Christ as one that transforms the lives of those who have received him as the ruler of their lives. He did not believe that God intends these transformed lives to be agents of change in the basic structures of society. He believed that God's intention for them is to be a sort of presence within society that changes the character of relations between people who occupy different positions within a social structure. He thought of Christ more as a transformer of lives and social relations than as a transformer of social order and its defining culture.

Other voices among the Christian Socialists pushed, with varying degrees of fervor, against the notion that the institutions of society were to be left as is. Though they shared the belief that the moral character of the nation was the key element in social reform, they nonetheless realized that social institutions were brought into their field of moral vision by the incarnation of Christ. For example, Scott Holland, in his work *Our Neighbours*, wrote this: "If we believe in the Incarnation, then we certainly believe in the entry of God into the very thick of human affairs ... God must be concerned with every scrap and detail that is human ... The Incarnation itself, then, is the decisive reason why Jesus Christ has a social and economic significance."[9] Scott Holland spoke eloquently about the social significance of Christ but rarely, if at all, of the implications of this significance for the practicalities of social reform.

Some went further to the left, however. Stewart Headlam, for example, following Maurice's view that all people are "in Christ," held that there is no distinction between the sacred and the secular because all work for humanity is God's work and all human experience conveys divine truth.[10] In a work entitled *Service to Humanity* he linked the church to this common human enterprise. Speaking of the church he wrote, "The Incarnation compels us to regard it as a great Co-operative organized institution for human welfare and human righteousness in this world."[11] These beliefs led Headlam to move in the direction of policy advocacy and then to join the Fabian Socialists.

As the examples of Holland and Headlam make clear, Maurice's doctrine of the incarnation left Christian Socialists with a theological charter for addressing the moral foundation of their country, but it also left them with an unresolved tension—a tension between their concern for the moral quality of the citizenry and the adequacy of the social structures and institutions in which the moral life of that citizenry was lived. Compelling as it might have been, the doctrine of the incarnation on its own could not establish a clear relation between the moral formation of the citizenry and the reform of social institutions. The tension was present almost from the beginning, and it remains with Christian citizens to this day.

Maurice's disciple, John Ludlow, provides a prime example of resistance to Maurice's social conservatism that existed among Christian Socialists from the beginning. Ludlow had been educated in France and was in touch with the French Socialists, who believed that changes in society would render changes in human nature and human relations. Nevertheless, he rejected their notion that society was to be regenerated by improved "social machinery." He did, however, see a need for the reform of social institutions, but he thought that institutional change apart from

---

9. Cited by Grimley, in *Citizenship, Community, and the Church of England*, 38.
10. Norman, *Victorian Christian Socialists*, 107.
11. Cited by Norman, in *Victorian Christian Socialists*, 107.

the transformation of character would in the end prove disastrous. In a letter to Charles Forbes he said this about the French Socialists: "They fancy that society is to be regenerated by an improved social machinery, as if a machine, however perfect, could ever produce any moral good, & were not productive of injury or benefit, exactly in proportion as the hand that moves it is evil or good. That is to say, their Revolution is practically godless . . . They are trying to manufacture a Paradise out of their own theories & imaginations, without thinking of God's will and their duties towards Him and towards their fellow-creatures. Indeed the word Duty seems forgotten among them; they speak only of Rights."[12]

This quotation is a clear example of Ludlow's reluctance to give the urgency of social reform priority over the importance of religious and moral values. Nonetheless, unlike Maurice, he believed fervently in the need for social reform. In addition to the French influence on his education, he was much taken by the work of Thomas Arnold. Arnold made a distinction in his social thought between preserving and improving principles. Clearly, Maurice's focus was on preservation, while Arnold's (and Ludlow's) was on improvement.[13] Arnold wrote these words, but they could just as well be from Ludlow's pen: "It seems to be that people are not enough aware of the monstrous state of society, absolutely without parallel in the history of the world—with a population poor, miserable, degraded in body and mind, as much as if they were slaves, and yet called freemen."[14]

Like Arnold, Ludlow believed that these conditions were unsupportable and that the accompanying gap between rich and poor portended tragedy. He was convinced that the nation must be made to understand the dire nature of its circumstance. Like Arnold, he also believed that the Church of England, despite its need for reform, was called to take the lead in a national moral revival. He even thought of the parish system as a means of doing so. In this reform effort, the church is to make clear that love is the governing principle of political and social life and that obedience to God's will is the only sound basis for social regeneration. Ludlow held that it is idolatrous to place one's hope in political and social mechanisms. These are tools meant to promote social wellbeing, but they must be founded on right Christian principles guided by love. On this

12. For this quotation see Christensen, *Christian Socialism*, 60.

13. For a helpful summary of Arnold's views, see Christensen, *Christian Socialism*, 52–53.

14. Cited by Christensen, in *Christian Socialism*, 52.

point, Ludlow and Maurice were in complete agreement. Nevertheless, in another respect they were not. Ludlow believed, in a way Maurice did not, that one ought not simply to acquiesce to given social structures. Though he was cautious when it came to the espousal of particular social reforms,[15] he believed fervently that one must be intolerant of social evils and one must seek to expose them. He held the view that all social institutions must be tested to see if they fulfill God's will on earth. Political institutions are, therefore, not sacrosanct. They have no right to exist if they do not give expression to the basic principle of the universe, love. He went so far as to say that if the monarchy, aristocracy, and established church block the way to progress they should be done away with.[16] Indeed, what is not in accord with the kingdom of God should be changed so as to accord with fellowship and cooperation. Thus, in the name of reform, he supported the extension of suffrage to "honest and worthy" workers. As a means of opening the political process to many who had for various reasons been excluded, he wanted suffrage to depend upon the "person" rather than their possessions. Ludlow was a supporter of democracy. Maurice was not!

Ludlow was also a man of action in a way that Maurice was not. In pursuit of this vision Ludlow considered moving to France and there starting a publication known as *La Fraternité Chrétienne*. He hoped for the birth of a community whose members would dedicate themselves to the reorganization of industry and trade on the basis of the principle of cooperation as an expression of brotherhood. Maurice refused to support such an effort on grounds that it would be an expression of party spirit. He believed that this sort of activity on the part of outsiders defied the order of fellowship because it usurped the responsibility of neighborhoods and local churches to respond in love and fellowship.[17] His drive to action sprang from moral sensitivity and a vision of the nature of the kingdom of God. He was convinced that this kingdom demanded a form of life in society that is in total contradiction to the selfish and contentious character of social life governed by the tenets of political economy.

Ludlow's difference in emphasis from that of Maurice is made plain by the following quote from an article Ludlow wrote against defenders of political economy:

15. See, e.g., Christensen, *Christian Socialism*, 88.
16. Christensen, *Christian Socialism*, 95.
17. Christensen, *Christian Socialism*, 120–22.

> And if anyone should ... say, "These evils are necessary ones—they are the natural results of competition, and competition is the law of human society"; this is what I have to answer—"If it be necessary in English society that from thirteen to fourteen thousand females should in London be engaged in slop-work, earning on an average two-pence-halfpenny a day, of whom one-fourth, being those who have no husband or parent to support them, have no choice but between starvation and prostitution—if this be necessary, I say, in English society, then English society is the devil's own work, and to hell with it as soon as possible!"[18]

Maurice would certainly have condemned these conditions and sought by means of virtuous activity to remedy them. But never would he have said that "English society is the devil's own work."

So it is that from the outset a tension existed within the ranks of Christian Socialism—a tension between principles and policies that was never fully resolved. Nevertheless, this brief review of the major tenets and concerns of the Christian Socialists reveals four things one can say about all expressions of the movement in its English guise. The first is that its adherents did not focus, in the first instance, on social institutions. The second is that they did not believe changes in social institutions alone would resolve the social inequality, misery, and degradation that so troubled them. The third is that they believed the moral regeneration of society was a *sine qua non* for improved social relations and healthy institutions. The fourth is that, because of their convictions about equality before God, the social nature of humankind and the central importance of moral reform rather than institutional change, they preferred to speak of social duties rather than rights. This fourth item, the primacy of duty over rights, constitutes a basic theme of their presentation of Christian Sociology, and much more will be said about it in due course.

As noted, the theological charter for all these convictions was, to the minds of the Christian Socialists, the incarnation of Christ. That said, they were often quite sketchy in spelling out either the theological content of the doctrine or its social ramifications. There were, to be sure, exceptions—in particular, bishops B. F. Westcott, Charles Gore, and William Temple. It would be fair to say that each of these men gave a fulsome account of the incarnation and its import. Nonetheless, their compatriots appear to have taken little note of their more extensive account of the

---

18. Cited by Christensen, *Christian Socialism*, 95.

doctrine. In a rather flat-footed way they simply took the incarnation as a charter for the Christian Sociology they sought to champion. It is, however, a grave error to do no more than assume the views upon which one's social principles rest. An adequate assessment of the Christian Socialists' view of a Christian society requires attention to its foundation. To my mind B. F. Westcott tried to do exactly this.[19] Indeed, his views are closer to those of Maurice than are those of either Gore or Temple, but at the same time he is more expansive in his account of the incarnation than is Maurice. His work shows just how far one can, or cannot, go by building on Maurice's views.

In the preface to his collection of addresses, *The Incarnation and Common Life*, Westcott notes, "The highest conceivable attestation of a divine revelation lies in its power to meet each new want of man as it arises, and to gain fresh force from the growth of human knowledge. The message of the Incarnation satisfies this criterion in unexpected ways, and our distresses enable us to feel its wider applications."[20] The "distresses" Westcott had in mind were those that accompanied the Industrial Revolution, and it was his belief that the incarnation speaks powerfully to these distresses and so is attested as revelatory of God's will.

The question is, To what exactly does the doctrine attest? According to Westcott, it attests that the incarnation is the central fact of the life of the world. That is, the incarnation of Christ discloses "the capacity and destiny of man, and of the creation over which man is set as sovereign and representative." Further, it discloses that the one through whom and for whom the world was created "took humanity to Himself and lived a human life." In doing so, Christ, the Word of God, "became not a man as one man of many men, but 'flesh.'" That is, "In Him humanity found its unity."[21] Prior to Christ's incarnation, humankind was "broken up into innumerable fragments." In and through the incarnation these innumerable fragments were gathered into Christ and so made one.[22] Though united in Christ, each person finds her own fulfillment, but she does so as part of a whole. That whole, along with each of its parts, realizes not as a hope or aspiration but as a fact one God as Father of all. Consequently, because each person is the child of one Father, each shares with all the

---

19. See especially Westcott, *Incarnation and Common Life*, and Westcott, *Christus Consummator*.

20. Westcott, *Incarnation and Common Life*, loc. 23 of 4679, Kindle.

21. For these claims, see Westcott, *Incarnation and Common Life*.

22. Westcott, *Incarnation and Common Life*, loc. 36 of 4679, Kindle.

others one origin and one destiny. What is more, because the Word of God has become flesh, it has been revealed to us that the material forms of the sensible world "have a Divine affinity and therefore correspond with a spiritual being." Because of this affinity "what we see becomes a sacrament of the unseen."[23] That the world served as a sacramental attestation to divine mysteries provided Christian Socialists with yet another powerful motive for participation in all dimensions of life in the world. At any turn, and at any cross in the road, what one sees might be revelatory of the mystery that lies at the heart of God's creation. Here is a powerful warrant for regarding the creation and the life of humankind with reverence. To bring their sacramental view forward into our time, one might well ask, What possible hope is there for the preservation of the natural order if it is not viewed with reverence? What possible reason is there for regretting the disappearance of species if their disappearance does not rob the world of a window that, possibly, opens onto the wonder of creation? The sacramental view of creation held by the Christian Socialists, tied as it was to the doctrine of the incarnation, should be regarded as an inheritance left to anyone who attempts in our time to give voice to a Christian social ethic.

In this brief statement of the meaning of the incarnation, Bishop Westcott says quite a lot. Christ is not simply a man. Christ encompasses all humankind united with God as God has intended from before time. All people, therefore, have a common origin, share one Father, enjoy a common nature, have a common status in the world as God's designated representative and ruler and share a common destiny, namely, to live eternally in the life of God. However, to these points must be added another of crucial importance. Christ does all these things as the "Sinless Head" of "the human race." It is through the *sinless Christ* that the human race is enabled to "realize the Divine Father."[24] One might take this statement as a move toward the Evangelicals, who saw Christ's sinlessness as the vicarious offering of an innocent life that procures atonement with God for a sinful humanity. It is, however, more likely a statement about how humankind comes to know the nature of God—that is, to "realize the Divine Father." It is more likely a statement about how we come to have a moral knowledge of God that can guide our behavior than a statement about how we know that we have been delivered. Here we have an

---

23. Westcott, *Incarnation and Common Life*, loc. 42 of 4679, Kindle.
24. Westcott, *Incarnation and Common Life*, loc. 42 of 4679, Kindle.

acknowledgment of the reality of sin, but that acknowledgment is countered by a moral vision rather than a salvific act.

It is likely that what we have in Bishop Westcott (despite his more extensive account of the doctrine of the incarnation) is another example of the Christian Socialists' tendency to downplay the importance of sin, atonement, and reconciliation and to overweight the power of love to change the world. From Maurice to Temple the Christian Socialists thought it their mission to awaken in the English people a moral vision whose ideals they believed to be utterly necessary if progress was to be made and anything done about the social conditions they so deplored. And so it was that Bishop Westcott, in the name of many, spoke of the importance of *ideals* that shape from below the social life of a nation in all its forms.

In March 1891 he gave an address to the Students of the London University Extension Society in which he said, "Ideals are . . . the soul of life. The simplest human act is directed to an end; and life, a series of unnumbered acts, must answer to some end, some ideal mean or generous, seen by the eye of the heart and pursued consciously or often unconsciously, which gives unity and a clue to the bewildering mazes of human conduct."[25] He then went on to say, "The inspiration of great ideals seems to be alone able to meet the intellectual distraction, the materialism, the critical indifferentism, and the consequent enfeebling of will which appear to be the dominant perils of our age."[26] He then concluded his remarks about the necessity of ideals for social reform with this prescription for rectifying the materialism and selfishness of his age: materialism results in inequality, no "enthusiasm" (desire) for service, and no stable peace. We accept wealth as the standard of success and skill as a means of overcoming an opponent, and the final appeal is to force. But "the contemplation of a great ideal" will constrain us to recognize that classes, nations, races rejoice and suffer together, that our possessions and powers are instruments of service.[27]

The chief concern of the Christian Socialists in England was a "Christian Sociology," a set of Christian ideals that might shape from below the common life of a nation. Social policy was to their minds a matter of knowledge and prudence. The mission of the church, through

---

25. Westcott, *Incarnation and Common Life*, loc. 1549 of 4679, Kindle.

26. Westcott, *Incarnation and Common Life*, loc. 1673 of 4679, Kindle; emphasis added.

27. Westcott, *Incarnation and Common Life*, loc. 1687 of 4679, Kindle.

its institutions, was to make better people rather than better policy. In his Enthronement Address in Durham Cathedral, Bishop Westcott put the point quite directly: Christians must bring back to all "that sense of true human sympathy" that gives dignity to labor and also hallows great possessions. He went on to ask, "How shall we check . . . the anarchy of unlimited competition, and enable each worker to feel that he is bound with all his fellow-workers in one brotherhood of common service?" The answer, he said, "must be spiritual and not legal, from within and not from without. Better men, and better men only, will usher in the better age."[28]

Bishop Westcott's treatment of the doctrine of the incarnation as the theological foundation of Christian Socialism is richer than that of Maurice but in the end does not stray far from Maurice's views. It remained for a student of Bishop Westcott, Bishop Charles Gore, both to build on this foundation and to be critical of it. It is Gore's work more than that of any other that qualifies Christian Socialism as a church tradition. Alasdair MacIntyre has famously argued that tradition develops in part by means of arguments internal to itself.[29] Jaroslav Pelikan, on the other hand, stresses the fact that tradition is more frequently "passed on in continuity rather than in conflict with what has gone before."[30] Gore's account of the incarnation shows there to be truth in both positions. On the one hand, he passes on and develops his predecessors' accounts of the incarnation, yet on the other, he identifies and addresses unresolved issues in the tradition he received. It will become clear that the same factors drive the work of William Temple and continue on into the twentieth century in the works of others influenced by the Christian Socialists. I have in mind particularly Rowan Williams and John Milbank.

But to return to Bishop Gore, in the first place his thought shows coherence with and development of what he received.[31] Like his predecessors, Gore shared a belief that the Church of England was failing to address the social issues of his time. In his response he gave primacy, as

---

28. Westcott, *Incarnation and Common Life*, loc. 149 of 4679, Kindle.

29. MacIntyre, *After Virtue*, 6–21.

30. Pelikan, *Vindication of Tradition*, 48. See also Turner, "Tradition in the Church."

31. Gore's theological output was truly extraordinary, and finding one's way through its many twists and turns is a job in itself. Fortunately, Prof. James Carpenter has provided an able summary of both his theology and his ethics. The following summary relies heavily on his work. See Carpenter, *Gore: A Study in Liberal Catholic Thought*.

did Maurice and Westcott, to the moral aspects of Christianity. To Gore's mind, the doctrinal and sacramental authority of the church are both tied to the social mission of the church. That mission is rooted in the historical Jesus as presented in the gospels. The key to understanding the incarnation of the Word lies in the humanity of the Son.

This focus on the life of Jesus led Gore to a particular understanding of the moral import of the incarnation, namely, the kenotic doctrine of the person of Christ. According to this account, in taking on life in the flesh, the Son empties himself of his divine status and power and becomes the servant of humankind. This act of self-emptying gives expression to the depth and breadth of God's love for his creation. It is a love that gives up its status and life for the life of the world. As with his predecessors, Gore's kenotic theory of the incarnation led him to two moral ideals—one is the fundamental equality of all people, and the other is universal love expressed in service. Gore's kenotic theory has many problems, but it does insist that divine love is not limited by the exclusionary classifications that define the peoples of the earth. The kenotic theory insists that, unlike human love, divine love knows no bounds.

To this point, Gore's account of the incarnation coheres with the view he received, but in important ways it also goes beyond and corrects what he received. As James Carpenter points out, Gore fought the liberal ideas of progress held by many of his fellow Christian Socialists. It is also the case that in giving particular importance to the doctrine of the incarnation, Gore did not ignore the doctrine of the atonement and so also the existence of sin.[32] In respect to the view of progress the Christian Socialists linked to Christ's incarnation, Gore insisted that the incarnation not be understood as the crown of natural or historical development. There may be or may not be progress in both nature and history, but Christ does not arise as the result of natural progression. He is born into history from above. He does not arise out of it from below. According to Gore, if one takes this second view, the Old Testament becomes irrelevant and redemption is reduced to an aspect of historical progress. Further, if one takes this view, divine love is equated with human love and divine judgment is jettisoned as an archaic, even barbarous notion. In giving priority to the doctrine of the incarnation, Gore did not deny the intractable, pervasive nature of sin and so also the need for an atoning sacrifice.

---

32. Carpenter, *Gore*, 149–89.

He insisted that, in discussing the incarnation, one give attention to the redemptive work of Christ.

With this shift in emphasis Gore not only develops the Christian Socialists' doctrine of the incarnation but also corrects it. As Carpenter points out, Gore does so under three headings—Christ as example, Christ as sacrifice, and Christ as new life.[33] As example, Christ calls his followers to obedience through a life of love directed to one's neighbor regardless of status or moral rectitude. Such obedience requires sacrifice that imitates that of Christ. The imitation of Christ's sacrifice, however, cannot be completely moralized. Christ's sacrifice is a victory over the power of sin both in each person and in the world. It is also offered in expiation for the sinful condition and sinful actions of humankind. By living a life of sacrifice born of love for one's neighbor, Christians not only act morally, they are also joined to Christ's once-given and all-sufficient sacrifice. In this way sacrifice takes on more than a moral meaning. It becomes an aspect of redemption.

It is the case that Christ's sacrifice puts everyone on a new foundation with God, and for Gore this new foundation, through the Holy Spirit, is life-giving. Thus, the example of Christ and the sacrifice of Christ are internalized in the life of believers through the action of the Holy Spirit. Redemption moves inward to a new life built upon a different foundation. The example of Christ and the sacrifice of Christ within the life of the believer manifest true righteousness, and this righteousness is manifest in an exemplary way in the common life of the church. It is also reflective of the nature of God's own life. This life is a communion of persons in a life of fellowship. So the imitation of Christ through example, sacrifice, and new life imitates the life of God and gives form to a community shaped by obedience and service.

With this account of the incarnation, Gore moves beyond the tradition that shaped him. To his mind, the Church of England could not rise to the challenges presented by the Industrial Revolution save by becoming an exemplary community. The Tractarians, whose view of the importance of the church he shared, had a static view that saw the church as a conveyer of divine truth and grace. Gore saw the church as a living organism that in its common life continues the life of Christ on Earth. He saw the church in a very real sense as the "extension of the Incarnation."[34]

33. Carpenter, *Gore*, 189.

34. For Gore's view of the church as the extension of the incarnation, see Carpenter, *Gore*, 222–43.

By this phrase he did not mean to imply that the life of Christ is united to that of the church as the Logos is related to the life of Jesus of Nazareth, without separation and without confusion. He meant only that the life of Christ is present in the lives of believers as they now exist—that is, as the crucified, risen, and ascended Lord who is now present in the lives of believers through the Spirit. This new life is mediated particularly through the presence of the Spirit and so of Christ in the life of the church.

The presence of Christ through the Spirit in the life of the church is of moral as well as soteriological significance. Properly understood, the doctrine of the incarnation allows for no separation between theology and ethics. Everything given the church through the Spirit has not only a soteriological but also a moral and social meaning. Gore believed, nonetheless, that the chief missionary witness of the church is its moral earnestness—an earnestness that generates social righteousness and so fellowship based on fellowship with God. Because the Christ has come in the flesh, he has fully entered into human life. For this reason, both Westcott and Gore insisted that Christians are duty bound to be concerned with all aspects of human life. Nevertheless, unlike Maurice and Westcott, Gore does not go so far as to say that the brotherhood of all humankind is a present reality that has only to be recognized. He only insists that because of the incarnation all Christians are duty bound to show concern for human life in all its variety of nature and circumstance.

Further, unlike Maurice, Gore sees God at work in the process of history to bring about beneficial changes in social organization. Unlike many Christian Socialists, he thought that government has an obligation to bring about beneficial social change. As an example, he wanted property laws changed so that property might serve not individual wealth but the development of character and the promotion of a good life for all people. These developments are to his mind always a morally mixed bag, but they do not fail to show progress. So unlike Maurice, he welcomed the appearance of democracy as a boon to the status of brotherhood and the development of personality. These developments must, he thought, be associated with the sort of equality rooted in the universality of God's love expressed in the incarnation; yet the equality he supported did not require that everyone get the same thing. Rather, it required that everyone have access to what is necessary for human freedom and the development of personality. Accordingly, he believed that socialism was a movement going in the right direction but that it contained dangers that only ideals rooted in the life of Christ could hold in check. Yet, with his fellow Christian Socialists, he believed firmly that the church ought never to support state socialism. Such a centralization of wealth and power most certainly would lead to disaster. In this respect, he also believed firmly that the incarnation makes clear the priority of communal claims over individual ones. In spite of all his nods to historical development Gore was no utopian. He vigorously opposed the cult of progress then pervasive in Christian Socialist circles. To his mind, even Scott Holland had fallen victim to this naïve view of human history. Gore looked out at his world in a different way. He did not see progress but a society under the judgment of God because of its love of wealth and power.

Part Two

The Incarnation:
How Firm a Foundation?

A. Social Ethics

WHEN BROUGHT INTO RELATION with the present circumstances of the churches in North America this all too brief account of the theological charter to which the Christian Socialists linked their social concerns is by virtue of its sheer difference arresting. A voice speaking of cooperation rather than competition, of brotherhood rather than warring tribes, cannot help getting a reaction from us. The question is whether or not the foundation they have laid by means of the doctrine of the incarnation provides an adequate platform for the sort of social ethic and account of the social mission of the church they championed. Indeed, the theological charter they provided for these goods, both social and ecclesial, has left us with four questions. First, is their account of the incarnation sufficiently robust to support, on its own, an adequate foundation for the social responsibilities of the churches? Second, how credible is their account of the common life and social mission of the church? Third, how adequate is their depiction of the ideals that define their social vision? Fourth, have they shown that ideals are of any real use in making concrete choices about the common good of either church or society? These four questions provide a starting point for an evaluation of the continuing relevance and so promise of this tradition. We shall address the first of the four in the remainder of this section of Part Two.

Is the doctrine of the incarnation as presented by the Christian Socialists a sufficiently firm foundation upon which to rest their account of the mission of the churches and the nature of their common life? It must be said, as previously noted, that all too frequently reference to the doctrine was made without much discussion of its content. For example, R. H. Tawney is content to reference the incarnation as a divine act that shows God's concern for the whole of human life, not only the state of the soul but also the state of social relations.[35] The implication of this citation is that because God's love revealed in Christ encompasses all humankind, it is the duty of all those who follow Christ to show that love to all people—rich or poor, kin or stranger, friend or foe. The Christian Socialists believed that the love of God shown to all people creates a fundamental equality within the entire human race. It is this kinship and fundamental equality that inscribes the boundaries and character of the love Christians owe their fellow human beings. In this respect, it should be noted that in no way did the Christian Socialists separate God's love shown in the incarnation from the fact that God has created all people and all things. By linking creation through the Logos to love for all shown in the incarnation of the Son, the Christian Socialists guarded fundamental human equality in a way that reference to creation alone might well not. One can imagine, and indeed many have imagined, that God did not create all people as equal. Throughout history many Christians have believed that some are created higher and others lower in the divine scheme of things. This belief provided moral cover throughout the Christian world for those who owned slaves and supported the institution.[36] By pointing to Christ's death on behalf of all people and his establishment of his kingdom for all people, the Christian Socialists sought to bar the way for such distinctions. To their minds, God, through the incarnation, has established a universal rule over the human community, whose members share God's image and are equally recipients of God's love.

Without question the first thing that must be said about the adequacy of the Christian Socialists' account of Christ's incarnation is that it lays down as a primary aspect of any social ethic the conviction that all people share a fundamental equality. However, unlike present accounts of equality, the one offered by the Christian Socialists does not rest upon some capacity inherent in human nature—reason, say, or autonomy. Rather, to their minds, human equality rests upon the belief that all human life is sacred because each and every life has sacredness bestowed upon it by the creative and redemptive love of God. Thus, in the eyes of the Christian Socialists, human dignity (a term they do on occasion use) is tied, as it is in the present day, not to human capacity but to the status of each individual in the eyes of God. This single point, if grasped, would change

---

35. See, e.g., Goldman, *Life of R. H. Tawney*, locs. 4066–4122 of 11074, Kindle.
36. See, e.g., Ruston, *Human Rights and the Image of God*, 65–98.

the ways in which present-day Christians address a number of social issues—from abortion to care of the dying.

The Christian Socialists' account of the import of the incarnation of Christ is worth considering for this reason alone. Nevertheless, for Tawney (and many others), the doctrine of the incarnation does not receive much critical attention. It simply hovers in the background of what they say as a general assumption. It was Bishop Westcott who gave a more robust account of its content and its relevance. In doing so, he provided an account that set the tone and content of much that the Christian Socialists had to say. Along with Maurice, he can be considered their representative theologian.

According to Westcott, God's love manifest in Christ extends to all people and, as a result, as F. D. Maurice proclaimed, all people are united in Christ. It should be noted that neither Bishop Gore nor Bishop Temple was willing to say that all people are in Christ whether they know it or not. Nevertheless, all Christian Socialists believed that the entire human race now exists within the love of God and the governance of Christ. This is so not simply because God loves all people. It is true also because Christ is not just *a man*. In Christ the Word became not *a man* but *flesh*. Westcott takes this to mean that Christ is the representative of all people. He carries in his human nature all people and so gathers them together into his life. In this way all people exist within the circumference of God's love and governance and so are called into fellowship with one another. As their representative and as God fully present in his life, Christ manifests the fact that all people have been created by the Word of God and that humankind has the same destiny as Jesus the Christ, namely, to live eternally in the Spirit in relation one to another and to God who is Father of all.

So it is that in the eyes of Westcott and many other Christian Socialists, humankind not only enjoys a fundamental equality before God; they are also called to a communal identity as children of God. The incarnation thus establishes not only equality but also fellowship as the primary markers of the life and destiny of human beings. In answer to the question, "Who are we?" the Christian Socialists said we are equally children of God destined to live in fellowship with God and with one another. Equality and fellowship, then, provide the foundation stones of the edifice the Christian Socialists sought to build.

These are noble ideals, but left to themselves they easily provide a justification for a form of Christian humanism that naively affirms both the goodness of human life in its various social expressions and its progression toward the kingdom of God on earth. For example, Maurice and his followers have had a pervasive influence on the more liberal expressions of Anglicanism. This focus on the restorative power of love, almost to the exclusion of the atoning sacrifice of Christ and the ongoing battle with sin, without question has produced within the Christian Socialist tradition an unbalanced account of both the person and the work of Christ, and it has most certainly led to a naïve and overly optimistic view of historical progress.

On occasion this optimism reached absurd proportions. Paul Avis has provided a jarring account of the extent of this naïve optimism in the thought and writings of Bishop Westcott.[37] Westcott preached frequently on the merits of self-discipline and sacrifice and seems to have believed that if people were self-restrained, content with their lot, and prepared to work hard and sacrifice for their fellows, then the world would become a better and better place. He believed also that the Church of England was progressive in nature and that the British Empire was divinely ordained with a vocation to shoulder "the white man's burden" and to carry on with its imperialistic expansion as a means of bringing about the fellowship of the peoples of the earth, in which each of these peoples would realize their special character. So he held that imperialism was the embodiment of the Christian Socialists' ideals of association and service; empire belonged to the destiny of the English people. In his view the great nations were not rivals but fellow workers. He believed that the British Empire would be spared the rhythm of rise and fall, that it would endure indefinitely because its foundation was benevolence. He even went so far as to say that progress is a law of life and creation. This brand of optimism is extreme but in more modest versions it ran through Christian Socialist thought until the time of William Temple, who, in his latter years, moved toward the theological center by seeking a more adequate balance between Christ's battle with the sin of the world and the power of his love to change the world.

That said, had more heed been given to what Westcott in fact did say about the incarnation, the account the Christian Socialists gave of the incarnation and its import might have provided a more adequate base for the social ethic they proposed. Westcott's presentation of Christ's incarnation in fact enfolds the entire life of humankind within a Trinitarian

---

37. Avis, "Anglican Social Thought Encounters Modernity," in Spencer, *Theology Reforming Society*, loc. 1104 of 3130, Kindle.

account of divine and human existence. Thus Christ, the Word of God, is the one through whom and for whom the world was created. Christ, the Word made flesh, is the one through whom we come to understand the nature of God. Christ, the crucified, risen, and ascended Son of the Father, is the one who brings reconciliation between God and humankind and human destiny to completion. Christ, who lives in the Spirit of his Father, gives us the same Spirit through whose agency we are conformed to the image of God's Son so as to fulfill God's eternal purpose for us.

What has been written above is in no way an adequate summary of all that Bishop Westcott had to say about the incarnation. However, enough has been said to suggest not only the limitations but also the possibilities of his account. It is inclusive of much of what Christians have to say. It refers back to our creation through the Word. It refers to God's self-revelation in the life, death, resurrection, and ascension of his Son. It refers to Christ's gift to us of God's Spirit in whose power our lives are conformed to the image of his Son. It refers to the final destiny that God has assigned us—namely, eternal life with God the Father through our unity in the Spirit with the Son, who intercedes for us with the Father.

Westcott's account of the incarnation says a lot. Nevertheless, it leaves out a lot as well. It does not say much about what the cross reveals about human beings' defection from their created status or about the depth of human sin. It does not say much about the way in which sin misshapes the cultures and institutions that form the contours of our lives. It does not say much about the way in which Christ's sacrificial death defeats the powers of evil and reconciles human beings to God and one another. It does not say much about what is left of God's creative ordering of the world after it has been distorted by humankind's fall from grace. It ignores God's judgment and Christ's final defeat of evil. Finally, it does not give an adequate account of the relation between creation and fall and the redemptive power of the cross and resurrection, or of what Christian beliefs have to say about last things.

In summary, the theology of the incarnation as propounded by the Christian Socialists said a lot—but by no means enough. Nevertheless, its deficiencies serve to remind subsequent generations that an adequate account of Christian social ethics cannot hang on any single Christian doctrine, even one as central as the incarnation. The Christian Socialists' theology of the incarnation certainly gave a robust account of the breadth and depth of God's love for the world. Nevertheless, an adequate account of Christian social ethics requires deployment not of one but of all the major topics of Christian theology—from creation through the fall, through the election of Israel, through the person and work of Christ, through the presence of God's Spirit in the common life of the church, through the present time of waiting on God, to the end time and God's final victory and the renewal of creation. Omission of the moral implications of any of these topics results in an inadequate account of Christian living.

These imbalances and distortions of Christian theology were most certainly connected with an overemphasis on the power of love to rid the world of its entrenched evils. To be sure, the First World War and the subsequent attack on the optimism of liberal Protestantism by Karl Barth and Reinhold Niebuhr reminded William Temple of this fact. Nevertheless, an undue optimism about the progressive powers of love lay deep within the hearts of the Christian Socialists and indeed remains with Anglican churches to this day.

With these comments in mind, what is to be said in response to our first question—is the Christian Socialists' account of the doctrine of the incarnation sufficiently robust to provide a theological charter for the social teaching of the church? After some reflection, one is bound to conclude that because of its heavy reliance on a single topic of Christian theology, it is not. Nevertheless, had the more expansive framework provided by Bishop Westcott been used and developed more widely so as to include the relevance of other topics of Christian doctrine, the Christian Socialists might have arrived at a theological charter for their social ethic that would have proved more enduring and more powerful. First, had the doctrine of the incarnation been linked more explicitly and in greater detail to God's creation of the world through the Word, the Christian Socialists, like the Roman Catholics, might have made more effective use of natural law as one pillar upon which to rest the social teaching of the churches. For a time, Bishop Temple moved in precisely this direction. He saw natural law as a means for the church to address an increasingly secular society in a form that might be convincing to those who did not share the faith of the Church of England.

Temple drew his chief example of the importance of natural law from that sphere of social life that was of greatest concern to the Christian Socialists—the capitalist system and the conflicts and inequalities that accompany it. He pointed out that within a capitalist economy natural law might provide the framework within which to determine how the tensions, endemic to capitalism, between love and justice, producer and consumer, haves and have-nots, are to be resolved. If one believes in a natural order, that is to say, an order that expresses the will of the Creator, then one will, he believed, recognize that by the law of our nature producers and consumers have duties and rights in respect one to another. That is, natural law teaches that the economic process is not an end in itself. Rather, it serves an end beyond itself. It exists as a means to enhance the life of humankind.[38] Thus Temple argues that the economic system is not by divine intent meant to serve itself alone. It certainly does not exist to enhance the wealth and power of a few. Rather, it exists to enhance the common life of human society as a whole. If this end is to be served, then producers of the products necessary for social wellbeing are due compensation for what they produce. Nevertheless, if the system, though efficient, "creates or intensifies divisions and hostilities between men, that system is condemned, not on economic but on moral grounds; not because it fails to deliver the goods, but because it is a source of wrong personal relationships."[39] He concludes with what he calls a "general position." He writes, "For economic production there *must* be profits, there *ought* to be regard for the consumer's interest, and it is wrong to sacrifice that interest to the increase of profits above a reasonable figure."[40]

Temple's account of the incarnation and its linkage to natural law is capable of doing more than most Christian Socialists allowed. It makes clear, as all forms of Christian Socialism professed, that God's love for humankind creates a baseline of equality shared by all human beings. However, it encompasses as well the fact that God, in his creation, laid down the laws of human flourishing. In this respect, it shows that God's concern for human wellbeing extends to the institutions that give form to their common life. Further, it takes account of the harmful effects of sin upon those laws and those institutions.

That said, under the influence of Reinhold Niebuhr, Temple moved away from his interest in natural law. He began instead to speak more frequently of principles coherent with Christian belief but meaningful to a secular audience. His reference point became Christian principles rather than natural law, but his goal remained the same, namely, to find a way for the church to address a more secular nation in a language that provides moral guidance but is at the same time "understandable to the

---

38. Temple, "Christianity and Social Order," 81.
39. Temple, "Christianity and Social Order," 79.
40. Temple, "Christianity and Social Order," 81.

people." His meeting with Niebuhr sobered his optimism about the ability of natural law to provide a way for the church to speak to the English people as a whole. Still and all, his idealism continued. Along with a number of other Christian Socialists, he continued to believe in and work toward a "return of Christendom." Granted, in doing so he placed restraints on his hopes. He came to see that the presence of sin renders both love and justice partial and often distorted in their expression. Nevertheless, these restraints upon the moral possibilities within history left a question. If, in a fallen world, love and justice exist in a never-ending tension, how is one to get the balance between them right? The question Temple asked remains with the churches to this day.

Thus, if the incarnation points forward, as he believed, to the fulfillment of God's purposes for the world, so also it points backward toward creation, toward God's original purposes and so to natural law. This law, though imperfectly grasped, is not utterly hidden. Indeed, the incarnation of the Logos through whom the worlds were created shines a light on the moral structure of the created order. It also shines a light on the future. It points to the future God intends and awakens hope in that future. In respect to both creation and redemption, the Christian Socialists' focus was on the positive implications of the incarnation. This focus on incarnation and so on God's love rather than Christ's atoning sacrifice led them to develop and defend an account of the social mission for the churches. Nevertheless, it also led them to overestimate the possibility of social advance and to underestimate the continuing power of sin within human affairs. It is well established that the Christian Socialists, in responding to an overemphasis on the fall on the part of Evangelicals, shifted the focus of their theology from atonement to incarnation and so also to moral advance. To be sure, as a general rule, the Christian Socialists, in their profound desire to introduce moral considerations into the discussion of political economy, paid insufficient attention to the way in which sin limits what can be said or done to remedy injustice. This sort of moral optimism also led them to flirt with the idea that if the moral state of humankind became coherent with the life and teaching of Jesus, then we could approach the kingdom of God within history by progression.

For them, the key to bringing about this happy confluence was to be found in education. It is fair to say, I believe, that idealism, when confronted with the uphill climb that always faces idealists, turns first to education rather than conversion as a means of joining ideal with real situations on the ground. So, for example, Bishop Westcott, in an address to teachers, expressed his optimism in this way: "Meanwhile, our office as Christian teachers is to proclaim the *ideal* of the Gospel and to form opinion. And if we do this, if we confess that our mission is to hasten a kingdom of God on earth, and if we ourselves move resolutely forward as the Spirit guides us, I believe we shall find through the common offices of our daily intercourse that peace which springs out of the consciousness of common sacrifice made for one end, and that assurance of strength which comes through new victories of faith." He then goes on to say, "The proof of Christianity which is prepared by God, as I believe, for our times, is a Christian society filled with one spirit in two forms—righteousness and love."[41]

This is indeed optimism on steroids, and the same virulent strain appears in an address to workers Westcott gave in 1891: "Our *work* is social, and therefore it must be organized: we are called upon to prepare and hasten the kingdom."[42] That preparation, he thought, would come in a very intellectual way—through the expression of an ideal. So, in 1900, in an address to the Christian Social Union, he said, "Progress is an advance towards an *ideal*. If we wish to estimate human progress we must fix the human ideal."[43] The ideal toward which the incarnation draws all people is the kingdom of God. Bishop Westcott's statement of an advance toward an ideal suggests that through a morally sensitized populace, we might approach that ideal asymptotically. With this move he links the incarnation to Christian eschatology, but he does so in a way that does not do justice to the biblical witness about the course of human history. That witness does not suggest a steady advance but an ongoing conflict between the will of God and the rebellion of God's creation. The witness of Scripture does not suggest steady advance but a struggle that carries on and intensifies throughout the course of human history. In this struggle, manifestations of the kingdom of God appear but are always fragile, incomplete, mixed with the alloy of sin. They are, in fact, always contested by opposing forces. These manifestations of the kingdom of God will, nonetheless, be vindicated and brought to completion by a final appearance of Christ. On that day, Christ will judge our rebellion and establish the saints firmly within the life and victory of God.

---

41. Westcott, *Incarnation and Common Life*, loc. 2484 of 4679, Kindle; emphasis added.

42. Westcott, *Incarnation and Common Life*, loc. 4398 of 4679, Kindle; emphasis added.

43. Westcott, *Life and Letters of Brooke Foss Westcott*, 2:327; emphasis added.

In a paper contributed to the Malvern Conference of 1941, Donald MacKinnon made an even more powerful criticism of the Christian Socialists' rendition of the doctrine of the incarnation than the one just mentioned.[44] Though he does not say so directly, he rightly understands their doctrine to be highly moralistic. Moralistic interpretations of basic Christian doctrine, he says, lead the church to understand its social function to be in large measure moral—that its calling is to encourage people to fulfill their obligations to their station and its duties. What a moralistic interpretation does not do is to "inspire novel social aims proportionate to its estimate of man's nature and dignity, and to the character of the existing situation."[45] Neither does it present the central significance of Christ's sacrifice, which is religious before it is moral.

MacKinnon suggests, as an alternative to the incarnation as a moral engine of progress, a religious rather than a moral interpretation of the doctrine. A religious interpretation begins not with Christ as a moral example or with Christ as the manifestation of God's loving interest in all aspects of human life, but with Christ as the savior of the world. Here MacKinnon moves toward the Evangelicals. He insists that Christ's incarnation can only be understood in the light of salvation, and that salvation can be rightly understood only in relation to the theological notion of sin. Sin, as a theological notion, is not the same as evil. Sin is a religious condition in which human beings have freely and openly turned their backs on God's grace. In their natural state they are created out of nothing. Their existence is one of suspension above an abyss of nothingness. Yet, in their natural state, they are upheld by grace. When God's grace is freely rejected human beings become "denatured." That is, in contradistinction to their true nature, they now have nothing between them and a fathomless abyss. Their reaction is to make a world for themselves—one that holds out a false promise of secure existence—one that represents a "synthesis" of human knowledge and practice. The problem is that "we can only hope to achieve a theoretically satisfying 'synthesis' if the limits of our understanding are coterminous with the limits of reality, if the world is our oyster."[46] If, however, we believe in God the Creator whose

---

44. See MacKinnon, "Revelation and Social Justice," in *Malvern 1941*, 81–116.
45. MacKinnon, "Revelation and Social Justice," 88.
46. MacKinnon, "Revelation and Social Justice," 92.

grace sustains us over the abyss of our origin, then this attempt to create a firm foundation for our lives becomes "the act of a Titan."[47]

Sin is, therefore, first and foremost "Titanism." It can only be overcome by one who becomes incarnate yet does not reject the grace of God that upholds him over the abyss. Christ strips our security away and shows us the abyss we so desperately seek to escape. He gives up the protections of the false platform we have built. He is despised, rejected, and crucified. As MacKinnon writes, "He passes ineluctably to nothingness, and therein is his Father glorified." On this point, MacKinnon agrees with Karl Barth, who said in essence, "There is no human possibility of which he did not rid himself and therein is he recognized as the Christ."[48] He returned humankind to its natural state as finite beings suspended over the abyss of their origin but upheld by the grace of God. In this way he opened the way whereby humankind returns to God. To be a Christian is, therefore, to join oneself in faith to Christ who, on our behalf, stood over the abyss, held up only by the grace of God.

The conclusion MacKinnon draws from this presentation of the saving action of Christ is not that we now have a platform on which to stand. In MacKinnon's words we do not have a "synthesis" we can rely on. Indeed, Christ shows us the inability of our self-created culture to protect us from the abyss of our origin. Nevertheless, in showing us the impossibility of our efforts at self-salvation, Christ makes this knowledge tolerable and he turns it into a principle of action. Our circumstances are tolerable because, despite the abyss, we know ourselves upheld by God's grace. This belief becomes a principle of action as a form of social criticism that refuses to identify any cultural achievement with the work of Christ. In MacKinnon's words, "It is his grace, and his alone, that permits the Christian social critic continually to discuss and continually to criticize."[49]

This permission grants freedom to each believer to be fully involved in her society, but always with a reservation. No matter what she accomplishes that accomplishment is part of what is passing away; and whatever may be accomplished cannot escape the Titanism to which humankind is addicted. MacKinnon insists that this stance in the world is not a retreat into pietism. It allows for full participation in the life of

---

47. MacKinnon, "Revelation and Social Justice," 92.
48. MacKinnon, "Revelation and Social Justice," 97.
49. MacKinnon, "Revelation and Social Justice," 97.

society, but always with a reservation. The social arrangements we have made to protect ourselves from the abyss provide what we need to sustain our lives from day to day, but, as W. H. Auden wrote, God allows these arrangements only for "the time being."[50] What they do not represent is a step toward building the kingdom of God on earth and within history. To frame the mission of the church in these terms is to fall victim to the same Titanism that ended in the crucifixion of the incarnate Lord.

In summary, it is fair to say that the link drawn by the Christian Socialists between the incarnation, on the one hand, and the day-to-day life of Christians, on the other, provides a powerful defense of the social ideals of equality and social fellowship. Nonetheless, it fails to take sufficient account of the power of human rebellion against God and his purposes, and it overmoralizes the person and work of Christ. Nonetheless, in the positive ledger, the view of the incarnation they supported has strong links with eschatology. As such, it could, if related more directly to Christ's crucifixion and Second Advent, decrease trust in human advance and increase trust in God's final victory over the forces that oppose him. Whatever their failings might have been the fact remains that the Christian Socialists' rather blanket use of the doctrine of the incarnation turned their focus to God's care for and entry into human affairs. It does not, however, speak with sufficient force of the Son as the Logos of God through whom the worlds were created. It says little, if anything at all, of the saving act of Christ as an act that can "inspire novel social aims proportionate to its estimate of man's nature and dignity, and to the character of the existing situation." It does not give adequate expression to the nature of Christ's atoning life and death. It does not speak forcefully of the fact that Christ will come to be a judge to whom we render an account of our lives and our feverish attempts at self-salvation by means of our economic and political systems. It does not speak much of the final victory of God over his enemies. Rather, it speaks rather blandly of moral advance.

That said, the incarnation, as presented by the most thoughtful members of the movement, suggests possibilities for robustness that exceed their original efforts. The Christian Socialists found a way through the incarnation to establish a basic equality among all people. Likewise they found a way to defend fellowship as a social ideal and to speak of how people ought to live one with another as the struggles of history

---

50. Auden, "For the Time Being: A Christmas Oratorio," in Auden, *Collected Poems*, 347–400.

unfold. They found a way through the incarnation to speak of a final destiny for the world and all its people. These are not small theological accomplishments, but they carry with them the weakness of any foundation for Christian social ethics that seeks its base in a single doctrine. A focus on atonement, the incarnation, creation, or judgment alone is in itself insufficient. To be adequate, the foundation of a Christian social ethic must be tied to all aspects of a complete Christology—God's creation through the Word, God's preparation for the incarnation of the Word through the calling of Israel to be his people, the life and ministry of Jesus, the Word made flesh, the crucifixion of the Word made flesh, the resurrection of the Word made flesh, the ascension of the Word made flesh, Christ's gift of the Holy Spirit to his people, and the final victory of Christ the King. Omission of any of these aspects of the person and work of Christ will inevitably produce an inadequate account of the mission of God's people in the world.

B. The Role of the Church in Society

DESPITE THEIR INCOMPLETE AND sometimes distorted nature, the theological accomplishments of the Christian Socialists were not inconsiderable. Nevertheless, they left a central question unanswered—the credibility of their account of the social mission of the church. The doctrine of the incarnation provided a foundation for a rich, though incomplete and often flawed, Christian social ethic. The problem was how this perspective was to be awakened or reawakened in the British people. It is this problem that brings to the fore the second question—one that serves as a means of assessing the relevance and promise of this tradition to the present circumstances of the churches. The doctrine of the incarnation gave further credence to the belief of the Church of England that its mission was to provide a religious and moral base for the common life of the English people. Accordingly, the Christian Socialists sought to call the nation back to an ideal, a moral vision that would change the way in which the various classes of British society viewed the world and lived one with another. In this way its exponents hoped not only to remedy morally unacceptable social conditions but also to counter what they perceived to be the claim of the advocates of political economy—that moral considerations, whether backed by the church or not, have no place in regulating markets.

This view of the calling of the Church of England was from the start hardwired into Christian Socialist thought and action. It was further a view accompanied by another, namely, that a clear distinction was to be made between the calling of the church and that of the government. Again, to use Bishop Westcott as an example, in his inaugural address to the Diocese of Durham, he clarified what was to be the role of government: In the "steady amelioration of life," both the church and the state have their "proper work." The state, the "temporal power," has a moral end; the true ruler works "to secure conditions of labor . . . favorable to the development of a noble character; to provide that all classes alike shall share in the fullness of the one life; to enforce by the sanction of law that which has been clearly proved to be for the common good; to organize protection for the weak; to aim at the well-being . . . of every citizen."[1]

Westcott describes the mission of the church in this way: as the "spiritual power," the church is to keep present to all the *ideal* that has been committed to its keeping. It is to enforce the social destiny of all conduct and all endowments, "of material wealth and intellectual power and personal influence," and to witness to "the larger fellowship by which class is bound to class and nation to nation." He concluded that the church is "to maintain and to vindicate the reality of 'the powers of the age to come.'"[2] He summarized his position thus: "It is, in a word, the office of the State to give effect to public opinion; it is the office of the Church to shape it. The Church educates and inspires society, which moulds the State."[3] In another place he refers to the church as "the spiritual organ of the nation."[4] He went on to say that it is the duty of the church to face social evils.[5] It is also the duty of the church to deploy the resources of faith to discipline the powers of capitalism.[6]

On the surface, this position has much to recommend it, not only in England but also throughout the churches of the world. Nevertheless, one does not have to look far below the surface to encounter problems. To what extent does the moral mission of the church become incarnate in a nation? Or again, to what extent do the citizens of the United Kingdom and the societies of the West indeed look to the churches to provide their ideals? In her comparison of Anglican and Roman Catholic social ethics, Anna Rowlands writes this: "We might note, then, that one of the remarkable features of the current situation is not the absence of an Anglican social tradition but rather a contemporary forgetfulness of the deeper roots of the Anglican social tradition, and if the sociologists of religion are to be believed, an increasing gap between the emphasis in

---

1. Westcott, *Incarnation and Common Life*, loc. 283 of 4679, Kindle.
2. Westcott, *Incarnation and Common Life*, loc. 283 of 4679, Kindle.
3. Westcott, *Incarnation and Common Life*, loc. 296 of 4679, Kindle.
4. Westcott, *Incarnation and Common Life*, loc. 322 of 4679, Kindle.
5. Westcott, *Incarnation and Common Life*, loc. 400 of 4679, Kindle.
6. Westcott, *Incarnation and Common Life*, loc. 336 of 4679, Kindle.

the church's public statements and the espoused beliefs on social matters held by its laity."[7]

It is now becoming obvious that neither English nor American society looks to the churches to serve, in respect to social issues, as an incarnate presence and/or moral tutor. A startling confirmation of the changed social location of the churches has been provided by recent polls. For example, it has been reported that the Pew poll finds that Americans are now more upset if their children marry a person of differing political persuasion than differing religious belief. Given the declining position of the Church of England in the life of the English people, it would not be surprising to encounter a similar climate of opinion there. Indeed, Malcolm Brown has provided a striking example of the extent to which, in the United Kingdom, church teaching has disappeared from the public mind. He writes, "I noted that the preliminaries to the introduction of the Marriage (Same Sex Couples) Act in 2010, whatever one's views of the morality of same-sex relationships, had demonstrated such ignorance and lack of interest about the church's perception of the social goods of marriage on the part of the then Coalition government, that we could no longer assume a fundamental basis of shared ethical perception that was even residually Christian."[8] To be sure, from the start, many Christian Socialists were fully aware of the changed social position of the Church of England, and many called for serious reform. As a key example of their doubts, Alan Wilkinson notes that as time passed William Temple himself came to see the world in which he lived as alien and shortly before his death predicted a post-Christian era.[9]

The change in social location of the Church of England, and indeed the churches of Western Europe and North America, raises several serious questions about the Christian Socialist view of the church's social mission and its dominant image of incarnation. Rowlands, noting that Roman Catholic social teaching has not been tied to national churches, has posed the first. She observes that Roman Catholic social teaching speaks not to particular nation-states but in more universal terms to all people of good will in all social and political circumstances. Roman Catholic social teaching does not give the same prominence to the nation-state as does Protestant social teaching. The question is whether or

---

7. See Rowlands, "Fraternal Traditions," 140.

8. Brown, "Anglican Social Theology," in Spencer, *Theology Reforming Society*, loc. 2248 of 3130, Kindle.

9. See Wilkinson, *Christian Socialism*, 117.

B. THE ROLE OF THE CHURCH IN SOCIETY

not a primary focus on the nation-state as the locus of the social teaching of the church does not both narrow the scope and distort the content of this teaching.[10] Is it indeed the calling of the church always to speak with a particular focus on the issues peculiar to each of the various nations of the world? Or is it the responsibility of the church to articulate a social teaching that can be applied locally but that, more broadly, applies to human society in all its variety?

The question Rowlands poses is one that the Protestant churches in America have ignored to their own peril. The Reformation settlements brought into being a number of established national churches. The nature of the times probably rendered these alliances between church and state inevitable. These local settlements no doubt brought many benefits to the churches and the nations involved, but they also brought about churches with a highly nationalist flavor. German Lutherans, English Anglicans, Swiss Calvinists, and Scots Presbyterians are branded by their national identities, and as a result are constantly tempted to be less than "catholic" in the vision they hold of their common life and their mission in the world. They are constantly tempted to speak to the nation in terms the populace can understand and accept rather than to speak to the peoples of the earth in more universal terms that apply to all people by virtue of the fact that they are human beings. It seems that in this attempt to become incarnate in the nation, the churches more often than not simply adapt themselves (without remainder) to their host culture.

As Rowlands notes, the Christian Socialists in England did not take the more universal route. Instead, their focus was on the British populace and their vision for the common life of the nation. They sought an answer to the question of what is to be done when a society (namely, the United Kingdom) that once might have looked to the church to provide its religious and moral foundations no longer asks for this sort of instruction and formation. Several responses were forthcoming. One was a turn to natural law as a medium of instruction acceptable across social divides. From Richard Hooker on, natural law played a major role in Anglican moral thought and teaching. It is, therefore, not surprising that at an early stage in his development (as previously noted), William Temple saw natural law as a way for the church to speak of the fundamentals of belief and morals in a language understandable to all people of good will. Nevertheless, as previously noted, as time went on he became more aware

---

10. Rowlands, "Fraternal Traditions," 133–74.

of the distorting power of sin and so also less certain about the ability of natural law either to be discerned or to provide a moral *lingua franca*.

This uncertainty led him to make a change of course. He began to speak of principles rather than natural law. These principles, derived from Holy Scripture, could be used by the citizenry in a rational process of dialectical reasoning that moves from moral principles to particular situations, and then back again from particulars to moral principles, and so on until individual citizens reach an informed moral conclusion about what course of action is right and good. To his mind, this way of tackling the problem of Christian moral vision works from the top down, from the moral teaching of the church to political debate among the citizenry and then back again to basic principles. It is hard to miss the fact that this mode of moral reasoning is thoroughly Platonic. Be that as it may, through this process, Temple believed, the Church of England could provide moral counsel to the citizenry without, at the same time, becoming an advocate in specifically Christian terms of particular measures.

Here it is well to note a development in what Christian Socialists had to say about the church's social responsibility. Maurice insisted that it was not the responsibility of the church to promote changes in social institutions. These had been provided by the grace of God and were to be tended and supported rather than reformed. So he maintained that it was the job of the church to cultivate a moral climate in the nation but not to reform its social and political institutions. Temple and later Christian Socialists were also reluctant to give the church *as an institution* a warrant to support particular measures. Their reason was not that social institutions were the product of providence but that the modification of social institutions was properly a matter of prudence and so a matter upon which reasonable Christian people might disagree. In promoting the morals that support a healthy society the church was not to invade the privacy reserved for individual judgment. The church is indeed duty bound to provide a moral vision and to denounce and struggle against evil, but it is not duty bound to invade the arena of particular judgments in respect to public policy over which Christians may reasonably disagree.

This vision of the social mission of the church is Platonic in nature in that it moves from a more to a less knowable moral source to an uncertain determination of a course of action. Other Christian Socialists sought to develop a Christian conscience within the English population that was based not in reasoned instruction from above but inductive learning from below. Many of the most notable of their number began not with reasoned discourse on the part of church officers and institutions but with a process of education offered by a well-educated elite to the working classes. Their hope was that these educational efforts would bring the populace once again into contact with the preexisting moral substratum of English society. Their focus was not on a process of moral reasoning but once again in good Platonic fashion on a process of moral education in the form of moral recall, particularly among the working classes. Believing in the power of education to shape society, they began classes and founded colleges for the education of working people. Their assumption was that basic Christian ideals still lay at a bedrock level among the English people, and that education would bring these ideals once more into the clear light of day. Education, to the minds of many Christian Socialists, was the way to bring about a "return of Christendom."

Time has proved this assumption false. The dream of many of their number of a "return to Christendom" was indeed a dream. Nevertheless, they continued to believe it possible, through education, to awaken a Christian vision within the populace. Such notables as Westcott and Tawney supported this view. In doing so they continued to operate within the legacy of F. D. Maurice. In a sense, they were "diggers" who wished to dig down to find the moral substructure upon which society rests. Once more, what they did not want was for the Church of England to become an active supporter of particular social legislation. Westcott, for example, argues that it is the job of the clergy to present to the public "the principles" of life in society derived from the incarnation. It is not, however, their responsibility to become advocates for particular measures. The latter, he held, is the job of the laity, whose task is to exercise practical wisdom in their various callings.[11] In accord with this view of the mission of the church he concludes, "It is not its office to discuss details or prescribe rules. These belong to men who have a practical knowledge of affairs."[12]

William Temple made the point in an even more pointed way. In *Christianity and the State* he states clearly that Christianity offers principles on the basis of which one may act regardless of circumstance, and it offers power to act on those principle. Nevertheless, he says, "the Church must never commit itself to any kind of political programme or unite itself to any political party. For programmes and parties are inevitably concerned not only with principles but with particular methods of

---

11. See, e.g., Westcott, *Incarnation and Common Life*, locs. 296, 481 of 4679, Kindle.
12. Westcott, *Incarnation and Common Life*, loc. 296 of 4679, Kindle.

applying principles to a given situation; and about this men of equally complete Christian loyalty may diametrically differ; for the question is partly, and sometimes wholly, one of expediency and judgment."[13]

He then goes on to make an observation that is particularly germane to the circumstances that now obtain in North America and Europe. He contends that if we apply "true principles, that is, apprehensions of ultimate verities concerning human conduct in all times," then we will tolerate differences of judgment and policy.[14] Now to this limitation on the scope of what today we call ecclesial pronouncements on policy issues Bishop Temple added two important qualifications. First, in warning against church teaching espousing particular policies, he did not discourage clergy and laity as individual Christians from expressing their views on these matters. They must make it clear, however, that they speak for themselves and not as official spokespersons for the church itself.[15] Second, he did not rule out the church through its offices and institutions pointing out areas in which society was in real need of reform. A prime example is his call for a reform of England's banking system. To this responsibility the Christian Socialists gave particular emphasis. They believed passionately in the duty of the church to speak against any and all appearances of evil within social and political relations. They believed that recognition of evil is a matter of spiritual discernment rather than prudential judgment, and as such its condemnation is a constitutive element of the identity of the church.

So it was that in search of a way for the Church of England to provide moral instruction to the nation some Christian Socialists focused on the teaching ministry of the church as an institution and others upon the provision of a general education. Bishop Charles Gore, however, pointed to a third way the church might provide a moral foundation for the nation. To his mind neither ecclesial instruction nor popular education would, on its own, do the trick. He believed that Christian values could not be revived apart from faithful examples on the part of individuals and intentional communities. Pursuant to this vision, he became one of the founders of a monastic community—the Community of the Resurrection. He was drawn, with undue optimism, to monasticism as an

---

13. Temple, *Christianity and the State*, 5.
14. Temple, *Christianity and the State*, 5.
15. Temple, *Religious Experience*, 10.

exemplary and historically successful form of life capable of influencing and shaping the life of an entire society.

Bishop Gore's move to an exemplary community (along with a similar move by John Ludlow) provides a third way for the church to address the moral foundation of the nation. It is a way that calls for the churches to take a step back from the world in order to build up orthodox belief, the practices of discipleship, and the strength of Christian communities. One way for the church to provide moral instruction in a secular society is to employ a form of apologetic discourse that might (but might not) be specifically Christian yet might nonetheless be convincing to the general public. Another is to provide educational opportunities, particularly to working people. A third way is to regroup and form a common life that is exemplary of the fundamental beliefs and practices of Christians. In one case Christian social teaching takes the form of an apologetic designed to appeal to the mind of a more secular culture. In another educational institutions are thought, through moral recall, to hold the key to a national moral revival. In yet another case exemplary communal living is seen as a historically validated and effective witness to an alien form of life. St. Benedict is a prime example of the third option. He did not win an argument. He did not seek to educate a peasant population. He provided an exemplary form of life that transformed European culture from top to bottom and from bottom to top.

This third way—the way of exemplary communal witness—is one that, in recent years, John Howard Yoder and Stanley Hauerwas have presented with both clarity and power. Books like Yoder's *Politics of Jesus* and Hauerwas's *Community of Character* have called the attention of many to the importance of community witness that stands in marked contrast to the forms of life that now comprise America's pluralistic culture. I have written a fairly long book presenting and defending this vision.[16] It is, however, a position that faces a severe challenge. In his response to Hugh Heclo's presentation of the relation between Christianity and democracy in America, Alan Wolfe states this challenge with particular force. He argues that American culture has in fact so subsumed Christian belief and practice that the two are now barely distinguishable. So he writes, "American culture, including secular culture, has so thoroughly shaped religion that, rather than constituting a danger to democracy, religion, in order to survive, has little choice but to adopt the trappings of modern

---

16. See Turner, *Christian Ethics and the Church.*

democratic cultural life. Subject to the dictate of the market in souls, it tempers its message to avoid turning off potential customers." Wolfe goes on to observe that religion and culture are indeed powerful forces that shape people's beliefs and actions. Nevertheless, he writes, "When the two conflict in America, religion yields more to culture than the other way around."[17] He worries, in contrast to many others, that in America the threat religious believers pose to secular, democratic culture does not stem from strong, sectarian beliefs and practices but from the fact that the religion they espouse is too weak and too lacking in content to make much of a difference.[18] Wolfe laments this descent into vacuity. Both he and Heclo note that there was a time in America when Christianity was "more intellectual, more demanding, more eloquent, more sin-focused." Then it produced "a certain kind of democratic citizen," the sort of virtuous citizens democracy requires, and in so doing offered what politics cannot.[19]

This observation prompts three remarks. First, it may be the case that the churches suffer from such a lack of integrity that they do not have the ability to make a communal witness other than one that sides with one trend or another in American culture. Second, this failure to abide in their own truth renders the churches no longer able to form citizens with the virtues that are necessary for a healthy democratic society. In a similar manner, the churches' loss of integrity apparently has rendered them incapable of forming an educated and exemplary elite that can provide social and political leadership. Third, it may be that the social mission of the churches in a modern secular democracy is not to be the moral tutor of the populace but to become a community capable of proclaiming the fragile character of all our social institutions and of forming men and women with the virtues and capabilities of leadership that empower others to be responsible actors in a society that is at the same time secular, democratic, and flawed. If this more modest vision of the social mission of the churches is indeed the present calling of the churches, the third way proposed by the Christian Socialists (barring their concern for the role of an established church) might have a lot to teach the present generation.

Wolfe and Heclo are certainly right to doubt the ability, at the moment, of the churches to provide their members with such ability and

17. Wolfe, "Whose Christianity? Whose Democracy?," 200.
18. Wolfe, "Whose Christianity? Whose Democracy?," 201.
19. Wolfe, "Whose Christianity? Whose Democracy?," 201.

such vision. They are certainly right to point out the devouring power of American culture that acts as a giant maw consuming all it comes in contact with. Nonetheless, their warnings cover hidden hopes held deep in their spirits. These dreams do not harbor a longing for the churches once more to become the moral tutor of a secular, pluralistic, democratic culture. Their dream is more modest. Their dream is that the churches will awake and follow a vision of their social mission that is like but not identical to the ones given to John Ludlow and Bishop Gore. That vision calls for the churches to take a step back from the world in order to become aware of the extent to which they have been compromised and to strengthen orthodox belief, the practices of discipleship, and Christian communities. This understanding of the social mission of the churches does not rest upon special social wisdom on the part of the churches. It relies on the exemplary character of its common life and the manifest virtue of its members. This way does not rest upon social position or expert knowledge, but it does provide society with what it most needs—not an established church but a community that provides society with a virtuous citizenry.

It may be that the churches so lack integrity that they are at present unable to escape the maw of American culture; but history shows that time and time again, against all odds, they have done just that. Indeed, there are hopeful signs even within the much-maligned millennial generation. Among their number small communities have begun to arise. These communities are forming around a question rather than a program. The question is not how we can restore a Christian culture. It is not how we can assure the adoption of progressive social legislation. It is this: Surrounded as we are with a culture based upon the desires of autonomous individuals, how can we become a community in which Christ is taking form?

This question is as relevant to present circumstances as it was to those in which the Christian Socialists found themselves. Both sets of circumstances are characterized by an atomized and highly competitive social order, an order in which social relations are breaking down and inequality is rending the social fabric. In both the churches find themselves at a loss as to how they are to make an effective response. The way out of their confusion is through addressing this question: How do we become a community in which Christ is taking form? I doubt very much that Bishop Gore's answer—a faithful monastic community—will do the trick on its own. The Community of the Resurrection still exists but it is languishing. Nonetheless, once more small intentional communities such as Chemin Neuf and The Community of St. Anselm hold exemplary promise as effective means of addressing this question.[20] The challenge is to transfer this vision of the communal character of Christian life into the life of congregations and parishes throughout the spectrum of Christian churches. It is only within localized, worshiping communities that this question of how to become a community in which Christ is taking form can provide an adequate and effective vision of the mission of the churches in the present age. It is only through the appearance of such worshiping communities, those seeking to be communities in which Christ is taking form, that the churches will find an adequate understanding of their calling in the present era. About this point, despite the social conservatism that accompanied it, Maurice was right. He insisted that neighborhoods and local congregations, not programs, had to assume responsibility for establishing a strong moral foundation for society.

A change of this magnitude assumes an enormous shift in social vision and moral commitment on the part of an entire population. Naïve as they might have been about the possibility for moral "advance" on the part of British society, they did know that they faced a daunting challenge. Public opinion had to change if their ideas were to gain social traction. To this end they followed four lines of action. First, they sought to change public opinion and gain social credibility, not through support of the labor movement but through a form of social experiment they termed "association." Second, they formed voluntary organizations open to clergy and laypeople with an interest in social issues. Third, they sought to raise public conscience through use of the media—in this case, through the only vehicles available at the time: the preached and the printed word. Fourth, they founded schools for the education of working-class people.

Under the influence of John Ludlow, who had experience of associations in France, a movement grew in Christian Socialist circles to found such organizations in England. The purpose of these associations was to encourage a new economic and social order that would abolish the distinction between capital and labor and at the same time eliminate the

---

20. Chemin Neuf is a Catholic community with an ecumenical vocation. It was formed from a charismatic prayer group in 1973. It now has two thousand permanent members in thirty countries and twelve thousand people serving in community missions. The Community of St. Anselm is a community, ecumenical in nature, under the patronage and direction of the archbishop of Canterbury. It abides by a rule of life and is open to people ages twenty to thirty-five. It consists of both residential and nonresidential members.

tradesman as the connecting link between producers and customers. The underlying purpose was to reconcile the interests of capital, producer, and consumer in a way that assured working people of the "whole fruits of their labor."[21] In 1850, as a means of encouraging these associations, Christian Socialists helped found the Working Tailors' Association. The aim of this association was to encourage noncompetitive joint work and shared profits. Later in the same year, the Christian Socialists formed the Society for Promoting Working Men's Associations. In 1852, John Ludlow sought to further such efforts by helping pass the Industrial and Provident Societies Act, which enabled the creation of cooperative societies in England.[22]

It is fair to say that these associations struggled and never proved to be very successful. More successful was the foundation of voluntary societies within the Church of England. The first was the Guild of St. Matthew (GSM), founded in 1877 by Stewart Headlam, a student of F. D. Maurice while at Cambridge and later the curate of St. Matthew's, Bethnal Green in London. Headlam's parish was in the midst of a very run-down section of the city, and there he sought to combine Christian Socialism with the sacramental theology of high Anglicanism. The aims of the guild were fourfold:

- to restore to the people the value which they give to the land;
- to bring about a better distribution of the wealth created by labor;
- to give the whole body of the people a voice in their own government; and
- to abolish false standards of worth and dignity.

Though the guild attracted great interest, its membership never exceeded four hundred. After a time, however, public interest waned and Hedlam dissolved the organization in 1909.[23]

Two Anglo-Catholic clergy at Oxford, Henry Scott Holland and Charles (later Bishop) Gore, in 1889 formed a more moderate group, the Christian Social Union (CSU). The goal of this group was to influence highly placed people within the Church of England, just as later the Fabians sought to influence highly placed people within the government.

21. Christiansen, *Christian Socialism*, 148–49, 155.
22. For a helpful summary of the practical efforts of the Christian Socialists, see Diniejko, "Christian Socialism in Victorian England."
23. Diniejko, "Christian Socialism in Victorian England."

Some claim that the leadership of the CSU was not socialist at all. It was, however, most certainly progressive. Following the lead of F. D Maurice, the CSU placed its emphasis on the moral and religious issues that lay beneath the surface of the social and economic issues of the day. Perhaps because of its more cautious stance, the CSU was more successful than its predecessor, the Guild of St. Matthew. At its height, CSU membership numbered three thousand, and it had no fewer than twenty-seven branches. Yet, it never attracted members of the working class, despite the fact that it sought to get their attention by beginning, in 1897, a sister organization known as the Christian Fellowship League. The CSU was most successful not in social advocacy but in establishing Christian missions in poor areas. Through these missions such notable persons as R. H. Tawney and William Temple were provided opportunity to encounter firsthand what life was like in the slums of England's cities. The most famous of these missions was Toynbee Hall.

Social experiments in association plus the formation of voluntary societies were the first two prongs of a fourfold attack. A third prong was the printed word, the dominant means of communication and persuasion of the time. John Ludlow and other members of the London Working Men's Associations founded a journal entitled *The Christian Socialist: A Journal of Association*.[24] In 1848 Maurice and Ludlow, along with Charles Kingsley, began to publish articles in a penny journal, *Politics for the People*. Here, for example, Maurice in the first issue argued that the virtues of liberty, fraternity, and equality, so basic to the French Revolution, are in fact basic elements of Christian teaching. This journal did not in fact reach a working-class audience and was closed down after seventeen years. Another effort was made in 1850 with the publication of *The Christian Socialist*. Ludlow was a chief contributor. The purpose of this journal was to promote a Christian version of socialist society, the chief characteristic of which was cooperation rather than competition in trade and industry. This effort was followed in 1889 by a series of pamphlets entitled *Tracts on Christian Socialism*. These pamphlets were aimed at both members of the working class and Anglican clergy. Their goal was to provide a manifesto for Christian Socialism. However, in no place do they advocate large-scale proposals for social reform. Their focus remained a moral reformation that would replace the rotten foundation of capitalist society.

24. Available on the Web and in electronic form in The University of Michigan Library.

A fourth and final prong of Christian Socialist attempts to give a renewed moral base to English society involved the foundation of educational institutions. In Little Ormond Yard, they opened a night school for working men and women. In 1848 Maurice began Queen's College, London. The college was the first school in England to offer higher education that allowed women to gain academic qualifications. In 1854 Maurice also opened the Working Men's College (WMC) in London. The WMC was the first college in England to offer evening classes. It was also the first to offer a liberal education to members of the working class. Its faculty included, among other notables, John Ruskin, Dante Gabriel Rossetti, and Thomas Henry Huxley. Its most popular classes were languages, grammar, math, law, politics and physical science. None other than John Ruskin began a drawing class.

It is difficult to assess the effectiveness of these efforts. It may be that serious social change does not occur apart from serious social crisis. My own view is that they helped prepare the way for changes that did occur after the two great wars that exposed the sickness of European society. Whatever the case may be, the mere mention of the importance of social ideals leaves a big question unanswered. If indeed it is not the mission of the churches to enter the political realm as advocates of particular policies, if they are no longer in a position to serve as moral tutors to society, and if they are to live a communal life that produces the virtues necessary for life in a democratic society, then just how, given these limitations, ought the churches to understand their role in relation to the economic, social, and political issues of the day? Though it was their position that the churches were not to become political agents or moral tutors of society at large, the Christian Socialists nonetheless believed it to be their responsibility as Christians both to give public witness to what they called a Christian Sociology (a view of the moral nature of life together in society) and to point out social evils whenever and wherever they exist. As we have seen, a Christian Sociology, like that advocated by the Christian Socialists, is comprised of the ideals that bind a populace together in the name of a common good. These ideals, when compromised, serve as well to expose social evils whenever and wherever they appear. Accordingly, it is not inaccurate to say that the present legacy of the Christian Socialists to the churches in this generation may well be a call to form exemplary communities whose common life bears witness to an alternative social vision.

It is now perhaps wise to pause for a moment and take stock of how things stand with our two initial questions. Enough has been said to establish that the theological focus of the Christian Socialists on the doctrine of the incarnation needs further development and qualification, but still, with expansion and correction, it can make a significant contribution to the development of a Christian social ethic. Enough has also been said to cast serious doubt on the Christian Socialists' devotion to the notion that, as established, the church is called to be the soul of a nation. This is not to say that it would be a bad thing for the church to be such a thing. It is only to say that neither in England nor in America do the churches any longer enjoy this sort of social charter. It is also true, however, that the Christian Socialists recognized that there was a problem and sought ways for the Church of England to become effectively what it was not in practice. Some emphasized general education, others ecclesial instruction. Still others emphasized provision of a living example of the ideals for which they stood. More recently, members of the Church of England have defended establishment by speaking of the church as a presence that, through its parish system, is coextensive with the boundaries of the nation. These proposals for the meaning of establishment, in the end, represent matters of emphasis only. The one rarely appears without mention of the other. No matter what the emphasis, however, all agree that the Church of England as an established institution is not to address the problem of the church's fading influence by espousing and fighting for particular measures. These are deemed matters for laypeople, guided by their own character and the social teaching of their church, to address from their various perspectives and in their various stations and callings.

This latter point will in all likelihood lead many to the conclusion that the tradition of Christian Socialism, as it developed in England, has little relevance to the political circumstances that now obtain in North America. I say this for the simple reason that the Protestant churches in North America, from the mid 1960s on, in lock step with the broader culture, have focused their political concern not on public debate and education but support for or opposition to particular policy proposals. This move to policy advocacy and institutional reform is exemplified both by the evangelical churches and the traditional "mainline" ones. The severe divisions that have accompanied the churches' move to political activism rather than teaching, example, and community formation on the surface lend weight to the insistence on the part of the English Christian Socialists that policy issues are matters of prudence—matters over which reasonable people might, as Christians, disagree.[25] These facts alone seem to validate the reluctance of the Christian Socialists to use the institutions of the church as instruments of policy advocacy. The root problem of the "politicization" of public speech and action on the part of the church as an institution is, however, not simply that good Christian people might have good reasons for disagreeing with the social pronouncements of their churches. It is not simply that in its policy advocacy it faults the conscience of fellow believers who are acting in good faith and in accord with their own conscience. The most severe difficulty posed by the church as policy advocate is that this stance invests temporary and imperfect social arrangements with eternal validity when they ought to be viewed as imperfect arrangements that exist as the best we can do for the time being.

In short, when the churches speak on public issues they are on firmer ground when they identify and denounce evil than when they seek a social program for the transformation of society. Second, too close a relation between religious belief and the political opinions of the day serves to compromise the integrity of religious belief itself. Hugh Heclo, in his study *Christianity and American Democracy*, reminds his readers that no less a figure than Alexis de Tocqueville warned the readers of *Democracy in America* to beware too close an association between the churches and the political issues of the day. Citing Tocqueville, Heclo writes, "Religion's sphere comprises the universal and permanent longings embedded in every human heart as it faces the ultimate questions of its own existence. Alliance with the fleeting powers-that-be in the world can only diminish this natural claim that religion has on human beings, turning it into something as fragile and changeable as those earthly powers. And in a democratic republic, those political powers are very changeable indeed. Religion with political power is not only prone to be intolerant, indolent, and unstable; it is prone not really to be religion."[26]

Now to return one last time to the first two of the four diagnostic questions directed to the tradition of Christian Socialism in England, we can say that the doctrine of the incarnation, with correction and expansion, does provide a promising starting point for a Christian social ethic. We can say also that the Christian Socialists' assumption that the mission of the church is to act as the moral tutor of society has, by the

---

25. For presentations of the problems of churches as churches supporting particular political measures, see Ramsey, *Who Speaks for the Church?*; Turner, "How the Church Might Teach," 137–59; and Turner, *Christian Ethics and the Church*, 254–56.

26. See Heclo, *Christianity and American Democracy*, 15.

changed social location of the churches, been rendered more problematic than most would allow. Nevertheless, we can say also that their attempt to express and resolve their doubts and uncertainties about the way the churches ought to address a secular society opens important lines of thought. We can say also that the hesitance of the English Christian Socialists for the Church of England to take sides in respect to particular policies is, at a minimum, a healthy warning about one of the primary ways in which attempts on the part of the churches to make a social witness can go awry. There remains, however, a third question. It seems uncontroversial to say that, no matter what the limitations may be on the social mission of the churches, they are called upon to teach and bear witness to those ideals that make for a godly society. Such a witness lies at the center of all that the Christian Socialists stood for. The question is how adequate and how applicable is their presentation of these ideals. That question is central to everything they said or did, and it is the question to which we now turn.

Part Three

Moral Ideals: Their Statement and Application

A. Statement

How adequate and applicable are the social ideals that the Christian Socialists articulated and in various ways promoted? The credibility of their movement depends in large measure upon the answer given to this question. Even a cursory review of Christian Socialist literature makes it plain that the inculcation of a set of ideals lay at the heart of their vision of the social mission of the church. The chief project of the Christian Socialists was, therefore, to articulate, defend, and spread abroad a set of moral ideals that were to provide an alternative to the competitive individualism they associated with political economy. As previously noted, political economy, as popularly understood, enshrined a view of the economic system that accompanied the Industrial Revolution and is alive to this day in, among others, the works of Ayn Rand. At present, what Milton Friedman termed "neoliberalism" has carried forward and enhanced the ideas of the *laissez-faire* capitalism associated with Adam Smith.

To this day many hold the view that production and consumption form an autonomous system that runs by laws internal to it—laws that allow no space for moral considerations. It was against this position that the Christian Socialists leveled their critical ire. They not only believed that common ideals are necessary for the fruitful operation of an economic and political system, they believed also that common ideals are necessary if a social order is to have an adequate moral base. In support of their position, the Christian Socialists addressed five questions that are even more appropriate today. First, how are the ideals held as necessary to be identified? Second, what are the ideals that serve to create a healthy society? Third, does idealism take into account the imperfections and downright evil to be found within any citizenry? Fourth, assuming that the requisite ideals for social flourishing can be identified and defended, how does one move from these ideals to particular social, economic, and political judgments? Fifth, how might these ideals actually serve to form the moral character of a citizenry? All these questions will, in due course, be addressed, but a brief comment at the outset on questions three and four will ease likely frustrations along the way.

In respect to question three, as noted, over the years defenders of political and social idealism have faced an oft-repeated accusation of irrelevance because they failed to take account of the degree to which the ineradicable presence of finitude and egotism renders political ideals impotent. Friend and foe alike have leveled precisely these criticisms at the defenders of political idealism. Even Bishop Gore, one of the most realistic of their number, failed to understand the difficulties that arise when moral principles are applied to the workings of industry.[1] It is fair to say that in their defense of cooperation over competition and in their promotion of social ideals over social realities, Christian Socialists often failed to understand the true complexity of social life, and they utterly failed to take account of the positive social effects of competition.

To find an example of these failures one need look no further than four of the chief social virtues Christian Socialists proposed as alternatives to the individualism and ruthless competition they perceived to be characteristic of their age. They held it to be a primary obligation of the Church of England to resist the "competitive individualism" characteristic of what R. H. Tawney called "the acquisitive society." At the center of the ideals they promoted as an alternative were the social virtues of "fellowship," "cooperation," "service," and "sacrifice." These ideals they presented as moral alternatives to the competition and social atomism they believed to be tearing apart the fabric of British society. The simple fact is that in proposing these other-regarding ideals they did fail to see that competition and individual striving often serve useful social purposes. They also failed to see that, given the pervasive and permanent presence of selfishness in human affairs, competition and social hostility are fixtures of social life that should not be ignored.

It is true that William Temple, probably the best known of those whose minds were in part shaped by Christian Socialist views, did come to accept Reinhold Niebuhr's point that in a fallen world provision of justice for one's neighbor is as close as one can come in social affairs to love of one's neighbor. It is also the case that in his later years Temple

---

1. See Carpenter, *Gore*, 255.

recognized the pervasiveness of competition and accordingly placed less emphasis on service as a guiding social virtue. Yet, despite the reservations with which he surrounded his ideals, he continued to hope for general acceptance of the social vision he thought implied by the incarnation of God in Christ. Even Temple, with all his doubts and uncertainties, until just before his death, hoped for the restoration of Christendom and so the triumph of Christian principles as guides for the social and political life of the British people. I mention this problem at the outset so that it will not be necessary to repeat the objection throughout.

It is also wise to mention at the outset the fourth question—the problem of applicability. How, if at all, do citizens move from ideals like fellowship and cooperation to particular judgments in, say, labor law or tax policy? This is an issue much discussed and debated by the Christian Socialists but never satisfactorily resolved. Their failure to find a resolution presents the most serious objection to their idealism. Indeed, failure to address the applicability of ideals to the problems of limited resources and limited altruism presents a most serious objection to any form of political idealism. It is simply the case that one cannot move from a basic premise like social fellowship to a moral conclusion like profit sharing apart from a process of moral reasoning that connects premise with conclusion. Failure to provide this connection in moral deliberation creates a direct connection between premise and conclusion. As a result the total context of fact and value involved in moral judgments is left vacant. Making a leap from an ideal to a particular moral or practical judgment produces a mind closed to reality. A leap from ideal premise to practical judgment always leaves open the possibility of the sort of fanaticism that is the besetting sin of idealists. Once again, it is best to get this worry on the table so that it does not lurk in one's mind in an obstructive manner.

Community, Love, and Equality

These criticisms of the idealism of the Christian Socialists leave defenders and critics alike with a simple question. Who has truth on their side? Does idealism in politics leave one with little but unsubstantiated opinion, or does it do real and necessary work within a political system? The best way to defend the relevance of the Christian Socialist project is to track carefully the normative view of life in society they proposed and defended while at the same time attempting to determine how well it holds up under scrutiny. As previously noted, the Christian Socialists held some ideals that we might classify as communitarian. These views provided the foundation for the "Christian Sociology" they hoped to articulate and defend. Indeed, the entire system of ideals they championed depends upon the primacy of the social nature and destiny of humankind. The communal foundation they proposed rested on two claims that they often ran together. The first is that the incarnation manifests God's love for all people. The universality of God's love establishes a fundamental and universal equality in that all people are of equal value in the eyes of God and so within his kingdom. The second claim is that human beings, created in the image of God, are therefore by nature social beings; and, because of their social nature, they share duties toward one another. These duties are reaffirmed and deepened by that fact that God has included all people within the circumference of his love.

Both claims can be found in the works of F. D. Maurice. Maurice's central belief was that in Christ God has shown his love for all people. He has come to us in a fully human life and so has sanctified all aspects of that life. It is also the case that through suffering Christ has established his kingdom among us. His kingdom includes all people and places them under his governance, whether they know it or not. The doctrine of the incarnation thus sets aside individualistic accounts of our life with God and one another and in their place proffers a more social one. This more social and divinely based account of human life and nature contains within it two beliefs—one based on the love of God and another on our created nature. With these beliefs in mind, Maurice notes, "We have often been obliged to ask ourselves, whether these distinct individual acts . . . must not depend at last upon some relation in which men stand to their fellows." This question leads him to another, namely, "whether we can take our start from individuals, and form a society out of them" and whether the existence of society is not implied by the existence of these individuals.[2]

This paragraph, abstracted from *The Kingdom of Christ*, rests upon a rather jumbled set of claims that require sorting out. One is based upon Maurice's understanding of redemption (rather than atonement) and another upon his understanding of Christ the Logos through whom all things are created. The claims that rest upon Maurice's understanding of Christ the Logos take a more central position when he talks about

---

2. Maurice, *Kingdom of Christ*, 139.

the orders of human society. Maurice sees family, school, and nation as aspects of a divine order that comes to full expression in a universal society, the church. Providence provides the peoples of the earth with many forms of this order, but they all serve to constitute their members as persons who, within these communal forms, realize their potential as human beings. More particularly, he asserts that within families the senses are disciplined and people escape domination by the world. In families, fraternity and equality are fostered and interdependence learned. In nations people learn to speak languages and so have the capacity to communicate one with another across social divides. Within nations they also live under law and so become personally responsible and loyal agents. Within the universal society of the church differences between nations and cultures can be reconciled. Thus, he concludes that it is best for church and nation to be in harmony.

For Maurice, family, nation, and church are divine provisions (that accord with human nature) within which the human project can be pursued.[3] He does not want to change this order. Rather, as noted, he sees himself as a "digger"—one who "digs down" under the differences so as to find the ground from which all forms of economy and politics grow.[4] This ground is a unity of love that mirrors the mutual love that binds into one the three persons of the Trinity. So he concludes that this order of family, school, nation, and church is sacramental in character. That is, it reflects and indeed participates in the divine order of the world and, in a sacramental manner, reflects the nature of God.

If we pause for a moment to reflect on Maurice's claims about the incarnation, its sacramental nature and the divinely established order of the world, then the content of his communal view of social life becomes plain. The first ideal of Christian Sociology is the unity of people in a community of love and their placement within divinely established order in the midst of which they can become fully developed personalities who live together peacefully, with all their differences. It is to this foundation that we are to dig down to find below the multiplicity of our differences. In this endeavor we are guided by the law of love shown us in Christ and by our created nature that can be fulfilled only in the company of others.

---

3. For a nice summary of Maurice's views on the order of God's creation, see Vidler, *F. D. Maurice and Company*, 161–65.

4. For Maurice's understanding of himself as a digger rather than an builder, see Wondra, "Introduction," xii–xvi.

We have thus been placed upon earth to enjoy fellowship with God and our fellow human beings.

It is this ideal that Maurice offers as an alternative to the atomistic and contentious view of human nature championed by the defenders of political economy. B. F. Westcott held a remarkably similar position. Like Maurice, Westcott argued that all people now exist in Christ and so find their unity in Christ. As Westcott says, Christ did not simply become a man, as one among many. He became *man*, and in this representative life gathered the innumerable fragments of humankind into a unity of love and fellowship with God and with one another. Within this fellowship of love each person finds her final destiny and fulfillment, not as an isolated individual but as a social being that is an essential part of a larger whole.

This account of the social character of human nature and destiny runs counter to the most common assumption of the present age, namely, that we understand ourselves first of all as autonomous individuals. Defenders of this more individualistic account of human nature and destiny often charge that communal views like those of Maurice, Westcott, Gore, and Temple submerge individuals in a collective and so, in the end, stifle human flourishing.[5] No less a figure than Tocqueville, in *The Old Regime and the French Revolution*, noted, "That word 'individualism' . . . was unknown to our ancestors, for the good reason that in their days every individual necessarily belonged to a group and no one could regard himself as an isolated unit."[6] Defenders of individualism argue against the charge that the birth of individualism destroyed the social ties that bind society's members one to another. Their contention is that the birth of individualism in the twelfth century was the result of a new respect for human possibilities.[7] They assert that allowing individuals to flourish contributes to the richness and variety of life and so enhances rather than diminishes life in society. The great defenders of this view are Wilhelm von Humboldt and John Stuart Mill. Von Humboldt argued that freedom and variety (rather than conformity to social expectation) produce human flourishing.[8] It was his belief that social union based on the wants and capacities of society's individual members allows each to participate

---

5. See, e.g., Smith and Moore, *Individualism*.
6. Cited in Smith and Moore, *Individualism*, loc. 60 of 2945, Kindle.
7. Smith and Moore, *Individualism*, loc. 370 of 2945, Kindle.
8. Smith and Moore, *Individualism*, loc. 421 of 2945, Kindle.

in the rich collective resources of all the others.⁹ So he concludes that the highest form of common life available to human beings is one in which each strives to develop herself according to her own nature and for her own sake.¹⁰

Mill mounts a similar argument. In his essay "Of Individuality, as One of the Elements of Well-Being," he insists that it is imperative "that human beings should be free to form opinions, and to express their opinions without reserve." He goes on to say that if this freedom is not granted the results are harmful to the intellectual and moral nature of humankind.¹¹ Mill provides a summary of his position, writing,

> As it is useful that while mankind are imperfect there should be different opinions, so is it that there should be different experiments of living; that free scope should be given to varieties of character, short of injury to others; and that the worth of different modes of life should be proved practically, when any one thinks fit to try them. It is desirable, in short, that in things which do not primarily concern others, individuality should assert itself. Where, not the person's own character, but the traditions or customs of other people are the rule of conduct, there is wanting one of the principal ingredients of human happiness, and quite the chief ingredient of individual and social progress.¹²

To this view, defenders of Christian Socialism had a double rejoinder. The first was that we can become individuals only insofar as we are shaped within and by community life. The second was that it is only within a community that individuals who are "persons" with a "personality" emerge. Indeed, for the Christian Socialists, the flourishing of individuals with personality and so also character constitutes the very purpose of social life. According to the philosophy of Personalism, which shaped the thinking of the leading Christian Socialists, the very purpose of social life is to support the development of each member of society as a personality—that is to say, a fully developed character that manifests consciousness, free self-determination, directedness toward ends, self-identity through time, and value retentiveness. In short, the Christian Socialists

---

9. Smith and Moore, *Individualism*, loc. 432 of 2945, Kindle.

10. Smith and Moore, *Individualism*, loc. 475 of 2945, Kindle.

11. Mill, "Of Individuality," in Smith and Moore, *Individualism*, loc. 516 of 2945, Kindle.

12. Mill, "Of Individuality," in Smith and Moore, *Individualism*, loc. 540 of 2945, Kindle.

sought the same thing as did von Humboldt and Mill—fully developed persons. Their difference from their opponents was simply that they insisted that this social goal could only be achieved within a society that passes on traditions that provide the foundations for the development of people who are defined by their "personality."

As previously noted, advocates of political economy tended to begin their discussion of social life in a very different place—with reasonable, free, autonomous individuals, each seeking her own happiness. In this search only the rights of other reasonable, autonomous individuals limit others in their search for happiness. The social ideal the Christian Socialists offered in opposition to the competitive individualism defended by the proponents of political economy began in a very different place—with human beings who are social by nature, bound together through the love and sacrifice of Christ in a community of love and destined for life in communion with God and all people. Both in respect to their beginning and their end, human beings must, they held, be considered as social beings created in the image of God. Further, by grace they should be understood as beloved citizens, either actual or potential, of the kingdom of God. The overarching ideal of a Christian society is therefore a community knit together by love of God and love of neighbor in which human personality can develop to the fullest extent.

Many, though not all, Christian Socialists gathered this ideal under an encompassing goal, namely, "the return of Christendom." In a collection of essays by that name, they explored the changes that would need to take place within the Church of England and the English people to make this ideal a reality.[13] In a signature essay entitled "The Idea of Christendom in Relation to Modern Society," Maurice B. Reckitt responded to the movement of workers that protested the inequalities and exploitive conditions brought about by the Industrial Revolution in this way: "Yet the primary need of the workers' crusade is not any practical programme but the inspiration of an all-sufficing *Idea* [emphasis added]. Only the conception of Christendom can supply this: in it men would find not only an ideal for the whole social order, but one which would restore to the individual the conviction of Vocation and a personal activity that could be offered to the glory of God."[14]

---

13. See, e.g., Group of Churchmen, *The Return of Christendom*.

14. Reckitt, "Idea of Christendom," in Group of Churchmen, *Return of Christendom*, 4.

Before passing on to the other ideals that comprise the social vision of the Christian Socialists, it is important to pause and contemplate a simple fact. The ideal of a restored Christendom was then and remains today a vain hope. At the end of his life, in the mid-twentieth century, William Temple declared that England was now a secular society. Latterly, Oliver O'Donovan notes that the era of Christendom lasted from the Edict of Milan until the date of the First Amendment to the US Constitution. From that time on, he says, we have lived in a "post-Christian era."[15] The world in which Christians now live was captured long before our time in the famous *Epistle to Diognetus*.[16] Speaking of Christians living throughout the Roman Empire, the author wrote, "Living in Greek or barbarian cities as it may be, following local customs in dress, diet and other daily matters, they display the astonishing, even perplexing character of their own citizenship." Taking a lead from First Peter, the author pictures Christians as "resident aliens" whose citizenship is different from the people among whom they live. This difference of citizenship is manifest most clearly in the fact that they are persecuted. But persecuted or not, their civic identity is defined first by the rule of God.

Christendom, says O'Donovan, refers to a historical idea—"the idea of a professedly Christian secular political order, and the history of that idea in practice. Christendom is an *era*, an era in which the truth of Christianity was taken to be a truth of secular politics."[17] Desirable as some form of Christendom may be, that era and that ideal have now passed beyond reach; but the churches have yet to grasp the significance of its passing. From both the left and the right come attempts to restore a "Christian nation." Even in America, the country of "no establishment and free exercise," churches from the left and the right long for a Christian America. The only difference (and it is a large one) is the way in which they picture a Christian America. Like the Christian Socialists, neither left nor right has grasped what O'Donovan terms "the ambiguities of Christendom." Neither has come to terms with the fact that "establishment," be it constitutional or by common consent, was accompanied by a loss of focus on the missionary context in which the churches always, and especially now, exist.

---

15. O'Donovan, *Desire of the Nations*, 193–95.

16. For this remarkable letter, see O'Donovan and O'Donovan, *From Irenaeus to Grotius*, 12–14.

17. O'Donovan, *Desire of the Nations*, 195.

To their credit the Christian Socialists realized that they were not fulfilling their social role as an established church. Their vision of a return to a previous era is at first glance extraordinarily naïve, but it was put forward with full realization of the daunting nature of fulfilling the assigned role of an established church. Despite his support of the idea, Reckitt said, "The subjection of the community to capitalist industry and the distortion of property by plutocracy have made the very conception of Christendom not only unrealizable, but for the majority of men today even incomprehensible."[18] Yet, despite the odds, Reckitt and his colleagues dared hope that their vision might become a reality. Why? They had hope because they viewed plutocracy itself as a religion, and they were firmly convinced that a renewal of the Christian foundations of the nation would bring with it a renewed vision of life in society both within England and beyond its borders. This vision would honor a different set of ideals than those lauded by capitalism. Fr. L. S. Thornton described the Christian Socialist vision of a renewed Christendom in this way. He wrote, "Society must be reintegrated upon a dogmatic basis, and . . . the common end which men must set before themselves is the Christian ideal of the Kingdom of God. Such a reintegration would be 'Christendom,' an international world-order bound together in a common allegiance to Christ strong enough to transcend all barriers. Such a Christendom would possess its own many-sided culture penetrating all grades of society; and the whole would be held together by a great common tradition of religious experience in which each individual has an intimate share."[19]

Equality, Fellowship, Duties, Rights, and Service

Time has revealed this vision as one that belongs to romantic dreamers. The dream of a Christian civilization stretching not only throughout England but also throughout the world belongs to the romantic optimism and pervasive imperialism of the nineteenth century. Nevertheless, the Christendom Group among the Christian Socialists offered their vision with hope not only for a re-Christianized England (along with its empire) but for a re-Christianized Europe as well. With full recognition that their

---

18. Reckitt, "The Idea of Christendom," in Group of Churchmen, *Return of Christendom*, 6.

19. Thornton, "The Necessity of Catholic Dogma," in Group of Churchmen, *Return of Christendom*, 55.

program required a dogmatic base, they set out to articulate not only the underlying beliefs but also the ideals of Christendom. R. H. Tawney developed an account of the necessary ideals with a breadth and depth unequaled by any of his confreres save perhaps William Temple. As with all the Christian Socialists, the basis of Tawney's vision was the incarnation. The key principle derived from this base was equality. What he has to say unfolds against the backdrop of aspects of English history and society he thought indefensible. It was his view that modern society was sick; its chief disease was inequality. To explain this social illness he propounds a secular version of the fall in which commercial forces destroy communal solidarities. With their destruction society as a spiritual organism gives way to society as an economic machine that operates by laws of supply and demand rather than human need and interdependence.[20]

With this development, capitalism is born, and with it came two phenomena to which the Christian Socialists were opposed—privilege and tyranny. Against privilege Tawney sets equality, and against tyranny he sets another form of equality—the dispersion and control of power. The question of course is: On what foundation does equality rest, and what exactly is its moral content and range of application? In the first instance, Maurice rooted his understanding of equality in the love of God shown to all people equally in the incarnation. This idea hovers in the background of much of what Tawney wrote, but his primary argument for equality does not reside in the incarnation. His primary argument is rooted in the idea that all people share the image of God, and for this reason all people are of equal value to God. Equality of status before God is the basis of the equality people enjoy with one another. Indeed, in a diary entry on March 6, 1913, Tawney wrote, "What is wrong with the modern world is that having ceased to believe in the greatness of God & therefore the infinite smallness . . . of *man*, it had to invent or emphasize distinctions between *men*."[21] It is this emphasis on distinction that lies at the base of capitalism. It is, in short, the emphasis on distinction that has allowed some people to live off of others and so treat them as means for the realization of their own purposes.

It is of crucial importance at this point to call to mind an observation made and supported in lavish detail by Lynn Hunt, namely, that equality before God has never, on its own, produced equality of value

---

20. For a summary of these concerns, see Wilkinson, *Christian Socialism*, 96–97.
21. Cited in Terrill, *R. H. Tawney and His Times*, 124.

and treatment in the eyes of the public apart from the birth of sympathy. Only in the presence of sympathy can regard for others be translated into equal evaluation that transcends social barriers and takes the form of equal consideration and treatment.[22] We will return to this point shortly because, as is clear, equality before God is of central importance to the Christian Socialists' case. So, for example, equality before God is the first ideal upon which Tawney rests his account of social equality. There are, however, two others ideals that are of foundational importance to him. One is that self-fulfillment, which is the *telos* of life together in fellowship, is necessarily linked to freedom. It is the link between freedom and fulfillment that serves to limit inequality. Too much inequality places inordinate limits upon the self-development of citizens, and self-development is the morally necessary purpose of life together. Freedom is then the second ideal upon which a principle of social equality rests. There is, however, a third foundational ideal—service. Because human beings can thrive only as social beings, they have duties one to another. These duties involve service to one's neighbors. If distribution of wealth and opportunity are allowed to fall out of relation to service, then inequality becomes inordinate. Within a Christian Sociology, the ideal of service serves to define morally acceptable ranges of inequality. One might say that the Christian Socialists promoted a service theory of value rather than a labor theory of value.

It was this focus on social obligation that led defenders of Christian Socialism to another ideal—a preference for "duties" rather than "rights." Indeed, one of their chief criticisms of capitalist society was that public discourse had devolved into claims and counterclaims about rights. Defining social relations on the basis of rights, they believed, pits one person against another from the start. Rights language is the language of "mine" and "thine." It is a language born of individualism, competition, and conflict. Duty, on the other hand, is a language born of fellowship, cooperation, and service. William Temple, Tawney's good friend, provided a pithy summary of this belief. He noted that objectively there seems little difference between rights and duties, but, he said, "The difference in the temper of a movement that rests on Rights will be aggressive, violent, contentious; and the temper of a movement that rests on Duties will be persuasive, public-spirited, harmonious."[23] It is important to note

---

22. See, e.g., Hunt, *Inventing Human Rights*.
23. Temple, *Christianity and the State*, 84.

this point. One thing ideals have the potential to do in society is to regulate the "temper" of social relations for the better. Temple's observations have been clearly demonstrated to be true by the character of political relations now ascendant in North America, England, and continental Europe. Political argument between nations and peoples is now most certainly carried on primarily in the language of rights. In the resulting cacophony of claims and counterclaims the tone is bitter and the results short-lived.

The view that conflict is imbedded from the start in rights language goes right back to the beginning of Christian Socialism. In *The Kingdom of Christ*, F. D. Maurice made clear his view that the contemporary focus on rights rather than duties had its roots not in fellowship and cooperation but in atomistic individualism. Individualism, he argued, leads to the view that will is superior to law. Elevation of the will leads in turn to the disruption of mobs insisting upon the right to make and unmake law. The battle cry of the mob is "we have a right," and this battle cry amounts to no more than an assertion that rights are not what duty confers and right demands but rather what we will.[24] So it was that the Christian Socialists held that rights claims are linked to conflict and espousal of duties to fellowship and service.

A little later, Maurice's disciple, John Ludlow, espoused a similar view in an article that appeared in the journal *Politics for the People*. He wrote, "Creatures of God, we live by Him and of His mercy. Of ourselves we have no right whatsoever; what He gave, that He may take—be it life, health, joy, riches, talents, esteem of others, power, love. But we have Duties. We have Duties to fulfill, and from those Duties spring the Rights of others, not as property in them, but as an obligation in ourselves."[25]

Some years later still, in the midst of the miners' strike, in an open letter to the *Times of London*, B. F. Westcott made a similar point. He wrote, "In our quiet moments we all recognize that the right conduct of life depends upon mutual trust and upon the endeavor to fulfill duties rather than to maintain rights."[26] Later, in an address to a conference on profit sharing, he gave eloquent expression to this preference for duties before rights: "Men cannot, even with a show of reason, press their 'rights' to the uttermost. They ask for forgiveness as they have

---

24. Maurice, *Kingdom of Christ*, 181.
25. See Christiansen, *Christian Socialism*, 78.
26. Westcott, *Life and Letters of Brooke Foss Westcott*, 2:118.

forgiven—forgiven, that is, real wrongs—forgone just claims. We have indeed 'no rights but duties'; and these can never be discharged in full. In strictness of account we must remain debtors to the end; and through the obligations of our Faith we are debtors to all who need us."[27] Once more, it is the doctrine of the incarnation that undergirds a basic premise of Christian Socialism, namely, the primacy of duties over rights. God's love in Christ and our created nature as image of God together bind all human beings in a fellowship of love, care, and duty. These ideals define the nature of human society under God, and within such a society social ties are rooted in duties to others rather than personal claims to have a right asserted in contradistinction to social duties.

It is the problematic relation between duties and rights that brings into focus the importance of the ideal of service held by Christian Socialists. In a society that gives priority to duty rather than rights, service to one's neighbor acts as a necessary and primary component of social interaction. Service is a social, indeed sacred, duty that binds together all classes in a fellowship of mutual care and help. In the case of Maurice, service was the ideal that allowed him to hold a belief that there was no need for altering the class structure of English society. It was his view that each class exists to offer a particular form of service to all the others. He firmly believed that the ideal of equality before God combined with mutual service would produce a peaceful and healthy society in which each and every person could find her place and fulfillment. So in the conclusion to *The Kingdom of Christ,* Maurice criticizes those who would set aside all the ranks of society by setting forth his hierarchical vision of a structured society in which mutual aid or service is the very form of social relations. He envisions a society in which "the middle classes may be brought to act upon the lower, so as to be their guides and not their tyrants; how the upper classes may be brought to act upon the middle, so as not to be their fawning slaves, and at the same time the betrayers of their consciences at elections—cold and distant, and the objects of servile imitations at other times; how each portion of the community may preserve its proper position to the rest and may be infused together by the spiritual power which exists for each, the minister of all, the creature of none."[28]

---

27. Westcott, *Life and Letters of Brooke Foss Westcott,* 2:135–36.
28. Maurice, *Kingdom of Christ,* 560.

The same emphasis on the linked ideas of equality, duty, and service appears a century later in the works of Archbishop William Temple. In *Christianity and Social Order* he takes full account of the way in which egoism limits a full expression of love. So he argues that in a fallen world "the most fundamental requirement of any political and economic system is not that it shall express love . . . nor that it shall express justice . . . but that it shall supply some measure of security against murder, robbery and starvation."[29] He goes on to say the church's assertion of original sin "should make the Church intensely realistic, and conspicuously free from Utopianism."[30] That said, he insists that despite the reality of sin, the fundamental principle upon which Christians should base their social commitments is the conviction that each human being is a child of God who is due respect and like all others is destined for fellowship with him. This basic principle implies three derivative ones—freedom, social fellowship, and service. Social life exists to further freedom and maintain fellowship. Fellowship and freedom in turn issue in the obligation of service.[31]

These convictions about the social nature of humankind, linked as they are to the ideals of fellowship, freedom, and service, place in bold relief the unbounded notions of freedom and the very attenuated notions we have of community and service present in the politics of identity now increasingly common in the West. In this political atmosphere rights language seems to be the preferred way we have to speak about social relations. The problem is that the language of rights is far too thin and exclusive an idiom in which to generate an idea of a common good. As Alison Milbank writes, "One problem of our society's perspectival, postmodernist attitude to truth and authority is that difference becomes purely agonistic as 'rights' compete, and another cognate problem is that we have no standpoint from which we might critique our own assumptions." We need, she says, a transcendent perspective and an anthropology based on solidarity and relation. Maurice and the Christian Socialists sought to provide precisely this point of vantage.[32]

---

29. Temple, *Christianity and Social Order*, 51.
30. Temple, *Christianity and Social Order*, 51.
31. Temple, *Christianity and Social Order*, 73.
32. See Milbank, "Maurice as a Resource for the Church Today," in Spencer, *Theology Reforming Society*, loc. 674 of 3130, Kindle.

Personality, Character, Freedom, and Property

Even this brief review of the relations between equality, fellowship, duty, and service makes clear that in deploying these ideals the Christian Socialists, in their emphasis on duty, fellowship, and service, often failed to take into account what I will call the limiting circumstances of scarcity and competitive egoism. Simply put, is it not the case that the legal establishment of a right may well be the only peaceful way to a more just social order when inequalities of wealth, power, and position destroy fellowship? In such circumstances, is charity enough and will duty prevail? Is it not the case, even granting the presence of love and fellowship, that rights are necessary means to bind people to the duties (born of love and fellowship) they have to their fellow citizens?

I take it as given that the answer to this question is yes. I also take it as a given that duty as presented by the Christian Socialists seems in large measure to flow down from the upper classes toward the lower and then from the lower up through the middle to the upper. That this is a correct understanding of the views of the leaders of the Christian Socialist movement will become plain as their position on the relation between the classes unfolds in the ensuing discussion. This blindness to the destructive character of the class structure is a major failing of an altogether noble and well-meaning social movement. Didier Fassin, in *Humanitarian Reason: A Moral History of the Present*, sums up the problem in this way. "When compassion is exercised in the public space, it is therefore always directed from above to below, from the more powerful to the weaker, the more fragile, the more vulnerable."[33] Those in a lower position, he says, live precarious lives. Their lives are not guaranteed. Rather, in a way, those above bestow their lives upon them. Those who have power over them define their condition.

The primacy the Christian Socialists assigned to duty over rights is questionable in a number of ways. Nevertheless, the primacy of duty as an ideal, essential as it is to the entire program of the Christian Socialists, is more than defensible. Is not the idea of social life ordered only by rights that exist prior to any claim of duty a chilling vision—one that posits one's neighbor as competitor rather than friend? And can a society that defines its denizens solely as possessors of rights possibly provide them, in their daily round, with peace, or rest, or satisfaction? Further, claims to have a right cannot possibly be sustained if asserted apart from a pervasive idea

---

33. Fassin, *Humanitarian Reason*, 3.

of duty to one's neighbors. It is certainly true that the dismissal of rights by the Christian Socialists exposes undue optimism on their part, but it rightly displays duty toward and service to others as necessary aspects of social health and human flourishing.

Duty and service to others are necessary ideals if social life is to prove fulfilling. Rights are necessary because people often fail in their duties. There were, however, other ideals whose importance the Christian Socialists insisted upon. Their moral vision was broad. They sketched an ideal society. It was not one in which possessors of rights struggle one with another. Neither was it one whose citizens were submerged in a collective that erased the significance of individual needs, aspirations, and talents. Their ideal was a society held together by a common vision of life that made possible the fulfillment of the lives of the individuals that comprise its membership. Their purpose was to link communal vision with individual flourishing. To this end, they employed two ideals. To their minds, life lived in fellowship with and service to others leads to the flowering of personality and the development of character. These two, personality and character, constitute human flourishing in its fullness, they believed. They further believed that the development of personality and character are tied to two other social ideals—freedom and property. The social vision of the Christian Socialists requires the fruitful interrelation of these four.

In his book on the modern state, John Neville Figgis provides a succinct statement of the crucial nature of the relation between community, character, and personality. "In the real world," he writes, "the isolated individual does not exist; he begins always as a member of something, and . . . his personality can develop only in society, and in some way or other he always embodies some social institution."[34] In his account of Christianity and the state William Temple lists "true principles" to which a state must conform. First among these true principles is "the sanctity of personality."[35] He goes on to say, "By common consent the first two principles in the Gospel as applied to social order are the Sanctity of Personality and the Fact of Fellowship. Society is, we find, essentially a Fellowship of Persons, and all the ramifications of social or political theory are articulations of that simple but far-reaching truth."[36]

---

34. Figgis, *Churches in the Modern State*, 88.
35. Temple, *Christianity and the State*, 4.
36. Temple, *Christianity and the State*, 89.

To the minds of the Christian Socialists, character and personality were more than welcome byproducts of social life. They were the divinely appointed *telos*, end or purpose of life together. Life in society is not meant to submerge individuals within a collective. It is meant to be the matrix in which the lives of individuals develop to their full potential. It was the term "personality" that summed up for them the good of personal development. "Personality" is a word that frequently appears in the writings of the Christian Socialists, but it is used without definition—as if the term is self-explanatory. This rather casual use of a key term remained undefined largely because, at that time, "Personalism" was the title of a popular form of philosophy—a term that floated in the air the Christian Socialists breathed. As a philosophy, it appeared in many versions, but in all its forms Personalism was an idealist school of philosophy.[37] Its proponents held that the basic features of personality, such as consciousness, self-determination, directedness toward ends, self-identity through time, and value retentiveness, make it the pattern of all reality. In its theistic form Personalism sometimes took a specifically Christian form, holding that the highest individual instance of personhood is Jesus Christ. It is important to note the content of this characterization of personality. The term has a wider sense than is normally now assigned. Presently, "personality" refers to the particular characteristics of an individual. The Christian Socialists used the term differently to refer, not to the particularities of individuals, but to the human capacities and developmental potential of each and every human being.

Thus, the Christian Socialists used the term "Personalism" as commonly employed in their time rather than in ours. It has been frequently noted that the Christian Socialists, on the whole, were not original thinkers. Rather, they made use, in various combinations, of a pool of ideas freely circulating within the reformist circles of their day.[38] It is easy to see from the above description of Personalism why it proved for the Christian Socialists to be such a useful and frequently used term. It sums up perfectly the goal of a society rooted in belief in God and participation in human fellowship rather than competition. That goal is for Jesus Christ to become the model for human development and fulfillment. In accord with this model, the fully developed personality will display

---

37. For an account of Personalism as a philosophy, see Williams and Bengtsson, "Personalism."

38. Of particular importance are the works of John Ruskin, Thomas Carlyle, and T. H. Green.

consciousness, free self-determination, directedness toward ends, self-identity through time, and value retentiveness. In addition the fully developed personality will show forth those virtues manifest in Christ's life.

A life that is self-determined, directed toward an end, and reflective of Christ's life is one with a recognizable character. Not surprisingly, in addition to the blossoming of personality, the Christian Socialists saw the development of character as the goal of a social life characterized by equality and fellowship. Further, the flowering of personality and the development of character do not level society. Rather they encourage diversity and increase social energy. Ross Terrill summarizes Tawney's view of the interconnectedness of equality, fellowship, personality, and character in this way: "A common culture is thus a new creation, not a leveling down to the existing working-class mentality or a leveling up to the existing middle-class or upper-class mentality. Individual character, diverse and even eccentric, will flower when personality, rather than wealth, is the badge of a man's social position."[39] Terrill quotes Tawney as saying, "Individual differences, which are a source of social energy, are more likely to ripen and find expression if social inequalities are, as far as practicable, diminished."[40]

Equality, personality, and character are interrelated ideals that arise out of a society rooted in faith and fellowship. Together these ideals support self-fulfillment among the citizens of any country. All three, however, presuppose another—freedom within the populace. To be sure, defenders of political economy and neoliberals like Ayn Rand, F. A. Hayek and (latterly) Milton Friedman also defend freedom. Nevertheless, their defense of freedom is tied to individually determined success, while the Christian Socialists' valorization of freedom was tied to self-fulfillment understood as a capacity to use one's moral capacities to do one's duty in respect to the treatment of others.[41] To put the matter in a slightly different way, for Tawney equality leads to greater freedom, and greater freedom supports greater individuation. Individuation, however, is to be distinguished from individualism. To be individuated is not to become a social atom. It is to become a partner with others in a common project. Where a fellowship such as this exists, individuals find self-fulfillment

---

39. Terrill, *R. H. Twaney and His Times*, 134.
40. Cited in Terrill, *R. H. Tawney and His Times*, 134.
41. Terrill, *R. H. Tawney and His Times*, 128.

because their personality finds a home within and contributes to a fellowship of equals.[42]

William Temple made a similar point in a succinct and clear way. In his great work *Christianity and Social Order*, Temple says this: "The primary principle of Christian Ethics and Christian Politics must be respect for every person."[43] This respect is due because each person is a child of God, one whom God loves and for whom he died. Further, respect for persons is of primary importance. Neither society nor the state takes precedence over the person. Indeed, the state exists for its citizens and not the citizens for the state. So "the first aim of social progress must be to give the fullest possible scope for the exercise of all powers and qualities which are distinctly personal; and of these the most fundamental is deliberate choice." Thus, for Temple, "to establish and secure freedom is the primary object of all right political action." Why? Because it is through freedom that people develop real personality, and personality is "the quality of one made in the image of God."[44] Temple then completes the circle of fellowship, equality, personality, character, and freedom by insisting that freedom requires training. Freedom is more than freedom from and freedom for. True Freedom is freedom to live a life directed toward its divinely determined end. These are moral qualities and goals that require moral formation. Moral formation requires fellowship. Apart from these constraints, persons will not enjoy the scope of genuinely free action; and that, he says, is the aim of all true politics.[45] Thus, it seems that moral formation is a social enterprise before it is an individual undertaking.

For the Christian Socialists, freedom requires both guidance and choice. Choice in turn requires both social imbeddedness and personal discipline. It also requires sufficient material wealth to create a social arena in which the important choices about the conduct of life are made. The importance Christian Socialists gave to social participation, self-development, and self-expression required them to give attention to social issues, particularly the extent of poverty and the vast inequality of wealth brought about by the Industrial Revolution. Their response was passionate but, to a contemporary reader, unexpected. In the sources I have searched there are indeed a few references to a fair or minimum

---

42. Terrill, *R. H. Tawney and His Times*, 134.
43. Temple, *Christianity and Social Order*, 67.
44. Temple, *Christianity and Social Order*, 67.
45. Temple, *Christianity and Social Order*, 68.

wage, but fair wages never formed the center of their concern. Far more attention was given to the distribution and use of property—what is its purpose, how it is acquired, and what its moral use ought to be.

The Christian Socialists were particularly interested in land tenure, in large measure because land was held by inheritance and used largely for private purposes. For example, Stewart Headlam, perhaps the most radical of their number, does say that in contracting for labor, those who do the work have a duty to insist that they should not be overworked or underpaid. This obligation, however, he considered a duty on the part of employers rather than a right on the part of those they employ. Indeed, in respect to wages Headlam insists, "Duty is a stronger motive power than right."[46] He then goes on to quote with approval a resolution inscribed by the English Land Restoration League in Trafalgar Square. It reads as follows: "That the main cause of poverty, both in the agricultural districts and in the great centers of population, is the fact that the land, which ought to be the common property of all, is now monopolized by a few; and that therefore those who want to cut away at the root of poverty must work to restore to the people the whole of the value which they give to the land."[47]

In retrospect, the fixation of Christian Socialists on the land question is hard for contemporary readers to understand. The major source of wealth was fast becoming not land but stock in limited liability companies. Nevertheless, the immediate problem the Christian Socialists faced was a *rentier* economy in which a very small group, whose wealth was inherited, controlled vast estates. The Christian Socialists saw land as a social asset, and so wanted to make it possible for land to be owned by many rather than a few. They believed that such a change would allow a wide swath of the population to benefit from ownership and so also remain on the land. Land reform for them was a primary means of promoting a wider distribution of wealth.[48] One must also say that land reform spoke directly to their obsession with an agrarian form of life. That said, their discussion of property is more often than not incisive and quite relevant, even today. I take as prime examples three works—R. H. Tawney's

---

46. Headlam, "Socialism and Religion," in Headlam et al., *Socialism and Religion*, 18.

47. Headlam, "Socialism and Religion," in Headlam et al., *Socialism and Religion*, 19.

48. For a contemporary account of the economic benefits of land reform, see Appelbaum, *Economists' Hour*, 275–84.

Acquisitive Society, published in 1920; a collection of essays entitled *The Return of Christendom*, published in 1922; and *Property: Its Duties and Rights*, also published in 1922.

In his treatment of property, Tawney moves the discussion out of an agrarian setting and into one defined by manufacture, wage labor, and modern finance. In *The Acquisitive Society* Tawney insists that states have no absolute rights. Indeed, he says that all rights "are conditional and derivative . . . They are derived from the end or purpose of the society in which they exist. They are conditional on being used to contribute to the attainment of that end, not to thwart it. And this means in practice that, if society is to be healthy, people must regard themselves not as owners of rights, but as trustees for the discharge of functions and the instruments of social purpose."[49] Duty once more takes precedence over rights. For Tawney this view allows a way to discriminate between various sorts of private property—which are legitimate and which are not.[50] So he draws the conclusion that property cannot rightly be viewed simply as a source of income. Property, he says, comes with duties because it has social as well as individual purpose. He concludes in a way atypical of the Christian Socialists, that nationalization is entirely proper if private ownership serves no function save personal gain.[51]

In his essay in *The Return of Christendom*, Maurice Reckitt takes a similar position. In doing so he puts on display a view of English society as a cooperative whole knit together by personal relations that cross social boundaries. Within such a group a return to Christendom might seem something reasonably to be hoped for. The members of this movement knew each other. They had studied the same subjects at the same universities and fit comfortably into the hierarchical structure of English society. That said, Reckitt was convinced that plutocracy had distorted the purpose of property within a commonwealth. Property is necessary for individual liberty and so is a prerequisite condition for the development of character and personality. As it is, Reckitt wrote, forty million citizens of Great Britain are deprived of property. Socialism, and in particular a return to Christendom, points the way to rectify this unacceptable situation, he believed. "The Christendom ideal points to that perfect harmony between personal freedom and social function in which

49. Tawney, *Acquisitive Society*, 50–51.
50. Tawney, *Acquisitive Society*, 51.
51. Tawney, *Acquisitive Society*, 103.

property becomes as much an organ of society as it does an expression of personality."[52] In such a society property would exist "to enable man to enjoy that independence which is a condition of his contribution to the common purpose being rightly made."[53] In such a society the possession and use of property serve to develop character. In another collection of essays, Hastings Rashdall makes the link between property and character with particular clarity: "Some liberty of action, some form of arranging one's own life in advance, some freedom of choice, and some certainty that a man will experience the results of his choice, are essential to the development of character; and this there cannot be unless there is some permanent control over material things."[54]

So for Christian Socialists there is a normative link between personal freedom, on the one hand, and the social function of property, on the other. Together, these provide the ideals to be realized in the kingdom of God. They become part of the vocation of all citizens and as expressions of freedom and vocation serve to prevent collectivism, on the one hand, and monopoly, on the other.[55] If, however, society loses its notion of common purpose, the relative nature of both liberty and property is lost and both become absolute rights. It is also the case that with the disappearance of this moral link, government rushes in to fill the vacuum and attempts to control everything. Government control seems the only way to curb unrestricted individualism and rampant greed. In these circumstances, property rights in private hands become a stimulus to antisocial greed and a means of exercising power over those who do not have these rights.[56]

The link between property and power is a prominent theme in a collection of essays on property edited by Charles Gore that appeared close in time to the publication of *The Return of Christendom*. In "The Historical Evolution of Property, in Fact and in Idea," Professor L. T. Hobhouse made a distinction between property that is used and property that gives

---

52. Reckitt, "Moralization of Property," in Group of Churchmen, *Return of Christendom*, 156.

53. Reckitt, "Moralization of Property," in Group of Churchmen, *Return of Christendom*, 157.

54. Rashdall, "Philosophical Theory of Property," in Gore, *Property*, 63.

55. Reckitt, "Moralization of Property," in Group of Churchmen, *Return of Christendom*, 157.

56. Reckitt, "Moralization of Property," in Group of Churchmen, *Return of Christendom*, 157-59.

control of one person over another. He insists, "These two functions of property, the control of things, which give freedom and security, and the control of persons through things, which gives power to the owner, are very different."[57] He notes further that modern economic conditions have all but abolished property for use. At the same time they have fostered the accumulation of vast masses of property for power and placed it in the hands of a relatively narrow class.[58] The result is that property as a means of self-development "is not available in the amount required by vast numbers." His conclusion is this: society that views property through the lens he provides would limit accumulation. It could not tolerate the present distribution of wealth. It would redistribute and it would hold that accumulation to this degree is not healthy for the soul or for society.[59] Thus, the control of property that makes for the control of others and not for self-development stands condemned.

Hobhouse believed, however, that there are ways, difficult as they may be, to mitigate this unhealthy set of social circumstances. That way is indicated by socialist principles. For socialists, "property is not common to all, but it is held in common for all."[60] This is the principle. The difficult matter is how property is to be assigned or apportioned on the basis of the principle. As in the case of Tawney, Hobhouse believes that property is to be apportioned on the basis of the social function it serves. The good of society is at issue. Apportionment is properly a matter of collective judgment. However, the difficulty socialists face is how this social judgment can be accommodated "to the free initiative and enterprise of the individual."[61] It is doubtful, he says, that the problem of apportionment is soluble on the basis of socialistic principles alone. The task is made even more questionable by the difficulty of determining the nature of the common good in a way that includes the general wellbeing both of society and of its individual members.

Hobhouse concludes with a rather elegant summary (which I will quote almost in full) of the dilemma and his statement of what he believes to be the way forward. The problem, he says, is "to find a method compatible with the industrial conditions of the new age, of securing to

---

57. Hobhouse, "Historical Evolution of Property," in Gore, *Property*, 10–11.
58. Hobhouse, "Historical Evolution of Property," in Gore, *Property*, 23.
59. Hobhouse, "Historical Evolution of Property," in Gore, *Property*, 30.
60. Hobhouse, "Historical Evolution of Property," in Gore, *Property*, 31.
61. Hobhouse, "Historical Evolution of Property," in Gore, *Property*, 31.

each man, as a part of his civic birthright, a place in the industrial system and a lien upon the common product that he may call his own, without dependence upon private charity or the arbitrary decision of an official." He goes on to say, "We have to restore the contact between the individual and the instruments of labour. We have to assure him of continuity in employment, and ... of provision against the accidents of life ... And for these purposes we have to restore to society a direct ownership of some things, but an eminent ownership of all things material to the production of wealth, securing 'property for use' to the individual, and retaining 'property for power' for the democratic state."[62] It is not much of a stretch to see in Hobhouse's search for an answer to the dilemma he poses an anticipation of Michael Walzer's notion of "spheres of justice" wherein what is just in one sphere of social life is not just in another. So, Hobhouse argues, let's keep property for power within the sphere of state activity rather than private life. It would not be difficult to show that there are other spheres of social life in which property for power has a legitimate place and that giving the state a monopoly of property for power might not be a very good idea. Still and all, Hobhouse posed a fundamental question that still awaits an answer.

---

62. Hobhouse, "Historical Evolution of Property," in Gore, *Property*, 32–33.

B. Application

1. The Way of Judgment

THE ACCOUNT OF PROPERTY, wealth, and freedom the Christian Socialists proposed brings with it a question. How does an industrial (or digital) society organize itself so as to ensure that wealth (property) is linked to social purpose and individual flourishing rather than simply acquisition, greed, and the exercise of power over one's fellows? Posing this question brings one face to face with a fundamental problem the Christian Socialists never fully resolved. Let us assume that the ideals they favored make sense and stand surety for a common good. One is still left with this question: How does one move from the ideals the Christian Socialists hoped might shape the common life of English society to concrete social policy? Put in this way the question reveals a very English view of politics "in which principles are thought of as a private affair, guiding politicians in the background, while the details of state affairs are largely to be governed by considerations of prudential expediency."[1] The imbedded nature of this view of the relation of ideals and politics in English tradition in part explains why Christian Socialists never found a satisfactory way of establishing the link between ideals and political judgment. Their view of the relation between ideals and particular measures was imbedded in time like an insect in amber. Nonetheless, this *aporia*, this gap between ideal and particular judgment, poses a threat to the Christian Socialists' entire project; and to it we will have to return on several occasions. It is simply the case that one cannot move, as the Christian Socialists were on occasion wont to do, from an ideal like social fellowship to a moral

---

1. I owe this observation to John Milbank. See Milbank, *Future of Love*, locs. 406–17 of 7928, Kindle.

judgment like profit sharing apart from a process of moral reflection that connects social ideal with facts on the ground and with a particular judgment. Failure to provide this connection creates a direct link between moral principle and practical conclusion. As a result, the total context of fact and value involved in moral judgments is left vacant. Making a leap from an ideal to a particular judgment produces a mind closed to alternatives. A leap from ideal premise to practical judgment always leaves open the possibility of fanaticism.

It may be the case that the reluctance of the leading voices among the Christian Socialists to prescribe specific forms of political action does not stem entirely from their respect for private conscience. It may be that their reticence to recommend particular measures was linked on occasion and in part to this failure to think through the difficult process of moral reflection that connects ideals with practical judgments. It may be simply that they thought the practical implications of their ideals were so clear that they had no need of such elucidation. No matter what its cause might have been, the immediate reaction to this diffidence by present-day Christian advocates of social justice will most certainly be negative. Nevertheless, there were good reasons, other than false certainty or the rigors of moral reasoning, for hesitancy on the part of the Christian Socialists to claim clear Christian warrant in support of particular measures of policy. What might be called the originating reason for their hesitancy is to be found in a firm conviction held by the founding father of the movement, F. D. Maurice. As previously noted, Maurice believed that God has provided the societies of the earth with social and political order. God's providence creates and sustains these orders—not human schemes and programs. The way to a healthy social order, therefore, is not through politically engineered social and political change but by lives lived in accord with the way of life made known in Christ. The development and deployment of Christian ideals, not political programs, is the way the church as an institution has to contribute to a healthy social life that benefits all citizens and all social classes. To be sure, the social mission of the church is to point out evil wherever and whenever it pops up. To be sure, it is the duty of Christians to take part in the common life of society and to do what they can to right wrongs. Nevertheless, in the face of injustice and strife, it is not the job of the church *as an institution* to give direct support to particular measures for their amelioration. Rather, it is the job of the church, as an institution, to cultivate social ideals among its members such as equality, fellowship, and service. These ideals, the Christian

Socialists believed, would guide the populace to practical measures that would in turn lead to a healthy society in which people can flourish.

Maurice's socialism had as its focus the responsibility of all citizens one for another. It was this foundational conviction that led to a second reason for the Christian Socialists' eschewal of social and political advocacy by way of official teaching on the part of the church. Their focus on mutuality and social harmony made them reluctant to deploy the claim to have a right. As employed in the context of labor unrest, rights claims were claims made on behalf of individuals or particular groups. As such, from the perspective of Christian Socialists, leading with claims of this sort contributes to social conflict rather than social harmony. The rights claimed by A potentially stand in conflict with the rights claimed by B. Thus, the Christian Socialists concluded that a society built upon rights claims is a society that, at its base, is atomistic and characterized by conflict rather than solidarity and cooperation. In response, as noted, they insisted that healthy social relations rest not upon rights but upon duties. It is mutual indebtedness along with service to others that lie at the base of healthy social life. It is interesting to note that none other than Gandhi, for the same reasons, insisted on the priority of duty over rights in his struggle with both British imperial power and the popular opinion of his time.[2]

The first two reasons for the Christian Socialists' aversion to social and political advocacy on the part of church governing bodies derive from core theological beliefs—Christ's rule over all people, the holiness of each life, and the social nature of humankind. An additional reason for their reticence, however, derives from the prudential and so uncertain nature of moral judgments themselves. Political judgments are fallible. What is right may well be other than the wisest heart might judge. Political judgment lies in the realm of freedom and reason rather than necessity and certainty. Consequently, it does not lie within the realm of ecclesiastical authority to invade the arena rightly left for the exercise of freedom and prudential judgment.

A third reason for reticence in respect to particular political measures might well be the difficult task of moral reasoning itself. Nonetheless, despite these impediments, some Christian Socialists like John Ludlow, Stewart Headlam, R. H. Tawney, and William Temple were pushed by their ideals and their personal experience to favor, *as individuals*,

---

2. See Redgrave, "It Might Be Us."

particular policy solutions. Nevertheless, they made these moves with caution and restraint. They understood that their commitment to certain policies was a personal commitment. In stating their personal commitments they did not claim the authority of official church teaching. What stood behind their views was not the authority of the Church of England but their character, their credibility, the power of their social vision and the cogency of their argument. Their commitments were coherent and well thought out but did not lead them to demand that the Church of England pronounce upon particular legislative measures. They believed, on the contrary, that it was sufficient for the Church of England to set before the populace not policy support but an interlocking set of social ideals. No matter how reasonable this sort of thinking might have been, their reluctance to "speak for the church" opened them to the charge of avoidance or irrelevance.

It was William Temple who, as archbishop first of York and then of Canterbury, best understood this problem. In response, he turned his vision of social ideals to the concrete problems of society and to the need (as he perceived it) for the Church of England to provide moral guidance to its members in matters of political importance. In *Christianity and Social Order*, after laying down his reasons for saying the church has a right, indeed a duty, to interfere in public affairs, he asks the key question: How should the church interfere? He begins by asserting the well-established position of the Christian Socialists: "It is of crucial importance that the Church *acting corporately* should not commit itself to any particular policy."[3] For this reason, he says, the church should be concerned with principles and not policy. Principles hold in all circumstances; policies do not.

In their role as citizens Christians are to judge, in the light of their principles, what is in the "best" interests of their country. The church, acting corporately, is to supply these principles, and they in turn will suggest areas of social life that require change. In setting forth these principles, Temple showed that he had taken seriously Reinhold Niebuhr's warning about undue optimism. Nevertheless, he did seek a way for the Church of England, as the established church, to provide for the conscience of Christian believers political guidance that, though concrete, did not amount to policy advocacy. This determination is to be made, says Temple, on the basis of Christian principles (supplied by the church)

---

3. Temple, *Christianity and Social Order*, 40; emphasis added.

that hold out promise for social advance, but advance that is always limited and flawed. Christian principles do not chart the way to utopia, but they do serve in the first instance to identify what is wrong and to suggest possible remedial courses of action.

What then are these principles, and what is the context in which they are to be deployed? The context is one in which God works to draw all people to him. That is, the goal of all things is the rule of God or kingdom of God. This is God's purpose for the world he created. Nevertheless, Temple insists, the kingdom of God is never fully present in history, though it does mark out the goal toward which history points. This knowledge of both the goal and limits of history provides Christians with a realistic but hopeful vision of the historical context in which they live. No matter what trials Christians face, they know God to be present and working in the course of history to establish his rule. It is this belief that gives Christians power to live with both hope and realism—hope that God is present in their time and place and that his kingdom will indeed come; realism in that the realization of God's purpose for the world within history is flawed and never complete. Hope and realism thus frame Christian participation in the political events of their time.[4]

Christians, no matter their time or place, live, as Simone Weil famously said, "waiting for God."[5] As they wait, no matter what the context, they are to be guided in practical affairs, says Temple, by both "primary" and "derivative" principles that the church can and must teach as incumbent on all believers. The primary principle is that human beings are created in the image of God, but this image is "stamped with an animal nature."[6] Between these two there is "constant tension resulting in perpetual tragedy." Despite this tension, however, all human beings, created in God's image, remain children of God. As such they all are to be treated with "dignity." It is important to note that Temple links the dignity of human beings not directly with the incarnation as an expression of God's universal love but to the fact that all people are made in God's image. This position is different from the more secular one received from Kant and now regnant within Western culture. This secular tradition locates human dignity in human reason.[7] For Temple the worth (and so dignity)

---

4. Temple, *Christianity and Social Order*, 61–62.
5. Weil, *Waiting for God* (1951).
6. Temple, *Christianity and Social Order*, 63.
7. For a discussion of the importance of this distinction, see Jackson, "Sanctity and Suffering," in Radner, *Church, Society and the Christian Common Good*, 45–62.

of a person is not rooted in what she is worth because of her capacities (say of reason) but in what she is worth to God. Thus, human worth is bestowed by God in creation and affirmed by God in the incarnation of his Son. Human worth is not rooted in a human capacity. The location of human value in bestowal rather than natural possession marks a fundamental point of difference between Christian Socialist thought and that of the present age.

Having distinguished between bestowal and possession as a basis for placing value on one's fellows, Temple continues his discussion of primary principles and in doing so shows the continuing influence of F. D. Maurice. Like Maurice, he moves from what is bestowed by God to what human beings are by nature. They are members of God's family. The natural expression of this metaphysical fact is the human family. By nature, people are social beings, created for fellowship with both God and one another. Temple concludes that the family is the initial and natural form of this fellowship. For this reason, the "preservation and security (of families) is the first principle of social welfare."[8] Further, the perdurable nature of nations through history indicates that they also are a part of the divine plan. In respect to families, he concludes that any ordering of society that injures the stability of the family is to be condemned. In respect to nations he concludes, "The aim within the nation must be to create a harmony of stable and economically secure family units; the aim in the world as a whole must be to create a harmony of spiritually independent nations which recognize one another as reciprocally supplementary parts of a richly harmonious fellowship."[9]

To anticipate one problem presented by this appeal to divine providence and natural order, it is well to note that it is far more difficult to establish the universality of the nation than it is to posit the family as the fundamental expression of the social nature of humankind. If by nation Temple means the various "peoples" of the earth, he may have a point. If, however, he refers to the nation-state, his position becomes highly doubtful.[10] The nation-state is a recent and fragile political institution, and the idea of a family of nations is both more recent and more problematic. For the moment, however, it is sufficient to note that, in making a move to the providence of God and the order of creation, Temple places himself

---

8. Temple, *Christianity and Social Order*, 63.

9. Temple, *Christianity and Social Order*, 64.

10. I say "doubtful" because Holy Scripture locates the division between peoples and languages of the earth in the fall rather than the creative intent of God.

within the Christian Socialist tradition. Nevertheless, his identification with this tradition is not without its qualifications. Though God's aim is fellowship within the family and between the nations, the human spirit is depraved. As a result, though we do not lose our social nature, we are never free from self-interest. Rulers, therefore, must appeal to self-interest even though people know that self-interest is not the real and final fact of their nature. So he concludes, "The art of government in fact is the art of so ordering life that self-interest prompts what justice demands."[11] Thus, against the views of the supporters of political economy, Temple is unwilling to allow markets simply to self-adjust on the basis of laws internal to themselves. There is a place for government interference, and so political and moral judgment, in market operations when those operations do not serve the common good. That intervention has the aim of reconciling self-interest with the demands of love and justice.

The art of government is necessary both for human flourishing and for determination as to what is best; but the best is never perfect. Within the context of the imperfection of social order, what is best is a matter of fallible judgment and flawed policy. Temple goes on to offer Christians three derivative principles that ought to inform our fallible and flawed social, economic, and political judgments. These derivatives flow from primary principles whose contents he summarizes as "respect for every person simply as a person" because they are created in God's image.[12] Reasoning from primary principles, Temple derives others as universally applicable aids to wise judgments. These are precisely those favored by Christian Socialists—Freedom, Social Fellowship, and Service.

Freedom is universally applicable because each and every human being is a child of God and as such each is created to develop as a person. This development is impossible apart from choice. Apart from choice people cannot develop the powers and qualities that issue in personality. For this reason, Temple says, "Freedom is the goal of politics. To establish and secure true freedom is the primary object of all right political action."[13] At this point it is well to note a difference between freedom as championed by Christian Socialists and freedom as posited by supporters of political economy. For the latter, freedom is a possession that is to

---

11. Temple, *Christianity and Social Order*, 65.
12. Temple, *Christianity and Social Order*, 67.
13. Temple, *Christianity and Social Order*, 67.

be encouraged and protected. For Christian Socialists it is a state to be achieved with the help of both society and good governance.

It was Temple's view that social fellowship flows naturally from freedom (and so personality) as the second derived principle. Human beings are created as social beings. It is within the fellowship of society that freedom is exercised and personality developed. By nature no one is fitted for life apart from the company of others. Our neighbors do more than contribute to meeting our needs. By their very presence their lives complement our own. As Temple says, "By our natural influence we actually constitute one another as what we are."[14] Further, we do so in small groups that are varied in purpose. A nation is, in fact, a community of communities in which freedom is exercised and fellowship developed and sustained. From this observation Temple draws an important political conclusion: "A democracy which is to be Christian must be a democracy of persons, not only of individuals. It must not only tolerate but also encourage minor communities as at once the expression and the arena of personal freedom; and its structure must be such as to serve this end."[15] This is a point of enormous ecumenical significance bringing as it does Temple's valorization of small groups into line with the Roman Catholic principle of subsidiarity. Sadly, Anglicans, along with other Protestant churches, have not in recent years made as much use of this principle as they might have, and in consequence have missed a great opportunity for ecumenical cooperation in matters touching the health of society.

Service is the third principle. It issues necessarily from the first two. From the combination of freedom and fellowship flows the obligation of service.[16] Within a society based in freedom and fellowship, duties precede rights. To see one's relation with others as one of obligation and so service rather than self-interested individual claim is to begin with the question, "What do I owe this person?" rather than, "What does she owe me?" In social relations, duty precedes rights! This maxim applies both in work and leisure; and in an economic system that more and more operates like a machine it serves to take the drudgery out of life. What one does, one does for others as well as oneself. Thus, the simplest task provides the opportunity both for self-development and social service.

---

14. Temple, *Christianity and Social Order*, 70.
15. Temple, *Christianity and the Social Order*, 66.
16. Temple, *Christianity and the Social Order*, 72.

For both labor and management, the ideal of service stands in the way of people becoming mere tools or freeloaders in a process of production.

Fully cognizant of the fact that the exercise of these principles takes place in a social context of limited resources and limited altruism, Temple insists we need an intellectual map that will allow people to weigh and balance these principles rightly. His view is that, within the changes and chances of social life, love and justice ought to regulate the order of the principles he has outlined. Love is "the predominant Christian impulse" but "the primary form of love in social organization is Justice."[17] So, for example, "Freedom must not be pursued in ways which offend against love, nor must service be demanded, or fellowship in any actual instance promoted, in ways that offend against justice."[18]

In deploying these principles, love and justice ought also to take account of the fact that we live in a natural order in which, as Tawney argued, everything has a divinely established "function." Following the tradition of natural law, Temple assigns reason the job of determining the function of a thing within an established order. For example, reason can show that within the economic field, goods are produced so that people "may satisfy their needs by consuming those goods."[19] From these observations he draws a practical judgment about economic systems, namely, that it is not possible to have a just economic system if its emphasis is on profit and not the meeting of human needs. The meeting of needs is so important because it makes possible family life, cultural development, and human fellowship. In other words, the provision of goods and services that address human needs promotes the true ends of life—"religion, art, science, and above all, happy human relationships."[20]

Temple's attempt to provide the guidance of the Church of England to the people of the United Kingdom takes one down a winding and highly intellectual path through the mind. It moves from an overall historical context to a primary principle, and then through derivative principles, and finally through a discussion of the complex matrix in which these principles are deployed. At the end, one is left with an intellectual, indeed Platonic, construct that hovers above the everyday world of social life. Nevertheless, he ends his treatment of political judgment with a

17. Temple, *Christianity and the Social Order*, 78.
18. Temple, *Christianity and the Social Order*, 80.
19. Temple, *Christianity and the Social Order*, 77.
20. Temple, *Christianity and the Social Order*, 81.

discussion of what his principles and their context imply for the concrete task of social betterment. In doing so he lays out a series of what the 1937 conference on "The Church and its Function in Society" termed "middle axioms." These are action guides that lie between basic principles, on the one hand, and specific policy proposals, on the other. Middle axioms "are an attempt to define the directions in which, in a particular state of society, Christian faith must express itself. They are not binding for all time, but are provisional definitions of the type of behavior required of Christians at a given period and in given circumstances."[21]

A number of the middle axioms he suggests concern what today we call family policy. He has established that the social nature of humankind finds its primary expression in the family; that any ordering of society that impairs or destroys the stability of the family stands condemned; and that to ignore the family is to injure both citizens and society. These facts imply certain middle axioms in respect to family policy. Family life requires leisure time, and leisure time requires a limited workweek and paid vacations. Family policy ought to support these things. Or again, because the chief expression of each person's status as a child of God is freedom to develop personality, social policy should not turn people into tools to be used simply for the profit of industry. Or again, because the development of personality requires education, arrangements for the education of the populace are a matter of priority. Temple ends his elaboration of middle axioms with an extended list of policy priorities that bear a remarkable resemblance to the platform of the Labour Party—adequate housing and education, secure income, a voice in the workplace, sufficient leisure, freedom of speech and assembly.[22] These "policy priorities" do indeed bear a remarkable resemblance to the platform of the Labour Party. It was no doubt for this reason that Temple listed them in an appendix rather than in the body of his text. He did so in order to make clear that in advocating these policy initiatives he spoke as an individual and not as the voice of the Church of England.

2. Walk as Wise

Temple's attempt to identify the content and limits of the Church of England's responsibility to provide political guidance to its members is

---

21. Visser 't Hooft and Oldham, *Church and Its Function in Society*, 210.
22. Temple, *Christianity and Social Order*, 96-97.

without question a *tour de force*—yet one that remains firmly within the idealistic tradition of Christian Socialism. In accord with this tradition he grounds his social ethic in the created order and the incarnation of Christ. The ideals he espouses—our social nature, the dignity of every person as a child of God, the importance of personal development, the fundamental equality of every person, the signal importance of fellowship and service, to name but a few—were all preceded by the valorization of a similar set of ideals on the part of the Christian Socialists. What Temple writes is both familiar and in many ways promising, but, if one stops for a moment's reflection, questions arise.

Temple moves from the primary principle of fundamental human equality and dignity to the derivative principles of freedom, social fellowship and service, and from there to hope and limitation within concrete circumstances, and finally to middle axioms that suggest guidelines for political judgment that take account both of the context of political judgment and of the principles and the limitations placed upon their application within particular historical circumstances. Temple is clear that he does not wish to lay down a template for a perfect social order.[23] Nevertheless, he does propose a template setting out a series of principles—axioms required by church teaching whenever one is confronted with a political issue. These principles, arranged as they are from primary to derivative, in Temple's mind constitute mandatory starting points for Christian moral reasoning about public issues. The very term "principles" suggests a path of deductive reasoning; and, though one would not want to gainsay their moral importance, left as they are, they do not adequately portray the way moral reasoning proceeds or the way in which political judgments are actually made.

When I had finished for the third time reading Temple's account of principles and middle axioms, Donald MacKinnon's comment, "The incarnation is not the disclosing of certain principles," came to mind.[24] So also did Oliver O'Donovan's portrayal of moral reasoning and moral judgment in the initial volume of his trilogy, *Ethics as Theology*.[25] He writes, "So practical reason is not deductive, which is to say, unidirectional, moving from a point established to a point still to be attained. It moves to and fro between the world of realities and the moment of action;

---

23. *Christianity and Social Order*, 59.

24. MacKinnon, "Revelation and Social Justice," 105. See also Wilkinson, *Christian Socialism*, 119.

25. See, i.e., O'Donovan, *Self, World, and Time*, 31–32.

it correlates a description of the one with a determination of the other."[26] Moral reasoning does not move simply from A to B—from premise to conclusion. It involves a long process of deliberation and reflection. This process moves back and forth until a judgment is reached. As O'Donovan says, "Any thinking-towards needs some thinking about as a springboard from which to take off."[27] So, for example, he writes, "One cannot think towards a policy of buying fair trade tea or coffee without thinking about the problematic balance of power in the world's tea and coffee markets. The question 'what am I to do?' means 'what am I to do in *this state of affairs*?' and so always presumes an answer to the question 'what state of affairs?'"[28]

In fact, Temple does not ignore the question "what state of affairs?"; but in *Christianity and Social Order* he does not make as clear as he might have done the way in which his principles interact with descriptive states of affairs. He might have done so had he made more use of the dialectical method that he affirmed in many of his other writings. Had he done so he might have made clear what it means to say that these states of affairs include more than principles, primary and derivative. Nevertheless, he did not and as a result, on occasion, gave the impression to many of his readers (this one included) that he had in mind a deductive process. As a result, many have reasonably understood his account of moral reasoning as a process that moves in deductive fashion from higher-level principles to lower-level principles that in turn suggest a right course of action.

In point of fact, however, when his better angel is present, his reasoning is more often than not dialectical rather than deductive. Throughout his career Temple emphasized the importance of dialectical reasoning that requires a process that moves back and forth between a number of factors, some of which are values, some principles, some accounts of particular circumstances, some estimates of results, some degrees of uncertainty, etc. In this back and forth, there is no predetermined starting point and certainly no conclusion hidden within any possible starting point. Moral reasoning is a process that goes back and forth between all these and many other factors. It has no necessary starting point. Its end point is not a conclusion drawn from a premise but a judgment made in the midst of uncertainty.

26. O'Donovan, *Self, World, and Time*, 31.
27. O'Donovan, *Self, World, and Time*, 32.
28. O'Donovan, *Self, World, and Time*, 32.

In his *Studies in the Spirit and Truth of Christianity*[29] Temple made clear his view of the way moral reasoning works in a more adequate manner than in *Christianity and Social Order*. This view is coherent (though not completely) with the views of Oliver O'Donovan set out above. In 1914 Temple wrote as follows, "All actual thinking proceeds in circles or pendulum swings. We approach a group of facts; they suggest a theory; in the light of the theory we get a fuller grasp of the facts; this fuller grasp suggests modifications of the theory; and so we proceed until we reach a systematic apprehension of the facts where each fits into its place. In the end we have not one universal and unquestioned proposition with other propositions deductively established from it, but a whole system—a concrete universal—in which each element is guaranteed by all the rest, and all together constitute the whole which determines each."[30]

This way of describing the process of moral reasoning does indeed involve a dialectic that moves back and forth between fact and value, value and fact. But, on occasion, Temple's description of the process presents its end as a conclusion, suggesting a necessary ending point. In this respect, his description is different and less accurate than that of O'Donovan. In point of fact, the dialectic between fact and value ends in a judgment based on discernment of what is right and good rather than a conclusion at the end of a rational process. The fact is that the principles Temple values are not actually starting points in a process of reasoning but aspects of a way of life that must be learned, lived out, and deployed in the midst of the testing fires of experience.

I wonder if in fact life in Christ is not so much a matter of attachment to principles that can suggest and frame problems and conclusions as it is an attempt to cultivate a manner of life that provides a way in which to view and react to the world. I wonder if the use of the notion of principles leads perforce to deductive reasoning. Perhaps it would be better to give up the term "principles" and speak rather, with the Christian Socialists, of ideals, ideas, and habits of mind and behavior that make up a worldview and provide "outlooks" that produce "on looks." In the interplay of outlooks and on looks ideals, ideas, and virtues (formed ways of behavior), along with the promptings of imagination, play their part, but more as perceptions and formed reactions to the world than as starting points in a process of reasoning that leads to a conclusion.

---

29. Temple, *Studies in the Spirit and Truth of Christianity*.
30. Cited by Suggate, in *William Temple*, 17.

This observation leads back to the unresolved question previously noted. Has the attempt on the part of Christian Socialists to make room for ideals in a political economy succeeded, or has it ended in an unnecessary, unrealistic, and inapplicable idealism?

In respect to the charge that ideals are unnecessary there is an easy and convincing response. History has shown again and again that left to its own devices a political economy does not produce the best results for society as a whole. These adverse results raise moral questions that people avoid at their own peril. As Ronald Preston has pointed out, there are a number of crucial moral issues brought about by the market system that the market system, despite its efficiency in allocating resources, cannot resolve. Among these there are moral issues connected with public health, pollution, social planning, periodic market collapses, and socially harmful inequalities in income and wealth.[31] All these are social and moral issues. They reach into the future and require remedial action that exceeds the reach of private action, and so there must be appropriate governmental action.

A world devoid of ideals has no way other than self-interest either to recognize or to address such issues. The Christian Socialists were right to insist that a world devoid of ideals is both cruel and destined for self-destruction. The point of their failure was not their insistence on the importance of moral ideals. Their most serious failure was rather at the level of moral reasoning—with an all too frequent failure to account for how moral ideals function within the process of moral discernment. I will call this issue the problem of insight and application.

Temple's attempt to find a way for the church to provide principles and middle axioms that can be applied by the faithful to public affairs is suggestive, but too little is said about moral formation, on the one hand, and the way in which people actually arrive at moral judgments, on the other. In respect to ideals, Temple's resort to principles does not give an adequate picture of what ideals are, of how they are instilled in moral agents, of what their limitations and dangers are, or of the way in which they actually work in the process of making moral judgments. Once again, the question is in what way ideals serve as necessary and effective action guides within the rough-and-tumble of political life. In respect to specific moral judgments, can they be applied directly to concrete issues? Or is it the case that apart from a complex process of moral formation

---

31. Preston, *Church and Society*, 46–47.

and moral reflection, they either simply idle like an engine that is forever in neutral or serve as blinders that shut out the complexity of life as lived in the world?

I have argued that ideals do not act like theorems, axioms, or postulates from which one can deduce political conclusions. Life within a social, economic, and political system does not lend itself to deduction, even at the level of Temple's middle axioms. How then do ideals serve as practical action guides in a world in which their expression is limited by scarce resources, limited altruism, even sin? What part do they play in the back-and-forth process of weighing and balancing characteristic of moral reason?

In the process of moral discernment, what if ideals serve not so much as principles from which others can be derived and from which conclusions can be drawn but more as defining characteristics of a view of the world and a way of life—characteristics that provide the way in which one views the world, understands it and seeks to behave within it? If ideals functioned in this way they would serve more as proverbs than principles. As Gerhard von Rad argued many years ago, proverbs name the standard circumstances of life and indicate ways in which one can live successfully within those circumstances.[32] Suppose the ideals of the Christian Socialists aren't really principles at all. Suppose they are best understood not as principles but as moral insights, virtues, values, and admonitions that provide the location from which to view the world and, in Paul's words, learn to walk "as wise [people], making the best use of time, because the days are evil" (Eph 5:15–16).

In short, it makes more sense to view the ideals professed by the Christian Socialists not as part of a political philosophy that makes logical connections between principles, axioms, and cases but as aspects of a way of life drawn from the exemplary life of a man whom they are urging people to imitate—a man who saw each person as a child of God, equally valuable in the sight of God, created in freedom to develop as a person with a given character, destined to life in a fellowship of cooperation and called upon to serve God and her fellows with her life and her wealth. In this case ideals have motive as well as cognitive power, and they encompass not only habits of behavior but ways of understanding that illumine life's circumstances as we pass through. In this case, ideals mark out aspects of a way in which, as citizens, Christians are enabled to

---

32. Rad, *Old Testament Theology*, 1:418–52.

"walk as wise rather than unwise" so as to make the best use of time, both for their neighbors and themselves. In this journey, Temple held that the possibilities for social advance are never absent, but they are limited. If understood as constituent aspects of a way of life, Christian ideals do not chart the way to utopia, but they do serve as enablers of Christian wisdom rooted in experience and expressed in ways that help believers "walk as wise rather than foolish."

In light of that admonition, a further comment on Temple's account of moral reflection is called for. In keeping with the tradition he inherited, Temple gave a distinctively moral—one might say "principled"—interpretation to the incarnation. As previously noted, it was this moral focus to which, at the Malvern Conference, Donald MacKinnon objected. His objection focused not on the adequacy of the moral reasoning he detected among his fellow conferees, but rather on the subject about which they were reasoning. He objected to giving Christology first a moral rather than a religious focus. Moralistic interpretations of Christian doctrine, he said, lead the church to understand its social mission largely in terms of morals. When this happens, Christians come to understand their social calling to be moral exhortation that urges people to fulfill obligations to their station and its duties. Such exhortation is by no means always a bad thing, but it does not "inspire novel social aims proportionate to its estimate of man's nature and dignity, and to the character of the existing situation."[33]

MacKinnon does not expound upon what he believes those novel social aims to be. He does, however, suggest what a religious interpretation of the incarnation has to say about judgments concerning "the character of the existing situation." A religious interpretation of the doctrine first of all provides a form of religious wisdom that lies beyond the reach of the standard moral wisdom of the Church of England. The moral wisdom of the Church of England first presents the incarnation not as a salvific act but as an engine of social progress. However, a religious interpretation begins with Christ, not as an agent of moral advance but as the savior of the world. As their savior Christ has liberated humankind from the power of sin. Sin is a religious condition before it is a moral state. It is a religious condition in which people have freely turned their backs on God's grace and in so doing have become, in MacKinnon's words, "denatured." That is, in our natural state, we are created out of nothing and so exist over an

---

33. MacKinnon, "Revelation and Social Justice," 88.

abyss, supported only by the grace and power of God. In refusing this grace and power, we have become "denatured"; we stand above the abyss of our origin with nothing to support us save our own wit and effort. Our reaction is to make a world for ourselves by means of which we seek to assure our continuing existence. This attempt at self-salvation is no more than the arrogant act of a Titan. MacKinnon suggests that it is from this perspective, as denatured Titans, that we should view our social wisdom and political activity.

MacKinnon does not mean to say that we should renounce our attempts to order our world so as to preserve life, to make peace with one another, and to establish conditions of human flourishing. He means only that if we view Christ as savior before we see him as moral example, then we recognize that what distinguishes Christ is not his rectitude and social message but his trust that only grace can prevent him (and us) from falling into the abyss from which we all come. And so it was that Christ, during his life and ministry on earth, turned his back on all human attempts to build a foundation that saves us from the abyss over which our lives are suspended. In this way he shows us the way to the Father. In faith we cast all our care on him. He shows us also that our attempts to provide for ourselves a foundation upon which to rest our lives are necessary but they are, in W. H. Auden's words, only "for the time being." They are a necessary means to sustain, perhaps even better, our lives, but they cannot deliver us from the abyss from which we have appeared. Only the grace of God the Father can do that, and if we invest saving significance in the fragile arrangements of our own making, then we become Titans, denatured human beings—perhaps even the beast speaking great things.

This is the specifically Christian message Christians have to deliver to the denatured inhabitants of God's world. This is the foundational wisdom the church has to speak and exemplify to the denatured inhabitants of God's earth. It is only from this foundation that any moral wisdom the church might communicate can escape the titanic pretense of human art and power. Only in the light of what might be called heavenly wisdom can we learn to walk as wise, making the most of the time. This is what Christians (as Christians) have to say to their fellow citizens about the moral judgments we make in respect to "the character of the existing situation" that amounts to more than a riff on the reasonable wisdom of the world. If our attempt to provide a self-made platform upon which to stand over the abyss of our origins is not shown to be a fragile attempt to deny our finitude, then even the Christian Socialists will in fact contribute to Titanism rather than the humble service we owe to God, our brothers and sisters, and ourselves.

Part Four

Assessment, Influence, and Promise

A. Assessment

FELLOWSHIP, COMMUNITY, COOPERATION, SERVICE, sacrifice, equality, duty, freedom, personality, character, and property constitute ideal forms of social vision that together comprise the Christian Socialists' alternative to the competitive and autonomous social relations championed by advocates of political economy. To find a theological warrant for their communal vision they turned to the doctrine of the incarnation. Upon examination, the weaknesses of this theological warrant, as they presented it, are apparent. Nonetheless, from what they believed to be the fact of Christ's full participation both in the life of the world and in the life of God they drew conclusions about the ideals that ought to shape the way in which the peoples of the earth live together. It is important to note that these ideals in fact form a coherent set of interlocking social goods that reflect the rule of God in human affairs, and provide a credible account of the social goals at which Christians and all people of good will ought to aim.

Indeed, the first thing to be said about their social vision is that the ideals that give it shape are interlocking, coherent, and appealing. The second thing to say is that these ideals, though suggested by Christian belief and practice, can resonate with people not formed by this religious tradition. They are firmly based in a claim about human nature (we are all created as social beings in the image of God) but also in a powerful account of who God, in the life of Jesus, has revealed himself to be. If, indeed, we have been created as social rather than solitary beings; if, as the image of God, we have indeed been created to enjoy fellowship with God and with one another; and if, indeed, God in Christ has shown his love for each of us equally, then it follows that we have been created for and called to forms of life together that carry on over time within the bonds of a common life wherein each person is accorded equal value.

This fundamental equality is to be recognized and sustained by the social ideals of cooperation, mutual service, and willingness, when called for, to sacrifice one's own benefit for that of others.

This account of the nature and destiny of humankind, no matter what its limitations and flaws turn out to be, provides a powerful rejoinder to the atomistic and competitive account of social relations proffered by the advocates of political economy and their latter-day neoliberal progeny. The counternarrative of the Christian Socialists is made up of several levels of argument that they often failed to distinguish. One line is based upon common sense and reason. It points out that one really can't bring about a society by the sovereign choices of individuals. In point of fact, one simply can't get to society by the concurrence of human choice. As previously noted, F. D. Maurice made this point clearly in his discussion of Methodism. There he asks, as noted, whether "distinct individual acts . . . may not, must not, depend at last upon some relation in which [people] stand to their fellows."[1] He wonders if, in accounting for social relations, we can take our start from the choices of individuals and then go on to build a society out of these choices. His rhetorical question is this: Is it not the case that individuals are born of social relations rather than the other way around?

In a recent book edited by Malcolm Brown, *Anglican Social Theology*, Alan Suggate, relying on Alasdair MacIntyre's work *After Virtue*, has made a similar point.[2] By nature we are bodies and as bodies we are social beings, having been born of parents in a community that gives one social identity. We must consider this communal belonging if we are to know who we are and how we are to act both as individuals and as members of society. As social beings we are introduced to practices that are socially established and to cooperative activities. It is within these activities that we learn the virtues necessary to achieve standards of excellence and realize the goods internal to those practices. These goods and virtues can be discussed. They are never simply arbitrary preferences. As Suggate concludes, we are never isolated individuals. Rather, we belong to ordered communities within which we seek the human good that is also the common good.[3]

---

1 Maurice, *Kingdom of Christ*, 139.

2. Suggate, "Temple Tradition," in Brown, *Anglican Social Theology*, 40–41.

3. Suggate, "Temple Tradition," in Brown, *Anglican Social Theology*, 41.

His point is not dissimilar to one made by Wittgenstein and his followers. They insist on the priority of social relations and language rather than individual choice when giving an account of social life. To take one example, Sabina Lovibond, in her book *Ethical Formation*, notes that the reasons we give for our actions do not exist simply in the hearts of individuals. Rather, the reasons we give for the sorts of people we want to be and for the actions we take are simply there in the cultural air we breathe. As she says, "The ethical, let us say, pertains to what people learn to value through immersion in a community acquainted with ideas of right, duty, justice, solidarity, and common social or cultural interests extending beyond the lifetime of the present generation."[4]

There is no distance between what Suggate and Lovibond say here and what Maurice wondered in mid-nineteenth-century England when he asked if individual acts do not depend upon some relation in which people stand to their fellows and if, in accounting for social relations, we can take our start from individuals and then go on to build a society out of their choices. The Christian Socialists were on firm ground when they took this contrary position against the individualism espoused by both Evangelical Christians and the advocates of political economy. The ideals of fellowship and community held by the Christian Socialists rest firmly upon the bedrock of fact. Apart from fellowship and community we cannot continue to exist as humans. That we are social by nature can be established by simple observation.[5] However, the status of the attendant ideals of cooperation, sacrifice, service, and equality are by no means so obvious. Do fellowship and community require also lives of cooperation, service, and sacrifice? Further, do they imply, as the Christian Socialists insisted, a fundamental equality between all members of the human community?

To be sure, social life is impossible without some degree of cooperation between its members. Years ago Colin Turnbull wrote a study of an East African tribe known as the Ik.[6] His study showed that it is possible that social tumult can so erode social solidarity that no single member of

---

4. Lovibond, *Ethical Formation*, 33.

5. Simple observation has recently found corroboration from evolutionary biology and social and economic analysis. Both attest to the fact that human beings, as a species, are born as communal, cooperative beings whose social nature is hardwired in their genetic makeup and in the process of their socialization. See, e.g., Collier, "Greed Is Dead."

6. Turnbull, *The Mountain People*.

a group any longer feels any obligation to any other member, including one's own children. The Ik, as described by Turnbull, exist in physical proximity but within that space enjoy the most minimal forms of common life imaginable.

With the example of the Ik, Turnbull describes human life at the very edge of what reasonably can be called a human existence; but what about social life rooted in fellowship and cooperation? In what way might the ideals of service, sacrifice, and equality be thought necessary components of a fulfilling form of social life? For fellowship and community to exist there must be some degree of cooperation between its individual members and subgroups. As Marcel Mauss and, latterly, John Milbank and Adrian Pabst have reminded us, social cooperation is carried on by means of multiple levels of social exchange.[7] These exchanges create and express alliances that make our desire for common life a possibility, but they also may become means of competition and dominance. Social exchanges create social bonds, but these bonds may be used as well to establish social hierarchies that render some parties subservient to others and possibly disadvantaged.

Notoriously, the Christian Socialists failed to recognize that cooperation, though a social necessity and social good, nonetheless has a dark side. Their blindness to the inbuilt exploitation connected with the class system provides a prime example of this failing. It is a failing they sought to overcome, if not eliminate, by linking the idea of cooperation with the ideal of service. A person's social place and standing, they argued, provide the location for giving one's life in service to others and so to a good in which all share. Further, this way of mitigating the negative aspects of unequal social exchanges called not for resistance but sacrifice—sacrifice on the part of both the more and the less powerful. Again, however, we must note with Didier Fassin that, like duty, service and sacrifice seem first to flow downward, from those in power to those in a lesser position, and then up from the bottom toward the top. In effect, this flow of social goods from top to bottom and then from bottom to top seems to bestow value on those below by those above that then must be repaid. Those of lesser estate receive their social place from superiors who are then to receive service and sacrifice from those who have had value bestowed upon them.

---

7. Mauss, *The Gift*, and Milbank and Pabst, *The Politics of Virtue*.

A. ASSESSMENT

Let us grant that the Christian Socialists' intentions were good—that they espoused the valorization of cooperation, service, and sacrifice as necessary counters to the valorization of competition and individual struggle on the part of the supporters of political economy. Still and all, the way in which they espoused these ideals is often frankly condescending, utopian, and seriously unfair. They are condescending because they call for service and sacrifice on the part of people who are disadvantaged by the very social position they occupy. They are utopian because they fail to recognize either the ever-present power of egoism to distort all social relations or the harmful forms of inequality engendered and sustained by many forms of social exchange. Finally, they are unfair because they fail to recognize the positive social benefits of competition. In respect to the charge of unfairness, it is enough to say at this point that the improvement of social conditions depends upon innovation, and innovation always competes with established ways and techniques. Winners and losers are woven into the very fabric of social change; but social change cannot be completely bad. For example, the changes brought about by capitalism have produced enormous wealth and, many would claim, have served to improve rather than lower living standards across the broad spectrum of populations. Nevertheless, despite evidence to the contrary, the Christian Socialists were reluctant to credit a competitive economic system with any form of social betterment. They remained staunch defenders of traditional social structures. Indeed, one cannot escape noticing once again a Platonic bent to their thought—a perspective that views change with great suspicion. In response to this worry, they fell victim to a desire to manage social relations from the top down. Hence, their call for the "return of Christendom"—a form of social organization that to their mind had a fixed social hierarchy governed by loyalty and sustained by the practice of virtues.

In response to these objections I suspect the advocates of Christian Socialism would point to the centrality in their thought of the ideal of equality. Above all else, equality serves to hold in check, even ameliorate, imbalances of wealth and rank. To the minds of Christian Socialists, all people, regardless of station or circumstance, enjoy a fundamental equality before God. They believed fervently that because all people share the image of God and because all people are recipients of the love of God present in the life of Jesus Christ, all are before God equal in worth. If all people are of equal value in the eyes of God, so should we be in the eyes of one another.

That there are problems is obvious, but there are also enormous strengths in the foundation for equality proposed by the Christian Socialists—strengths they could have deployed but failed to do so as effectively as they might have. The strength of their account of equality is that it rests on the status of each and every person before God rather than upon some quality, most commonly "dignity," that one possesses as it were on one's own. It is dignity that the Universal Declaration of Human Rights ascribes to every person, but as Ruth Macklin wrote in the *British Medical Journal*, "Dignity is a useless concept. It means no more than respect for persons or their autonomy." She went on to say, "Appeals to dignity are either vague restatements of other more precise notions or mere slogans that add nothing to the understanding of the topic."[8] Given the prominence dignity now enjoys in discussions of human rights, this is a strong statement, but the fact is that "dignity" is a term with a dubious history. Joel Feinberg notes, "Respect for persons may simply be respect for their rights, so that there cannot be one without the other; and what is called 'human dignity' may simply be the recognizable capacity to assert claims."[9] And as Michael Rosen points out, skeptics contend that dignity has no coherent meaning of its own. Rather, it is given content by a range of extraneous convictions for which it serves as a mere receptacle.[10]

Michael Rosen provides strong support for this view. In his study of the meaning and history of the term he mentions that dignity has been used to refer to the particular character of various (nonhuman) aspects of the world. He notes further that dignity has been used in Roman Catholic thought to justify a fixed social hierarchy. That is, each "station" in a social system has its own dignity, as do the people who occupy that station. It does seem that in the course of history dignity has indeed taken its meaning from aspects of the social environment, among them being high social status, a human quality (capable of expansion to all people) that demands respect and a worthy character. After Kant, its primary meaning has been the possession of freedom and reason by means of which individuals becomes moral agents and so "persons." Through that history the meaning of the term "dignity" has moved outward in expanding circles from social elites to a circumference that includes humankind as a whole.

8. Cited in Rosen, *Dignity*, 4.
9. Cited in Rosen, *Dignity*, 5.
10. Rosen, *Dignity*, 6.

At a minimum one must admit that the term "dignity" at best has an unstable meaning whose imprecision serves as much to generate argument about the extent of its meaning and application as it does to establish a firm foundation for universal human rights. The Christian Socialists were keenly aware of the problematic nature of rights claims, rooted as they often are in the internal capacity for autonomous action. They foresaw clearly that rights claims rooted in human autonomy rather than the image of God would issue in endless argument and social conflict. That their concerns were both prescient and well founded has been vindicated by current social dynamics wherein society is locked in irresolvable arguments over whether the unborn or newborn, the mentally defective or the dying are indeed autonomous beings who, by reason of their autonomy, have "dignity" and so also are "persons" with inalienable rights.

As presently employed, "dignity" is a term that refers to autonomy, and autonomy refers to the possession of freedom and reason. In insisting that the value of human life is rooted not in some capacity persons may possess to varying degrees but in the position each person enjoys before God, the Christian Socialists were on firm ground. For them each human life has value not because of something it possesses and may lose but because of a fact of its existence it cannot lose—the value each holds before God. In short, the Christian Socialists could have pressed the point more than they did that the value of a life does not depend upon some capacity or another (which to varying degrees may or may not be present) but upon holiness that is always present because bestowed and guaranteed equally by God.

For the Christian Socialists, God is the one who stands surety for the equal value of each human life. It was this fundamental equality before God that for them implied the equality of all people regardless of capacity, station, or circumstance. Firm as the foundation they provided might have been, that foundation in and of itself did not make clear the implications of equality before God for the ordering of common life. Equality before God is not an insignificant status to occupy, but how far do claims for equality reach when used to measure the quality, character, and justice of social structures and relationships? Clearly it does not establish equality as the measure of all forms of human interaction. We have seen that for Maurice, equality did not apply to the hierarchical structure of English society. It applied only in respect to members of each class treating members of all other classes as recipients of God's love and so rightful recipients of the love of Jesus expressed in their own lives. So, for Maurice, the class structure remained unchanged but the members of each class were bound together by mutual affection shaped by the love of God revealed in Christ.

Despite Maurice's influence, his conservative view of the relation between equality and social structure did not rest easy with a number of his followers. R. H. Tawney, for example, believed that the inequalities of the class system posed the most severe problem of what he termed the 'the acquisitive society." His view of divinely bestowed equality led him to hold that inequality was the most serious social and moral problem the nation faced. He argued that with the Industrial Revolution came inequality, and with inequality came privilege and tyranny. Equality is the basis for rejecting both. So it was that against privilege Tawney set equality and against tyranny he set another form of equality, the dispersion and control of power.

At a minimum Tawney's view of equality exposes the privilege, wealth, and power of the upper classes as a violation of a God-given feature of human nature. Accordingly, on the basis of human equality, he called for fairer distributions of both wealth and power. Such redistribution he viewed as a necessary implication of human equality before God. The question remains, however, as to what, on the basis of fundamental equality, constitutes a just distribution of privilege and power. It is obvious that it is nonsensical to say that equality means that in every distribution of wealth and power everyone gets the same. These observations suggest that the ideal of human equality may well serve to call attention to the negative aspects of other ideals like fellowship, cooperation, service, and sacrifice, but unless there is further elucidation of the range and manner of its application it does little to mitigate the negative possibilities of these social goods. Indeed, a failure to provide such elucidation is perhaps one of the greatest failures of all attempts to deploy ideals in the midst of the push and pull of public life. Apart from the hard moral reasoning and social sympathy required to make the right connections between ideals and everyday life, ideals unmeasured by additional moral reasoning and sentiment beckon their supporters to rash, absolutist, and destructive conclusions about the conduct of life in society. As Michael Walzer has argued in respect to justice, what is just in one sphere of social life may not be just in another. Something similar can be said about equality. The way in which basic human equality rightly applies in one set of social circumstances may not be the way in which it applies rightly in another.[11]

So also is it with privilege and power. Their just distribution, one that is fair and yet honors fundamental human equality, yields no single answer. What is right in one set of circumstances may well not be right in another. What is clear is that appeals to fundamental equality provide no satisfactory answer to the question of their just distribution. Aware of this problem, Tawney turned to another ideal, service, as a way to address the question of the just distribution of wealth. Monetary reward, he believed, should be distributed not on the basis of supply and demand but on the basis of value for service rendered. The problem here, of course, is who should judge the value of service rendered and on what basis. It would take Plato's philosopher king to render a just decision in such a matter, and since no such judge (save God) ever has existed or ever will exist, one must judge Tawney's proposal as no solution at all. In fact, the market seems as good a mechanism for judging the value of service rendered as lies within human reach. Yet the market, by its own operations, can measure only popular demand and not intrinsic value. This simple fact reveals another. The most efficient and fair way of determining the values of a society lies in the standards by which social rewards are meted out.

Nevertheless, it is fair to ask, On what basis should society value the services its members render to the commonweal? Can ideals provide an answer to this question? One possible candidate among the ideals favored by the Christian Socialists is the purpose of social life itself. Society exists, in their view, to provide the culture out of which well-developed personalities possessing a good character can grow. For the Christian Socialists, well-developed personalities with a formed character constitute the *telos* of social life, but social life is variegated. It is made up of various groups and various individuals doing different sorts of things. Given the cooperative nature of society, the social product of these variegated forms of social life and these variegated forms of service comprise the elements that serve the development of personality and character. Thus, one way to determine what constitutes a just reward for service rendered might be the importance of that service for the common good of society. This solution assumes some agreement about the social value of service rendered along with a fundamental equality among the members of society but it does not assume an equal worth in the contribution of each member.

11. See Walzer, *Spheres of Justice*.

Fundamental equality requires that all people be rewarded appropriately for their service, but it does not require that all be rewarded equally.

Fundamental equality requires that all people be recognized and properly rewarded for their service to the common good, and so to the development of strong and healthy personalities that manifest sterling character. However, it also requires an inclusive notion of equality that governs the various dimensions of social life. This means that equality cannot be measured by one standard—say financial reward or academic ability. Indeed, if a society were to reckon equality only by the measure of monetary return or academic ability, it would produce hierarchies of wealth and power of the very sort Tawney condemned. As Mickey Kaus has pointed out, equality within a society can and should be measured in relation to a number of factors other than wealth (the present standard of equality).[12] For example, equality can be measured by access to the various forms of education that lead to personal development in a variety of activities. It can lead to access to basic health care. It can lead to access to suitable housing. Fair distribution does not mean that everyone gets the same salary, or education, or house, or medical care. It means only that everyone has access to the necessities required, in their case, for a fully developed personality and character.

The sort of equality I am speaking of has been well summarized by L. T. Hobhouse in his essay "The Historical Evolution of Property, in Fact and in Idea." The challenge in respect to wealth and the distribution of other social goods, he says, is "to find a method, compatible with the industrial conditions of the new age, of securing to each man, as a part of his civic birthright, a place in the industrial system and a lien upon the common product that he may call his own, without dependence either upon private charity or the arbitrary decision of an official."[13] It is this equal access to the various goods that make possible the development of personality and character that is the sort of equality the Christian Socialists advocated. For Hobhouse the sort of equality the Christian Socialists sought is not one in which everyone gets the same thing but one that secures for each person "a lien upon the common product that he may call his own, without dependence upon private charity or the arbitrary decision of an official."[14]

---

12. See Kaus, *The End of Equality*.

13. Hobhouse, "Historical Evolution of Property," in Gore, *Property*, 32–33.

14. Hobhouse, "Historical Evolution of Property," in Gore, *Property*, 33.

In support of their use of a qualified ideal of equality as a defense against undue inequality of wealth and power, the Christian Socialists also marshaled the ideal of freedom. The sort of freedom they advocated was neither freedom from undue restraint nor freedom to pursue individually chosen social goals. It is true that some forms of restraint are necessary for human flourishing. In the same way freedom to pursue private ends, beneficial though it may be, can also take a course that is damaging to social health, personality, and character. What the Christian Socialists wanted was a society whose forms of life honored basic human equality and promoted the sort of freedom that allows people to pursue the divinely appointed ends of all people, namely, to honor God and love one's neighbor as oneself, to share a common form of life, and to develop fully as a personality. For the Christian Socialists the goal of human life, and so of a Christian society, had become incarnate in Christ Jesus, who fulfilled the law of life—to love God with all one's heart, soul, mind, and strength and one's neighbor as oneself. For them the true measure of human personality and character is to be found in Christ Jesus, and their aim was a society whose ideals promoted such an end.

A society ordered to promote the flourishing of personality and character fashioned after the pattern of Christ's life, to their minds, cannot be pursued apart from sufficient wealth to allow for the exercise of freedom. So it was that they engaged in a rigorous discussion of the place of property within a social order. Property was necessary for the exercise of freedom, the development of personality and character, and the fulfillment of one's duties to God and neighbor. So they published a collection of essays by leading intellectuals of the period setting out what they called the "duties and rights" of property ownership.[15] Charles Gore, then bishop of Oxford, wrote an introduction that well summarizes the content of these essays. In keeping with the goals of the Christian Socialists, Bishop Gore states correctly that the purpose of the essayists is to provide principles that have power to form the conscience of the nation and so promote reform of an economic system that does not reflect Christian principles in respect to the possession and use of property. In particular, Bishop Gore is concerned that concentrations of wealth mean that wealth is taken away from its proper use and devoted to the accumulation and exercise of power.[16] To his mind, this is a destructive situation because, as

---

15. Gore, *Property: Its Duties and Rights*.
16. Gore, "Introduction," in Gore, *Property*, xv.

Aristotle pointed out, property is necessary for the free development of the higher life of an individual and at the same time is the most effective stimulus there is for personal effort and the development of character.

The very success of a civilization can be measured by the degree to which cognizance is taken of this fact. So Gore writes, "The success of a civilization . . . must be measured not by the amount and character of its products or material wealth, nor by the degree of well-being which it renders possible for a privileged class, but by the degree in which it enables all its members to feel that they have the chance of making the best of themselves, to feel that an adequate measure of free self-realization is granted them."[17] On the basis of this principle he notes that "our civilization is open to the most serious indictment" because there is too little property for use and too much for power.[18] Too little property for use means too many people are unable to control their destiny. They become tools in the hands of others—mere "hands" in what ought to be a social enterprise wherein everyone occupies a space for contributing to the common life and by the use of freedom developing a full personality and a good character.

Accordingly, Gore insists we are social beings. It is common life that makes property possible. We realize ourselves in communities, and in these communities the state has a profound responsibility. It exists "to enable its members to make possible a worthy life."[19] Thus, the state is free to alter laws and methods to secure a better distribution of wealth. Given the dominant individualism of the age, it is wrong to claim, as did the supporters of political economy, an almost unlimited right of "acquiring, retaining, and perpetuating property."[20] Bishop Gore concludes, "The tenure of property in any community must be judged by its tendency to promote what alone is the real end of civil society—that is, the best possible life for man in general and each man in particular."[21] For this to happen, every citizen must be afforded his personal share. Property for power must be transformed and given a communal function governed by these principles.

---

17. Gore, "Introduction," in Gore, *Property*, xiv–xv.
18. Gore, "Introduction," in Gore, *Property*, xv.
19. Gore, "Introduction," in Gore, *Property*, xvi.
20. Gore, "Introduction," in Gore, *Property*, xx.
21. Gore, "Introduction," in Gore, *Property*, xxi.

So wrote Bishop Gore. The proper use of property is an ideal that ought to govern social relations within a society guided by Christian belief and practice. Property use, along with fellowship, community, cooperation, service, sacrifice, equality, duty, freedom, personality, and character development, form a coherent and mutually supportive set of ideals. These ideals in turn serve as a guide to the citizenry of England for shaping a society that reflects both the creative intent and profound love God has for each and every person. Fellowship produces community and leads to cooperative relations that are sustained by service and sacrifice. These ideals make possible and encourage the development of personality and character. The development of personality and character is made possible also by social conditions that encourage and support freedom. In turn, freedom along with the development of personality and character are in part made possible by a financial base (property) that supports the exercise of freedom by all segments of society.

These are the ideals that the Christian Socialists believed were present in Christendom, and they are the ideals the Christian Socialists hoped, through the church, to awaken in the British public. All of these guiding principles were, however, dependent upon a sense of duty (not rights) on the part of the British public. As previously noted, the Christian Socialists opposed the prominent place given to rights by supporters of political economy. They would no doubt oppose the same valorization of rights common among neoliberals and progressive liberals of the present age. To establish the primacy of duty over rights is central to their whole project. Indeed, their entire effort to establish Christian Sociology depends upon their account of duties and rights. It is difficult to imagine the complex set of ideals that make up their social vision having much traction apart from a populace already shaped by a strong sense of duty to the members of the community and/or commonwealth of which they are a part.

As previously noted, the initial point of the Christian Socialists is that the primacy of duty over rights rests upon the social nature of all forms of human life. To their mind, there must be a "we" if there is to be an "I." Because we are social beings, they held that we, from the start, incur debts to those whose life together makes human agency possible. Apart from such indebtedness, we become unbounded, free individuals who at best can claim rights in the face of social incursions by other unbounded individuals. From the start the Christian Socialists insisted that to begin with rights is to begin with individuals in conflict rather than individuals engendered, shaped, and bound by communal ties. These ties are established by exchanges of goods, services, and language that create forms of mutual understanding and indebtedness and so also cooperative social life sustained by the duty of service and, on occasion, sacrifice. To this argument, rooted in human nature, the Christian Socialists added a religious foundation apart from which they believed their argument from nature would not prevail. So they argued that God, who created humankind as mutually dependent, also, in Christ, showed his love for each and every person. This divine love establishes a fundamental equality that renders us duty bound both to God and to our neighbors.

In their minds, duty provides the glue that holds together the social ideals they championed. It is clear that present opinion runs directly contrary to this fundamental conviction. In our time, as in theirs, rights establish duties. It is not the other way around. To put it another way, for the Christian Socialists, human freedom is to be exercised within the constraints of duty. At present, the basic assumptions of neoliberal and progressive liberal thought surround the exercise of freedom first with the fence of rights that define the range and content of our duties. If some version of the Christian Socialist program is to be credible and effective in this age, then it is necessary now as it was then to establish the primacy of duty over rights—no small task!

The difficulty of the task is immediately apparent. Duty can be understood in many ways, and one primary interpretation on the part of the Christian Socialists was this: each person has a station in society, and her obligation is to fulfill the duties that attach to that station. This very conservative view of social organization was held by Maurice, Westcott, and to a lesser extent Gore. Ludlow, Tawney, and others worried about the support given by many to the notion that it was a person's chief duty to fulfill the duties that went with her station. The thought immediately comes to mind that in the face of such a use of the notion of duty, it would prove obvious and necessary to deploy a notion of individual rights that holds apart from the obligations attendant upon duty. If, for example, one man's duty precludes his freedom or the freedom of another to develop his personality and exercise his talents, it is easy to see that the assertion of a right that exists prior to duty to pursue personal goals in freedom makes sense. This observation, when coupled with the Christian Socialists' account of duty that flows downward from the higher to the lower ranks of society, seems sufficient to undermine their account of duty from the outset.

There are, however, considerations that speak against too cavalier a dismissal of their views. Chief among these is the fluid notion of the nature and function of a right. Recent studies in the history of "rights" have revealed that no less than three understandings of rights have appeared since the time of America's Declaration of Independence.[22] One, connected with that declaration and the French Declaration of the Rights of Man, has as its focus the rights that accrue to autonomous individuals because of their possession of freedom, reason, and so dignity. Immanuel Kant famously defended freedom and reason as the seat of human dignity and so individual rights. In contemporary terms, these individual rights provide certain entitlements that defend human dignity and allow for the justifiable exercise of autonomy. As John Milbank and Adrian Pabst have pointed out, the notion of individual or subjective rights now current stands behind both the economic views of neoliberals and the views of personal autonomy held dear by social progressives.[23]

A second view of rights, one that has its roots in the classical natural law tradition, rose to prominence (particularly in Europe) during the 1930s and 1940s. This account of rights has as its focus not the autonomy of individuals but the ideals and character that provide the identity of a given society and its form of government. It is an account of rights that gives them a more corporate meaning and locates them within a political system. This account of rights declares that the citizens of a commonwealth, as citizens, have a right to freedom of speech, freedom of movement, freedom of religion, freedom to choose those by whom they are governed, and access to equal consideration and treatment under law. This more communal view of rights was made popular in Europe after World War II by Roman Catholic thinkers like Jacques Maritain who saw the need, in the face of atomistic individualism and after the collectivist reactions that appeared in the rise of National Socialism and Communism, for a social alternative to individualism, on the one hand, and collectivism, on the other.

A third view can be found in the Universal Declaration of Human Rights, passed by the United Nations in 1948. Its supporters sought to establish a list of rights that apply to human beings as such, independent of their membership in a nation-state or ethnic group. Jimmy Carter was the first political voice to make such rights an aspect of a nation's

---

22. See, e.g., Moyn, *The Last Utopia*, and Moyn, *Christian Human Rights*.
23. See Milbank and Pabst, *The Politics of Virtue*.

foreign policy, but even so the declaration remains just that—a declaration without concrete embodiment or political form. This view rose to prominence with the decline of the imperial powers, the instability of many new nation-states, and the pervasive poverty and depredation that were the result of this instability and its attendant corruption. It was a way, by means of a universal declaration, to call the nations of a new world order to a higher moral place. The trans-political reference of this catalogue of rights constitutes its strength. Its lack of grounding in particular political and social systems is its weakness. Apart from such political and legal grounding the list at best expresses aspiration and at worst sheer hypocrisy.

This all too brief historical sketch clearly displays the fact that it is a form of the first understanding of rights (not the second and third) that so troubled the Christian Socialists. They saw the assertion of individual rights rather than duties (particularly on the part of the working class) as inevitable aspects of political economy and its attendant social inequality and disorder. Many of their number were convinced that the assertion of rights untethered from duties produces only conflict and strife. Nevertheless, they failed to see another possibility for the assertion of rights, namely, a corporate one that focuses on the social conditions necessary for the sort of life that fosters what they believed to be the most profound goals of social life, that is, freedom, harmony, and the development of personality and character. As previously noted, fellowship, community, cooperation, service, sacrifice, equality, duty, freedom, and private property constitute ideal forms of social life that promote personality and character within a population. Had they turned to this more classical notion of rights, the Christian Socialists might easily have converted their communal ideals in respect to duty into rights guaranteed by a society, resting upon mutual responsibility, that exists for the development of the sort of personality and character worthy of people created in the image of God and loved equally by their Lord and Creator.

History reveals that human rights mean different things to different people in different times and places. No doubt the ideal of equality before God presses in the direction of social equality and so also to an equal dispersion of duties, rights, and benefits among a populace. Nevertheless, in and of itself equality before God is not a strong enough warrant to produce changes in the way people behave toward one another. The persistent practice of slavery among Christians is sufficient testimony to the fact that this is indeed the case. In her study *Inventing Human Rights:*

A History, Lynn Hunt makes this point and supports it with massive detail.[24] Her argument is that human rights claims rest upon the claim of self-evidence. As America's Declaration of Independence states, "We hold these truths to be self-evident." For rights to be self-evident, however, they must be perceived to be *natural* (inherent in human beings), *equal* (the same for everyone), and *universal* (applicable everywhere). They must also be undergirded by human sympathy. She writes, "Human rights are not just a doctrine formulated in documents; they rest on a disposition toward other people, a set of convictions about what people are like and how they know right and wrong in the secular world. Philosophical ideas, legal traditions, and revolutionary politics had to have this kind of inner emotional reference point for human rights to be truly 'self-evident.'"[25] So she concludes that social and political change come because of social interactions that evoke feelings—sympathetic, empathetic interactions that produce changes of heart, mind, and behavior.[26]

John Ludlow's account of a dying woman living in a closet and Henry Mayhew's description of the street people of London provide graphic examples of the sort of experience that served to create within the English populace a new social vision—one defined by identification of other people as, though different, in some way "just like me."

It is at this point of social awareness that the ideals championed by the Christian Socialists come into view once again and recommend themselves, not as immediately associated with rights but as indicators of duty and social responsibility rooted in human sympathy. The implication of Hunt's argument is that, on their own, ideals do little work. Nevertheless, when linked with empathy and sympathy for others, they draw people who hold them to both thought and action. They may even draw citizens into a communal discussion of duties and rights—individual, social, and universal. Indeed, it might be fair to say that apart from sympathy ideals idle, but apart from ideals sympathy has no guide for its appropriate expression in duty, and apart from rights neither sympathy nor duty can silence the voice of self-interest that drowns out the voice of sympathy and conscience.

In short, if the Christian Socialists' valorization of duty over rights is placed within the history of the notion of human rights, then one can

---

24. See especially Hunt, *Inventing Human Rights*, 42.
25. Hunt, *Inventing Human Rights*, 27.
26. Hunt, *Inventing Human Rights*, 34.

easily see the shortcomings of their dismissal of "rights." At the same time one can see that contemporary discussions of rights, be they individual, social, or universal, cry out for a more communal understanding of human nature, a more adequate account of the ideals and social goals that define a healthy social life, and a wider circle of human sympathy that links the nations and peoples of the earth in a common project that promotes forms of life in which people can flourish. This is the sort of world the Christian Socialists sought, and no matter what their shortcomings, it is a world in which the ideals and duties they defended still have a place. Indeed, apart from these ideals, the contemporary idiom of rights will, as the Christian Socialists surely saw, produce social conflict, dull sympathy for those different from oneself, and shrink the range of social duties to those established by law. The Christian Socialists are justifiably accused of always standing on the edge of utopianism. Nevertheless, apart from a social vision like theirs, it is easy to imagine a dystopia wherein human sympathy shrinks to the narrowest of circles and duties apply only within a circumference drawn by self-interest. With an operative notion of social duty rooted in human sympathy, however, it is easy to imagine, as did Archbishop William Temple, political exchanges being carried on in a very "different tone" than the one to which we are now becoming accustomed.

The history of human rights thus reveals that when linked to the social experience of sympathy and empathy, ideals have power to establish duties that lead to the self-evidence of certain rights, sometimes individual, sometimes social, and sometimes even universal. History also brings to light another insight. Apart from favorable historical circumstances, no matter the strength of sympathy and empathy that might support rights, they still lack power to become imbedded in political discourse and action. The pioneering work of Samuel Moyn makes this point with extraordinary clarity. From Jorge Luis Borges, Moyn gets the idea that in history there are no precursors. As Moyn writes, "If the past is read as preparation for a surprising recent event, both are distorted. The past is treated as if it were simply the future waiting to happen. And the surprising event is treated as less surprising than it really is."[27] In this way, along with Borges, Moyn does away with what might be called a Whig interpretation of ideals whereby they develop into full flower by means of their own latent meaning and internal force. He argues instead that

---

27. Moyn, *Last Utopia*, 11.

our present notion of rights is a construction—a bit of *bricolage* that took place in the midst of a particular set of circumstances, namely, the rise of the nation-state and the collapse of an old order. Again, as Moyn writes, "In the realm of thinking as in that of social action, human rights are best understood as survivors: the god that did not fail while other political ideologies did. If they avoided failure, it was most of all because they were widely understood as a moral alternative to bankrupt political utopias."[28]

Moyn provides a number of examples of this hypothesis. Chief among them is his account of the appearance of rights language in Europe during the 1930s and 1940s. In his Christmas address of 1942, in the midst of World War II, Pius XII said something new about dignity, rights, and human persons. He wrote, "He who would have the Star of Peace shine out and stand over society should cooperate, for his part, in giving back to the human person the dignity given to it by God from the very beginning. He should uphold respect for and the practical realization of ... fundamental personal rights."[29] Moyn notes that the pope's statement was a departure in the history of political discourse. In so speaking, the pope "gave Christian 'personalism'"—a term much loved by the Christian Socialists—"a broad hearing, attaching supreme ethical significance to human beings agonizingly caught between individualist atomism without community and 'totalitarian' statehood without freedom."[30]

The pope's focus on dignity, persons, and rights makes clear the historical context in which this departure in the history of political discourse took place. The background is the social atomism of capitalist society and the collectivist response to this atomism in the rise of fascism and communism. The popes, and with them Catholic Christianity in Europe, were after a new moral foundation for society—one that strikes a balance between individual rights, on the one hand, and common life and common good, on the other. As Moyn notes, attention to public discourse in the 1930s and 1940s "shows that the birth of human rights was not so much about new individualist schemes of protection as communitarian investment in moral order."[31] In giving prominence to dignity, rights, and persons, Christians in Europe provided a foundation for a conservative view of liberal democracy. They captured the notion of "the rights of

28. Moyn, *Last Utopia*, 5.

29. Pius XII, "The Internal Order of States and Peoples," Christmas Message 1942, cited in Moyn, *Christian Human Rights*, 2.

30. Moyn, *Christian Human Rights*, 3.

31. Moyn, *Christian Human Rights*, 13.

man" and gave it a conservative, more communal meaning—one whose foundation was not individual autonomy but a transcendent moral order. Popes Pius XI and XII, and along with them the Catholic faithful, came to realize that "rights" are compatible with conservative forms of moral government, and their aim was precisely this form of governance. This form of governance provides a communal setting that locates individuals within a social setting but does not submerge them into a group identity. So, with the conclusion of World War II, rights language was employed to affirm the importance of individual persons while at the same time affirming the social nature of humankind and placing limits on the hyperbolic state.[32] And so, in Europe, Christian Democracy became the regnant form of governance. This social compact remained intact until another historical shift occurred—the growth of secularism and the unparalleled collapse of the churches that accompanied secularism. This shift brought with it a shift of social focus, from communal identity to the autonomy of individuals, and so also a focus not on communal identity but on the subjective rights of the individual.

It certainly appears that the world is now in the midst of another historical shift—one that is exposing the bankruptcy of the cultures of the West, grounded as they are in the autonomy of the individual, and one that is calling for an account of human nature that is rooted in its social character. It is within this shift that the ideals championed by the Christian Socialists find a favorable social location and so the promise of rearticulation in a different age with analogous yet distinctively different challenges.

---

32. Moyn, *Christian Human Rights*, 108–10.

B. Influence

WITH THESE REMARKS, THIS investigation of an almost forgotten tradition returns to its original question. In the present age, characterized as it is by social dislocation, social atomism, competitiveness, inequality, and plutocracy, can Christian Socialism provide a religious and moral compass for a relevant and faithful Christian response? Two of the leading Anglican theologians of the present era, Rowan Williams and John Milbank, believe that the answer to this question is a resounding yes! To be sure, in speaking as Christian Socialists, they speak only as individual thinkers. They do not pretend to speak in an official capacity for the Church of England. Nonetheless, what they have to say is of fundamental importance because the content of their response to the present condition and possible future direction of our society owes a great deal to the tradition of Christian Socialism. Their *ressourcement* of a tradition of social thought places in bold relief both the pathos and the promise of their efforts. The pathos stems from the unpopularity and seeming impossibility of any form of socialism finding acceptance by the public. The promise stems from the relevance of what they have to say about the ever-hastening collapse of the reigning social, economic, political, and moral beliefs and practices of liberal society. The promise also stems from a belief on the part of a significant number of younger people that something like the sort of socialism the Christian Socialists defended constitutes "the only way left"[1] for a society whose common life seems to be in free fall. To put the matter in a different way, the crisis of the times has exposed to a rising generation the gods that have failed and, at the same time, created a social space that can be occupied by a very different view of life together.

---

1. I owe this phrase to George MacLeod, founder of the Iona Community and author of *Only One Way Left*.

Rowan Williams's account of the root problem of secular society, coupled with his discussion of human rights and the role of government in civil society, shows both his debt to Christian Socialism and the promise that is woven into the fabric of this tradition. Williams's foil is not, as was the case with the Christian Socialists, political economy. His foil is secularism of a certain sort. He does not object to the sort of secularism he terms "procedural." Indeed, he believes that Christianity played an important part in its emergence. Procedural secularism is not antireligious. It simply "declines to give advantage or preference to any one religious body over others."[2] It operates on the principle that the job of the state is not to establish a religion but to oversee a variety of religious communities and, when necessary, to take steps to insure that these communities, though free to express their views, live in peace one with another without any one of them assuming a privileged position. There is, however, another form of secularism to which Williams does object—programmatic secularism. The aim of programmatic secularism is to rid the public square of religious content altogether. Consequently, it forbids "any and every public manifestation of any particular religious allegiance."[3] Programmatic secularism, like its predecessor political economy, though for a different reason, effectively bans fundamental moral convictions and religious beliefs from public political discourse.

Even though Williams is an archbishop within an established church, he has no problem with procedural secularism. He has, however, taken up arms against programmatic secularism. He has done so for obvious reasons. Programmatic secularism effectively excludes religious content from public discourse. This ban, he argues, inevitably leads to what he calls "functionalism," and functionalism leads not to public tranquility but to conflict. If religious beliefs and values along with related moral convictions are relegated to the realm of private judgment and personal opinion (and so barred from public argument), the tendency will be to look for "final and decisive accounts of what things are good for in terms of profit and functionality."[4] A thoroughly secular account of public attitude and argumentation requires that these matters not be settled by reference to "agencies or presences beyond the tangible."[5] In an

---

2. Williams, *Faith in the Public Square*, 2.
3. Williams, *Faith in the Public Square*, 3.
4. Williams, *Faith in the Public Square*, 5.
5. Williams, *Faith in the Public Square*, 12.

environment of this sort, differences of attitude and opinion must be negotiated and successfully sustained between individual agents and groups but without reference to transcendent values. On occasion differences between these attitudes and opinions can't be successfully negotiated. If such is the case, ways must be found to find a common language that allows for the reconciliation of differences. Secular society thus exists by agreeing to a truce within a feud. In this case, writes Williams, "Social equilibrium is a state in which all significant participants are adequately satisfied that others are serving or at least not obstructing their goals."[6] So, he concludes, "secularism in its neat distillation is inseparable from *functionalism*; and if so it will generate a social practice that is dominated by instrumental or managerial considerations, since the perspectives that would allow one to evaluate outcomes in other terms are all confined to the private and particular sphere."[7]

According to Williams, to view social life as a sort of peace within a feud presided over by government creates a severely limited view of the responsibility of government. It serves only as a referee in a contest between rival forces. Williams's view, taken from the writings of J. N. Figgis (especially *Churches in the Modern State*) and William Temple, is both more expansive and more nuanced.[8] In a 2008 lecture at St. James's Church, Piccadilly, he insists that the state is to recognize in every citizen something superior to its own authority. Such recognition leads necessarily to the conception of a welfare state. The welfare state, he says, exists not for itself alone but for the sake of its citizens. The welfare of its citizens is the *telos* or moral purpose of the state. By this he means more than the state has a duty to provide for its citizens. He means that in recognizing in the citizen something superior to itself the state is required to seek the welfare of its citizens in its fullness. This means, he says, that the state, limited by the principle of subsidiarity, has a duty to deal with human beings "in their *freedom*, not just in their *need*."[9]

Williams's view of the political institutions of secular society clearly implies that secular society is inherently unstable. It does not bring to the world the sort of peaceful order and human fulfillment it promises. Far worse, these institutions and the beliefs upon which they rest rob the

6. Williams, *Faith in the Public Square*, 12.
7. Williams, *Faith in the Public Square*, 12–13.
8. Figgis, *Churches in the Modern State*.
9. Cited by Spencer, "William Temple and the Temple Tradition," in Spencer, *Theology Reforming Society*, loc. 1761 of 3130, Kindle.

world of certain capacities it desperately needs. First among these is a grasp of human limitation and dependence. Religious belief in its various forms has a grasp of this truth and so it "delivers us from aspiring to mythic goals of absolute human control over human destiny."[10] Williams notes in passing that this point is of enormous significance if we think of its bearing on environmental challenges. In a similar manner, because programmatic secularism excludes the restraining power of religious belief and practice from the public square, it robs the world of the resources provided by religion that hold in check the incessant search for limitless economic growth. In so doing, secularism threatens our very existence. In keeping with the legacy of Christian Socialism, Williams terms this loss the loss of a "sacramental" understanding of God's creation. Like the Christian Socialists before him, Williams does not believe the world is simply there. Our world is not merely "stuff" to be used. Rather, it is a divine gift that serves as a sign or sacrament of God's glory and goodness. As gift, the world becomes redolent with meaning. As such, it is not to be exploited. Rather, it is to be treasured and cared for.[11]

Continuing in this same line of thought, Williams makes what he takes to be the central points in his political thought. In the first instance, programmatic secularism looks for "final and decisive accounts of what things are good for in terms of profit and functionality."[12] In the course of this search, programmatic secularism excludes "an attitude to the world that acknowledges that there is more to anything and anyone I encounter than I can manage or understand."[13] One might say that programmatic secularism strips the world of all mystery. From a religious perspective, however, "what I see is already 'seen' by, already in relation to, some reality immeasurably different from the self I know myself to be or even the sum total of selves like me."[14] In this instance one might say that programmatic secularism strips the self and other selves of holiness—the sort of sanctity only God can bestow upon his creatures.

The Christian Socialists were concerned that political economy robs the world of its moral foundation. It excludes the "ideals" that render social life livable. Rowan Williams is concerned that programmatic

---

10. Williams, *Faith in the Public Square*, 4.
11. Williams, *Faith in the Public Square*, 4–5.
12. Williams, *Faith in the Public Square*, 5.
13. Williams, *Faith in the Public Square*, 5.
14. Williams, *Faith in the Public Square*, 5.

secularism has rid the world of its religious foundation. In so doing, it has reduced human relations to pragmatic estimates of profit and loss. As previously noted, programmatic secularism also renders it difficult, if not impossible, to let go of the fiction of control. Faith, however, renders it possible to "let go." This capacity, he says, "opens up the possibility of taking responsibility for meaningful action, action that announces the presence of the fundamental *giving* on which the world rests and entails also taking responsibility for the other, for the suffering, for those experiencing meaninglessness."[15]

Thus, faith renders it possible to see that the original state of the world is not one of conflict and competition but of giving—of communion and reciprocity. Faith of this sort creates space for particular lives that show what it means to make room for God and one's neighbor in extreme situations—in the most extreme situations one can imagine. Precisely in such situations, faith brings forth individuals whose lives are not governed by calculations of profit and loss. Such people, he says (no doubt overstating his case), do not arise in societies in which Christian imagination has "atrophied to [the] vanishing point."[16]

Defenders of programmatic secularism will, with considerable justification, object to this claim. They might be willing to credit the statement that the world will have been robbed in significant ways if notions like holiness, mystery, and sacramental potency disappear from public consciousness. They will, however, most certainly deny that estimations of profit and loss are impotent and without positive social effect. They will also object strenuously and justifiably to the claim that people who put others before themselves and who devote themselves to promotion of a common good will not arise in a secular society that operates simply on the basis of profit and loss. It is empirically verifiable that such is not the case. To make his point, Williams overstates his case. Nonetheless, he makes a point of enormous importance. Christian belief and practice do indeed add notions like image of God, equality before God, holiness and reverence to the social imaginary. These notions add a degree of depth and power to the way in which one looks at the world that the self-regarding notions of profit, loss, dignity, freedom, and reason do not.

The views set forth above are presented in the introduction to *Faith in the Public Square*. They do more, however, than provide a summary

---

15. Williams, *Faith in the Public Square*, 6.
16. Williams, *Faith in the Public Square*, 6.

of Williams's political theology. They show clearly his debt to Christian Socialism. Each in its own way seeks a Christian Sociology grounded in the gracious generosity of God and the social nature of humankind. Nowhere is this debt to tradition clearer than in Williams's discussion of human rights. In an address entitled "Reconnecting Human Rights and Religious Faith," he says this:

> In what follows, I shall be suggesting some ways in which we might reconnect thinking about human rights and religious conviction—more specifically, Christian convictions about human *dignity* and human *relatedness*, how we belong together ... I believe this reconnection can be done by trying to understand rights against a background not of individual claims, but of the question of what is involved in mutual *recognition* between human beings. I believe that rights provide a crucial way of working out what it is for people to belong together in a society. The language gets difficult only when it is divorced from that awareness of belonging and reciprocity.[17]

He then goes on to say that the "world of 'rights'" is best anchored in "habits of empathy and identification with the other."[18]

The influence of Christian Socialism upon Rowan Williams is obvious in this discussion of rights. In the work of John Milbank we have a full-blown retrieval of the Christian Socialist tradition. Though significantly modified, Christian Socialism provides the source for his attack on the basic premises of both conservative neoliberalism and progressive liberalism. His charge is that the liberal picture of human nature as atomistic and conflicted has not contributed to human flourishing. On the contrary, it has served only to hollow out the substance of liberal institutions and in the process done catastrophic damage to the quality of individual life. The basic assumption of the present age—that we are first of all autonomous individuals—has created what Milbank and his coauthor Adrian Pabst call a "metacrisis" in the way we view ourselves as social agents, the way in which we are governed, the way in which our economy works, and the way in which our culture does or does not provide a basis for human flourishing. This attack is accompanied by an extensive and positive account of the ways in which Christian Socialism offers a path forward for Western society and its inhabitants. In presenting this alternative, Milbank acknowledges the pathos of his proposals,

17. Williams, *Faith in the Public Square*, 161.
18. Williams, *Faith in the Public Square*, 161.

but at the same time notes that what he calls the "metacrisis" of liberalism makes room for the very real promise of a society built not upon competitive individualism but upon the communal character of human nature and a cooperative social vision.

The works of John Milbank are extensive, complex, and often obscure; and for these reasons it is difficult to know exactly where to start unpacking them.[19] I have chosen to begin with his extensive critique of the liberal assumptions about human nature and human society that, at present, are shared by both progressive and conservative thinkers. In reaction to similar views, the Christian Socialists insisted that the society they inhabited—a society dominated by the individualistic tenets and practices of the supporters of political economy—rested upon a "rotten foundation." The alternative they proposed for that rotten foundation was one that rested upon what they held to be the firm foundations of moral ideals, offered not to a society built upon the autonomous choices of individuals but to a community with a shared life shaped by common ideals. What the Christian Socialists offered in response to "political economy" was a devastating criticism of the rotten foundation of their society and a positive alternative to it. John Milbank's project is exactly that. He wants modern, liberal society to jettison a rotten form of life and replace it with one that is in accord with human nature and so also human flourishing. Milbank advocates a revolution in social thought and practice that will produce dramatic changes in social relations and social institutions. He and his coauthor, Adrian Pabst, make this proposal in what can only be called "a big book," *The Politics of Virtue*. The alternative society they propose rests not upon the sovereign choices of individuals but upon a set of virtues that are shared by a community of persons jointly seeking a common good.

I. The "Metacrisis" of Liberalism

Milbank and Pabst begin their criticism with the observation that liberalism is now manifested in two forms. There is, first, the social-cultural

---

19. John Milbank's body of work is indeed large, complex, and not always easy to understand. The critical presentation of his work that follows does not pretend to be a critical study of his extensive writings. It is designed only to show the significant correspondences between his work and that of the Christian Socialists. Its purpose is to present the work of John Milbank as having a place within a tradition that dates back to the mid-nineteenth century.

liberalism of the left and, second, the economic-political liberalism (neoliberalism) of the right. The relation of the two is ironical in that both, though different in focus, share the same underlying assumption, namely, liberalism in all its forms rests upon the moral and social prominence given to autonomous individuals whose freedom is defined largely in negative terms. That is, for champions of both forms of contemporary liberalism, liberty is not based upon mastery of the self but upon freedom from constraint. As did the Christian Socialists before them, Milbank and Pabst note that this assumption, *ab initio*, sets human beings in conflict one with another. These autonomous actors seek to resolve their conflicts by utilitarian calculations (what Williams calls functionalism) that find resolution in transactional contracts. It is becoming increasingly obvious, however, that these transactional relations are failing in important ways to produce beneficial social results. Recent crises in liberal democracies have exposed the weakness of both left-leaning liberalism and right-leaning liberalism. In tacit alliance they have managed to produce unacceptable concentrations of wealth and power, along with social fragmentation and decline accompanied by the rise of authoritarianism. The cruel irony is that liberalism has brought about the very conditions it was supposed to remedy.[20] The rise of these conditions out of the very social agreements and institutions designed to thwart them constitutes the "metacrisis," that is, the crisis within the crisis that accompanies liberalism.

The question is, what might be the meaning of this "metacrisis" and how has it come about? According to Milbank and Pabst the chief reason for the failure of liberalism is the assumption that most of reality has nothing to do with good or evil. The world is simply there without any superabundance of meaning. As a result human behavior, in the final analysis, has nothing to do with good or evil. Good and evil are simply pasted by human will onto a morally neutral world. They have no fixed place in the scheme of things. In such social circumstances behavior is not grounded in the reality of good. It is basically amoral. They write, "The ethical is not seen, as it was for previous Western traditions, as self-grounded in the reality of the good, regarded as the real factual *and* valuative object of human pursuit."[21] This moral vacuum leaves only utilitarian bargaining as a means of resolving social conflict. The most typical form of this conflict, as the Christian Socialists foresaw, involves battles over "rights claims."

20. Milbank and Pabst, *Politics of Virtue*, 1–2.
21. Milbank and Pabst, *Politics of Virtue*, 4.

Once more, the argument of Milbank and Pabst parallels that of the Christian Socialists. As was the case with supporters of political economy in the past, in the present both cultural liberals and their economic-political cousins, because of their attachment to the primacy of freedom and the dominant position of rights claims, are forced to give priority to political and economic solutions to social conflicts rather than to social ones. In this world, justice is no longer a matter of judgment that accords with shared perceptions of the good. On the contrary, justice is reduced to procedural rules that govern the adjudication of social conflicts. Due procedure supposedly renders just judgment, but in fact these procedures render judgments determined by the exercise of power. Consequently, disputes over rights lead to settlements that disembed politics from a broader network of social relations governed by judgments of good and evil and re-embed them in a world governed by utility rather than the obligations that mark social relations in everyday life.[22] The problem is that political and economic processes in liberal society, because of the supreme value assigned to personal choice, are unable to provide a final resolution to its endemic disputes. As a result the combatants that inhabit liberal society inevitably turn to technocratic control on the part of the state to resolve their disputes. This analysis leads Milbank and Pabst to the conclusion that the elevation of political and economic relations over social ones results in the centralization of power, the concentration of wealth and, worst of all, the "commodification" of all aspects of life. Once again, the terrible irony of liberalism is that it brings about the very conditions it was designed to prevent. It turns out that liberalism encourages not liberty but the limitless expansion of power, wealth, and inequality.[23] This situation constitutes an accompanying crisis for all forms of liberalism.

Milbank and Pabst's presentation of the metacrisis in which liberalism finds itself may be summarized in this way: its inability to resolve conflict produces a metacrisis that *cannot be remedied*. The heart of the problem is the promotion of the economic and political over the social and so the subordination of both social bonds and civic ties to abstract standards of law and contract.[24] They go on to track the effects of this eclipse of the social nature of human beings. Society, they say, has been

22. Milbank and Pabst, *Politics of Virtue*, 13–15.
23. Milbank and Pabst, *Politics of Virtue*, 16–17.
24. Milbank and Pabst, *Politics of Virtue*, 58; emphasis added.

eroded from two directions, with the result that human beings as individual actors are degraded. On the one hand, everything we think of as human is reduced to an animal level. We are no more than "a bunch of greedy apes with bigger brains." On the other hand, "everything human is declared entirely artificial, just stuff that we have made up such as the social contract, which reflects nothing other than the arbitrary whims of human volition and can be simply undone by other acts of will."[25] It is well to note that F. D. Maurice made similar observations about political economy. The result of this eclipse of all that is distinctively human (both now and then) is that, on the one hand, we are reduced to our lowest instincts (greed, fearfulness, and enmity) and, on the other, we are made subject to post-human forms of control by a cybernetic future that will, we think, control desire and produce a "peace of a sort."[26]

II. The Postliberal Alternative

In response to the metacrisis of liberalism, Milbank and Pabst propose what they call "a postliberal alternative." Postliberalism, they argue, "suggests that a more universal flourishing for all can be obtained when we continuously seek to define the goals of human society as a whole and then to discern the variously different and in themselves worthwhile roles that are required for the mutual achievement of these shared aims." They go on to say that "the respective freedoms of these roles and their rewards will be variegated: not literally equal in terms of wealth, power or command and yet equitable and so capable of sincere general acceptability."[27] The starting point of this postliberal alternative to liberalism is precisely that of the Christian Socialists' response to the supporters of political economy. As did the Christian Socialists before them, supporters of the postliberal alternative begin not with individuals in conflict but with moral agents embedded in a shared way of life within which individuals find their particular role as valued contributors to a common enterprise.

Naturally, liberalism in all its forms stands in contradiction to this possibility. Respect for the autonomy of others coupled with an assumed inability on the part of individuals to reach agreement on values leave both social liberals and economic-political liberals skeptical about appeals to

25. Milbank and Pabst, *Politics of Virtue*, 58.
26. Milbank and Pabst, *Politics of Virtue*, 58.
27. Milbank and Pabst, *Politics of Virtue*, 69–70.

a common good (save as a term that refers to the full panoply of goods produced through the freedom of individual actors). In the place of social bonds that establish moral agreement they substitute a strong sense of fairness that honors the freedom of each social actor. By way of contrast, the postliberal alternative rests upon faith in a common good that promotes a search for shared ends that express "the truest goods that we share together, such as intimacy, trust and beauty, whether momentarily with strangers or continuously with friends."[28] This sense of a common good comprised of basic and universal human values is embedded in the practices of honor and reciprocity on the part of an entire society.

Milbank and Pabst are quick to add that a common good embedded in practices of honor and reciprocity requires time, the establishment of tradition, wise leadership, and the prudential adoption by all of previous example (i.e., tradition). At this point it is important to notice both similarities and differences between the agenda of the Christian Socialists and the Milbank-Pabst account of a "postliberal alternative." They are in agreement that apart from a strong religious and moral foundation, society cannot promote genuine human flourishing. Indeed, freedom unanchored in a strong and shared religious and moral tradition issues in the "increased criminalization of political and economic power."[29] Political and economic powers join in a criminal cabal guided neither by right nor by wrong but by what one can get away with. Indeed, capitalism, as presently constituted, consists of a union of political and economic power that, with no internal moral guidance system, becomes little more than a criminal oligarchy. Thus, promoters of "a postliberal alternative," along with earlier Christian Socialists, insist that a "new internal ethos" is needed if we are to avoid this sort of dystopia.[30]

Important differences appear, however, when one compares their respective accounts of this internal ethos. The Christian Socialists were advocates of a set of moral ideals they sought to reestablish as the foundation of a society in which persons could grow and mature. As noted, most prominent among these ideals were community, love, equality, fellowship, duty, service, personality, character, freedom, and property. Undergirding all of them lay the assumption of the social nature of humankind. Milbank and Pabst certainly share this fundamental assumption. Nevertheless, the

28. Milbank and Pabst, *Politics of Virtue*, 70.
29. Milbank and Pabst, *Politics of Virtue*, 72.
30. Milbank and Pabst, *Politics of Virtue*, 73.

Milbank-Pabst account of the virtues that form the foundation of their postliberal alternative is markedly different. In place of the elaborate account of social ideals proposed by the Christian Socialists, they put forward a strikingly short list of desired social attitudes and practices—honor and gift exchange built upon trust. A postliberal society honors the moral excellences of its members and thrives on the accomplishments of its citizens. These excellences and accomplishments are shared through social exchanges by means of which all are enriched. Postliberalism aims to create a society marked, first, by an honor culture and, second, by a system of trust-based exchange that promotes "the virtuous provision of social benefit, and genuine distributed wealth of all kinds."[31]

What then is an honor culture? Honor serves first of all as a form of self-restraint that directs one away from goals that do not promote "the virtuous provision of social benefit, and genuine distributed wealth of all kinds." Honor requires that one look at the whole person and assess what promotes human welfare. The sort of welfare honor promotes involves a unity of mind, body, and soul rather than material success.[32] Its chief focus is social health rather than economic or political advance. Its chief reward is self-worth that comes from social recognition that acknowledges one's contribution to the welfare of one's fellows. Thus, in an honor culture, wealth and power are connected with symbolic meaning. They are joined to public benefit rather than private possession. Further, in an honor society, built upon exchange rather than agonistic struggle, each person is honorable in her own way. As such, each is recognized as honorable because of the contribution each makes to a common good.

"Honor," therefore, is a term whose meaning derives from its function within a network of social relations. Various forms of exchange that establish and maintain the links that constitute life in society govern these relations. Following the pioneering work of Marcel Mauss, Milbank and Pabst build their case for the social nature of human beings on the universal practice of exchanging gifts. Exchange rather than competition constitutes the basic form of human relationships.[33] As Levi-Strauss in his *Structural Anthropology* later noted, these exchanges take place on three significant levels—the exchange of goods and services, the exchange of language (and so meaning), and the exchange of marital partners between

---

31. Milbank and Pabst, *Politics of Virtue*, 74–75.
32. Milbank and Pabst, *Politics of Virtue*, 77.
33. See Mauss, *The Gift*.

social groups. Milbank and Pabst add to this analysis the observation that honor is also exchanged through the recognition of what each person in their own place and in their own way contributes to the common good of human flourishing. The postliberal assumption is that society is bound together more by mutual generosity and honor than contract and conflict.[34] Social bonds are not voluntary, occasional acts of will. Rather, they are endemic to the human situation. They are created and maintained by mutual recognition expressed as the attribution of honor. Honor is given to those who, regardless of social position, contribute to a common good. In this way honor is reciprocally exchanged and in that exchange shows itself to be the exemplary form of mutuality that includes each and every member of society.

There are significant differences between what the Christian Socialists, on the one hand, and Milbank and Pabst, on the other, have to say about the moral foundations required for a healthy society. Nevertheless, their views about social change run parallel to one another. Both are quite suspicious of the benefits many expect from engineered changes in social structures and institutions. From F. D. Maurice, the Christian Socialists inherited the Augustinian notion that social order and social institutions are the work of divine providence. As such they are to be maintained rather than reformed on the basis of human wit. The conservatism of the Milbank-Pabst proposal is similar but stems from a different source—the necessary link they perceive between place, time, and tradition. Stability requires tradition, and tradition requires a society that honors place and is perdurable over time.[35] A society that honors the differentiated character of social space (in Milbank and Pabst's case a class structure) acts to preserve that diversity. Accordingly, it requires also a strong sense of one's station and its duties as the basis of equitable sharing. In turn, equitable sharing requires a valid hierarchy along with cooperation between members of the various social states. These exchanges between persons of differing social states do not give priority, as is now the case, to social mobility, rights claims, and conflict. They are cooperative rather than competitive activities that are necessary aspects of a healthy society rather than tools employed for competitive advantage.[36]

---

34. Milbank and Pabst, *Politics of Virtue*, 80–81.
35. Milbank and Pabst, *Politics of Virtue*, 77.
36. Milbank and Pabst, *Politics of Virtue*, 74–75.

Milbank and Pabst provide the following summary of the sort of changes postliberals wish to see. In a way, they do support social change. Nevertheless, the change they support points to the past rather than to the future. It is one that deconstructs and undermines the basic character of all forms of liberalism. Postliberalism, they say, seeks social change that combines "a working-class search for restored community with the new middle-class search for more holistic fulfillment in work and the search of both classes for combining work with the needs of family and community."[37] Once more, there is nothing in this statement with which F. D. Maurice would be in disagreement. The only difference between them is that Maurice wanted to keep social structures as they were, but with the ameliorating condition of cooperation rather than competition between the classes. On the other hand, the Milbank-Pabst proposal seeks to return social order to the way it once was, but this time with the substitution of a cooperative, virtue-driven alternative to a class-structured, conflict-ridden social order and with a greater ability to change one's social location.

There are other ways in which the Milbank-Pabst promotion of a postliberal alternative channels the program of the Christian Socialists. Both support a form of "organic pluralism" that makes room for various sorts of association. Indeed, as we have seen, the creation of craft associations formed the centerpiece of Christian Socialist attempts to provide an alternative to the unacceptable concentrations of wealth and power they so bitterly opposed. In a similar manner, postliberalism seeks an "organic pluralism" that creates "multiple sources of sovereignty" that are graded yet organically linked. They seek a form of constitutionalism that protects these corporate bodies from the expansion of centralized authority and in doing so mediates between citizens and centralized sovereign power.[38] Associations also protect against the sort of atomism that gives individual choice priority over social duty. The postliberal alternative to liberalism seeks a polity that consists of a "nested, interlocking union of persons, families and communities who are bound to one another by social ties and civic bonds."[39]

At this point the "postliberal alternative" to liberalism shows yet another link to Christian Socialism. Both view the promotion of

37. Milbank and Pabst, *Politics of Virtue*, 76.

38. For a discussion of "association," see Milbank and Pabst, *Politics of Virtue*, 80–82.

39. Milbank and Pabst, *Politics of Virtue*, 82.

"personhood" as the primary goal of social living. Both understand a society built upon a common good to be one that leaves room for difference. Human difference, they hold, is best understood under the heading of personhood. As with the Christian Socialists, Milbank and Pabst view persons as both more and less than the social whole. They are less because they can come to be as persons only in relation to a social body, and they can acquire personal roles only in relation to the totality of the relations present within that body.[40] Persons are more than the social whole because the point of social relations is to foster the growth of personality. Thus, the position of each person within a social whole provides each one a unique identity that is essential to the whole. As Milbank and Pabst note, personal roles exist only within a totality of social relations. Persons are situated in a chain. One's presence at a particular location makes the chain, but the chain is what gives one a particular place.

At this point the Anglican tradition of Christian Socialism brought forward and supported by postliberalism invites fruitful conversation with Roman Catholic social teaching, particularly with the principle of subsidiarity. This principle holds that if a smaller unit of society can accomplish a task, it ought not to be assigned to a larger one. Subsidiarity requires devolution of some powers to the smaller units of society. It may, for example, require giving smaller economic bodies more responsibility—a move Milbank and Pabst believe would curb the criminal distribution of wealth now so common in late capitalism. Their primary point, however, is that the dynamic relation between persons and the social whole they favor can only be sustained by a "complex and overlapping series of partial societies or intermediary associations that compose 'civil society.'"[41] These smaller associations are of various sorts—political, economic, and social, even religious. Their existence and strength are of crucial importance for reminding the state of its limits while at the same time tempering possible excesses of individual liberty. They are also necessary if persons are to avoid being swallowed by the social whole. As Milbank and Pabst observe, these smaller associations secure "reciprocal justice and the always specific virtuous flourishing of each of [their] members."[42]

---

40. For a discussion of the meaning and importance of "persons," see Milbank and Pabst, *Politics of Virtue*, 83–84.

41. Milbank and Pabst, *Politics of Virtue*, 83–84.

42. Milbank and Pabst, *Politics of Virtue*, 85.

As we have seen, personalism for the Christian Socialists provided a defense against the charge that socialism submerges individuals in a collective. Personalism plays an identical role in the thought of Milbank and Pabst. There is more than sufficient evidence to establish the fact that the postliberalism of Milbank and Pabst is in fact a late development in the earlier Anglican tradition of social ethics associated with Christian Socialism. There is, however, what Milbank and Pabst term an *aporia* that stands between the views of the Christian Socialists and their own. The gap lies between the account of ideals that stands at the foundation of Christian Socialism and the notions of honor and gift exchange that form the core of the Milbank-Pabst proposal. To put the question in another way, do the ideals of community, love, fellowship, duty, service, personality, freedom, and property, so dear to the hearts of Christian Socialists, have any place in a social ethic based on the exchange of honor and various gifts? Milbank and Pabst do not ignore this issue, but they turn to it only much later in their discussion of moral formation in liberal societies. In this discussion they establish the central importance of virtue within a political system and so suggest links between the ideals championed by the Christian Socialists and the notions of honor and gift exchange that characterize postliberal society.

Nevertheless, they do not do so by the elaboration of a set of ideals. Indeed, they apparently reject the entire notion of ideals. The Milbank-Pabst proposal for an alternative to liberalism requires first of all not ideals but readmitting "participation in transcendence."[43] Here they are in complete agreement with Williams. They argue that the only way out of the mess produced by liberalism "is to assume a cosmos that shares in a transcendent principle that indicates an overarching unity that binds nature and culture."[44] We must come to see ourselves as a part of a reality that is not defined by our own ideals. Rather, in a way reminiscent of the Christian Socialists' insistence on the sacramental nature of the universe, we must learn to see "all worldly realities, including cultural ones, as symbolizing something higher and hidden."[45] We must learn to see the world in which we are called to participate as a world that is, in the deepest sense, defined not by ideals but by something like Plato's

---

43. Milbank and Pabst, *Politics of Virtue*, 291.
44. Milbank and Pabst, *Politics of Virtue*, 258.
45. Milbank and Pabst, *Politics of Virtue*, 307.

Ideas—patterns that lay down the structure of the world.[46] Ideals, they hold, are values we invent and then paste on to a morally neutral world. On the contrary, ideas or patterns are aspects of a transcendent reality that is larger than any set of ideals we might invent. Ideas of the Platonic sort beckon us to a transcendent world not of our making in which nature and culture are part of a single whole—a world in which we can flourish if our lives are brought into conformity with the ideas or patterns that define the very shape of the world. Ideas are transcendent and so call us beyond our own inventions. Ideas are not invented. They are transcendent realities that must be approached respectfully and explored. As such, our relation to them requires of us constant investigation and testing. Ideals, on the other hand, are self-enclosed and so lead to closed-mindedness and fanaticism.

The question, of course, is how a moral transformation of this magnitude is to take place. Milbank and Pabst are well aware of the difficulty of the task they set for themselves. Moral perspectives are not private inventions. They are the product of moral formation. They are socially passed on rather than individually invented. The problem is that the moral perspective of the present age is embedded in the moral tradition of liberalism, and this tradition insists that culture is simply pasted on the reality of nature. The worlds we inhabit are in no way sacramental in nature. They do not participate in transcendence. They are self-created and self-enclosed.

Moral formation in liberal society does not concern itself with human destiny or the "metaphysical basis of life and existence."[47] Neither, as was the case with the *paideia* of the ancients, is it concerned with producing "philosophic and political virtue" in a citizenry.[48] Ancient moral formation had as its focus the formation of virtuous citizens. Liberal society, however, has given up moral formation as a social goal and left in its place the strange assumption that morality will emerge spontaneously from nature. It has also handed over to the state the authority to teach what, in the end, enhances the state's own power.[49] What emerges is a utilitarian view of what is necessary for social life and a romantic notion of the arts and humanities. What emerges is not *paideia* but a form of

46. Milbank and Pabst, *Politics of Virtue*, 292.
47. Milbank and Pabst, *Politics of Virtue*, 266.
48. Milbank and Pabst, *Politics of Virtue*, 260.
49. Milbank and Pabst, *Politics of Virtue*, 262.

education that produces not a virtuous citizenry but a population prepared to be consumers and functionaries.[50] Milbank and Pabst conclude that liberal education is "middle brow" in that it destroys both "high and folk culture." That is, liberalism "rids society of an exemplary elite and the time-honored patterns of folk life."[51] So they conclude, "Without a popular inculcation of virtue and without virtuous elites that lead by example and command popular assent precisely because they uphold and hyperbolically fulfill ideals that are open to all, culture becomes debased and descends into the empty vacuity of bourgeois, middle-brow pietism."[52]

The Milbank-Pabst account of liberal education poses an apparently insurmountable obstacle to the sort of formation required for a postliberal social order. Noting the severity of the obstacle, one is forced to ask if there is a way out of this mess. In their response, Milbank and Pabst point, in the first instance, somewhat vaguely in a direction rather than toward a concrete proposal. Noting that the main element of human association is psychic and that human association has more to do with friendship, benevolent sharing, and sharing in a common good than it does to law and the distribution of material goods, Milbank and Pabst insist that politics requires a "psychic community." So they say that today we need a revival of this psychic function *in the mode of* Christian *ecclesia*, "which most of all discovered and enacted the preeminence of the person and of relationality within a fluid sense of the organic whole, beyond the twin atomisms of Occidental egotistic individualism and Oriental static, rigid, hierarchical organism."[53] The Milbank-Pabst suggestion of a way around the obstacle of liberal culture seems to be a society that is "churchlike." Their way ahead requires a body politic within which a culture of honor and benevolent sharing and a shared commitment to a transcendent common good shape common life. If Bishop Gore were present in this time of a postliberal alternative to liberalism, he would without question say, Why not the church itself? Do you not need the church if you are to have a society that is formed by its beliefs and values?

Milbank and Pabst, in their own way, say, "Indeed we do." They note that after the triumph of the Enlightenment focus on self-interest and utilitarian morality there remained a "Christian residuum." The church

---

50. Milbank and Pabst, *Politics of Virtue*, 262–63.
51. Milbank and Pabst, *Politics of Virtue*, 266.
52. Milbank and Pabst, *Politics of Virtue*, 267.
53. Milbank and Pabst, *Politics of Virtue*, 284.

continued and kept alive "the future of the soul, mutual charity and reconciliation in excess of the legal coercion of the state."[54] What is more, as a social body, the abiding church interrupts an overemphasis on the state by reminding society that men, women, and children remain citizens of heaven. Further, it retains a governing structure that further reminds society that both adults and children must continue to learn and be formed in virtue. Thus, from Milbank and Pabst's perspective (and in agreement with Williams), the church remains a vehicle for opening the way for participation in transcendence and so also the passing on of skills and habits associated with virtue and tradition.[55] Indeed, in his introduction to a collection of essays entitled *The Future of Love: Essays in Political Theology*, Milbank writes, "I believe, along with Radical Orthodoxy in general, that only the Church has the theoretical and practical power to challenge the global hegemony of capital and to create a viable politico-economic alternative."[56]

There are finally two other ways in which the church can provide a way around the obstacle of liberal education. First, a focus on the virtue of many involves also the virtue of a few who provide a model of the good life. Virtue is learned in part by example. Like Williams, Milbank and Pabst believe that a virtuous society requires the example of people who are, in a way, the truth. The church through the ages has provided such exemplary persons—persons whose very lives embody truth, beauty, and goodness. This is the first way. There is also a second way in which the church can and does provide a path through the obstacle of liberalism. It can provide not only noble souls but, on a more quotidian level, faith-based schools that nurture citizens in virtue.

These prescriptions for replacing the "rotten foundation" of liberal society are precisely the ones the Christian Socialists proposed as alternatives to political economy. Thus, the Christian Socialists argued that a healthy society requires both a "dogmatic foundation" and a "Christian Sociology," wherein individual persons have an identity and a particular calling. The Milbank-Pabst proposal for the revival of a psychic body having to do with friendship, benevolent sharing, and sharing of a common good is reminiscent of Bishop Gore's call for an exemplary community that can provide the seed from which a healthy society can grow. Such a

---

54. Milbank and Pabst, *Politics of Virtue*, 286–87.

55. For this discussion of the contribution of the church, see Milbank and Pabst, *Politics of Virtue*, 286–91.

56. Milbank, "Introduction," in Milbank, *Future of Love*, loc. 84 of 7928, Kindle.

society would also comprise a school for the formation of virtuous citizens, and it would encourage faith-based schools that aid in that effort. Milbank and Pabst summarize their view of a way through the impediment of liberal education in this way: "It is hard to see how we can sustain the genuine Western legacy unless we revive, more democratically, its archaic idiom. This is required to uphold the absolutely incomparable value of both the person and of relational reciprocity in free association. We need both the mysticism of the individual soul and the spiritual and liturgical community of souls, in whatever sense."[57] They go on to complete their view of a postliberal alternative to liberalism by insisting that we must learn to see all realities, both nature and culture, "as symbolizing something higher."[58]

Milbank and Pabst provide a stirring vision of a way ahead for a postliberal alternative to liberal culture. They envision a form of moral formation that opens the way for a renewed contact with transcendent reality within a culture formed by reciprocal honor along with personal and socially constructive forms of exchange that contribute to a common good. This is indeed a stirring social vision, but does it not require the presence of two more mundane characteristics within the citizenry? Must not ideals like community, love, fellowship, duty, service, personality, freedom, and (sufficient) property inform in some way the exchanges that contribute to a common good and so are due honor? And must not there be present among the citizenry people whose lives manifest what the Letter to the Ephesians terms "a life worthy of the calling" to which these citizens have been called (Eph 4:1–3, 32)? This list of virtues (or, as I prefer to say, graces) is far more extensive than the rather truncated one offered by Milbank and Pabst, and includes humility, gentleness, patience, forbearance, kindness, tenderness of heart, and forgiveness. Milbank and Pabst entitle their work *The Politics of Virtue*, but the virtues they list boil down to honor, love, and trust. These virtues are indeed necessary for peace and tranquility in a society built upon various forms of exchange rather than competitive settlements the participants regard as fair.[59] Yet,

---

57. Milbank, and Pabst, *Politics of Virtue*, 307.

58. Milbank, and Pabst, *Politics of Virtue*, 307.

59. Milbank and Pabst mention love and trust as crucial virtues that sustain and strengthen social exchanges within societies whose governing structures reflect the ontological structure of the one, the few, and the many that is necessary for a well-ordered society. See, e.g., "Introduction," in Milbank, *Future of Love*, loc. 113 of 7928, Kindle.

where would these virtues be apart from the more modest graces listed by Paul? Apart from these everyday ways of relating to others, would not honor be without recipient, love vacuous and trust inconstant?

That said, following the lead of Bishop Gore, the Milbank-Pabst proposal for a postliberal alternative to liberal society requires the presence of a form of life. It also requires exemplary people who embody the vision and virtues found in the church. Milbank and Pabst are fully aware that many will view their proposal as utopian. They insist, however, that their views appear utopian only within current capitalist logic and liberal ideology.[60] Their argument is that capitalist logic and liberal ideology are palpably failing and capitalist economics and forms of government are in free fall. Capitalist economics and liberal ideology, because of their rapid decline, stand exposed as gods that have failed. As was formerly the case with human rights, time and tide created circumstances in which human rights could emerge as a central political idea. So it is that capitalist economy and liberal ideology are being revealed as failed gods whose failure opens the way for an alternative social vision and way of life.

III. Milbank and Pabst's Vision

Milbank and Pabst believe the failure of these false gods creates space for a different social, economic, and political vision. They are convinced that the time for a postliberal alternative has arrived. This possibility leads them to take a step beyond the idealistic proposals of the Christian Socialists. Not only do they point out, as did the Christian Socialists, ways in which the central assumptions of liberalism serve to undermine the economic, political, and social relations of liberal society, but they also go beyond their predecessors to propose the elements of a practical alternative. The additional steps they take toward a practical solution lead them directly into policy advocacy. The specificity of their proposals goes well beyond even the most progressive of the Christian Socialists. Nevertheless, they do not take these steps as representatives of the Church of England. In no way do they pretend to speak for the church. Rather, they speak simply as Christians, but as Christians who stand as advocates of a "politics of virtue." They speak only as ordinary Christian advocates of a postliberal alternative open to all people of good will. Viewing the world from a "postliberal" perspective, what do they see and what do

60. Milbank and Pabst, *Politics of Virtue*, 171.

they propose? Their focus is panoramic. It includes accounts of liberal economic, political, and social systems. The Milbank-Pabst diagnosis includes assessments of what has gone wrong in each of these dimensions of social life and what specifically is demanded by way of corrective thought and action.

First, from a postliberal perspective, what does one see when examining late modern capitalist economic systems? Not surprisingly, having seen the "metacrisis of liberalism," they see also what they call the "metacrisis of capitalism."[61] The crisis stems in a most immediate sense from the patent inability of late capitalism to balance the growth of wealth with a concrete demand for commodities and from a consequent inability to sustain economic growth and profit. They see also an increasing inability to generate socially productive wealth that serves the genuine good of meeting human needs. In combination, these trends lead to increased pressure to maximize profits and so also to cut labor costs. They also lead to gross inequalities of wealth coupled with the subordination of the long-term needs of the populace to short-term returns on investment.

It is the view of Milbank and Pabst that late modern capitalism is less and less able to generate productive capital that produces genuine social good. They contend also that capitalism "abstracts from the real economy of productive activities."[62] Money now circulates in its own world—a world in which money is employed simply to make more money. The result of this abstraction is that economic relations are stripped of human meaning. The economic sphere, stripped of human meaning, is reduced to "bare, abandoned materiality."[63] In the swirl of money chasing money both land and labor lose their moral significance. The link between "thing and value" is cut. The result of this severance is that economic activity in a late capitalist economy is carried on without regard to tradition, communal association, duty, or purpose. The fact is that late capitalist economies are not instruments for pursuit of a common good. Rather, they rest upon financial speculation and material aggression. In quest of profit, they move from interest to interest and in this constant movement render capitalism a system of destruction rather than preservation. Indeed, because consumption is the sole purpose of production

---

61. See especially Milbank and Pabst, *Politics of Virtue*, 93–95.
62. Milbank and Pabst, *Politics of Virtue*, 94.
63. Milbank and Pabst, *Politics of Virtue*, 94.

and because of a voracious appetite for new products, capitalism moves incessantly toward destruction of what is.

The downward pressures on the general populace caused by declining profits and declining income bring with them three other baleful results. First, the crisis of declining economic strength is addressed by "financialization" or "the creation of credit" as a means of supporting consumption rather than the creation of work and valued good.[64] Milbank and Pabst label this a failing strategy for a simple reason. They claim that society cannot go on forever on credit rather than work, compensation, and profits.[65] Second, a speculative economy produces vast inequalities in wealth. Inequalities in wealth are accompanied by class struggle. In this struggle late capitalism has produced the super-rich and the supper-super rich. These beneficiaries of financial speculation and aggression join hands to form a society of oligarchs—a new aristocracy that is defined by wealth rather than honor. The wealth of this increasingly small group does not trickle down. Rather, it trickles up and out of social usefulness. As time goes by, the winners in this economic struggle more and more blame the victims of their own greed. Indeed, they come to despise the indigent poor and regard their poverty and low social status as "their own fault."[66] Class struggle becomes, in fact, a necessary aspect of late capitalism. Once again, the basic flaw of liberalism, its assumption that the original situation of humankind is one of war and struggle rather than cooperation, raises its ugly head and brings with it the very difficulties liberalism was supposed to remedy.[67] Further, as the Christian Socialists learned from bitter experience, normal political processes cannot remedy the destructive effects of inequalities in wealth and power. As Milbank and Pabst note of the super-rich and the super-super rich: these folk have power and they are not about to turn it over.[68]

This negative judgment about the human condition brings into focus the third negative result Milbank and Pabst attribute to the inequalities of late capitalism—the centralization of economic and political power. In response to the exigencies of international finance, oligarchies seek to compromise the freedom of governments to respond in an adequate

64. Milbank and Pabst, *Politics of Virtue*, 94.
65. Milbank and Pabst, *Politics of Virtue*, 95.
66. Milbank and Pabst, *Politics of Virtue*, 108.
67. Milbank and Pabst, *Politics of Virtue*, 106.
68. Milbank and Pabst, *Politics of Virtue*, 112.

manner. In moments of crisis, oligarchs always seek to subordinate the long-term needs of a populace to short-term economic gains.[69] Domestically, similar destructive forces are at work. In the interest of increased acquisition and profit, oligarchy fuses state and market power to protect short-term gains.

Looking back over the Milbank-Pabst account of late capitalism one cannot miss the fact that the economy they describe is built upon the premise that the original situation of social life is one of war and struggle rather than cooperation.[70] They conclude that war and struggle are endemic to liberalism in all its forms, and particularly to what they call the capitalist and statist power structure.[71] The question they must answer is how this merger of economic and state power can be broken apart and replaced with something better. Their answer is by making fundamental changes in each. First, the economy must be re-embedded in social relations rather than purely economic ones, and second, the ontological structure of the one, the few, and the many must be restored to political relations in a way that is governed by relations of honor, faith, and trust. Once again the postliberal proposal for social renewal shows a remarkable resemblance to that of the Christian Socialists.

What, first of all, is their proposal for a postliberal economy? It is extensive and complex, but all their proposals serve one purpose, namely, to relocate the market within the realm of civil society and the moral virtues of civil life.[72] At present, economic relations subordinate everything to the accumulation of abstract wealth. As such these relations are intrinsically agonistic. Since there is no concrete common purpose, disparity of economic interests insures a continued and slow-burning struggle between classes. Social struggle that is pervasive and persistent presents society with a question about the purpose of government. Is it to increase human freedom and market choice, or is it to promote human flourishing or *eudaimonia*?[73] Milbank and Pabst pose this question in a particularly pointed way. Can the invisible hand coupled with state action produce stability apart from agreement about a common good? Their answer is clearly no. Human flourishing cannot come to be apart

---

69. Milbank and Pabst, *Politics of Virtue*, 94.
70. Milbank and Pabst, *Politics of Virtue*, 106.
71. Milbank and Pabst, *Politics of Virtue*, 107–8.
72. Milbank and Pabst, *Politics of Virtue*, 123.
73. Milbank and Pabst, *Politics of Virtue*, 130–32.

from sharing a common good, and a common good is impossible unless economic relations are re-embedded in social relations that share a common purpose. The re-embedding of economic relations within a wider range of social ones constitutes what Milbank and Pabst term "the civil economy alternative."[74] This alternative requires society to "relocalize" the economy. Relocalizing the economy, they believe, will result in the establishment of trust. Like the Christian Socialists before them, they contend that the means to this end lie in the empowerment of small groups. In smaller groups the focus shifts from the need to balance self-interest with the needs of others to shared needs that can only be satisfied through mutual assistance that is built upon trust. Trust makes possible reciprocity rooted in human sympathy. Reciprocity built on sympathy and trust combines freedom with personal flourishing—yet another theme central to the social thought of Christian Socialists.[75]

Once again, the defenders of liberalism will reply that proposals for a "civil economy" are utopian. Citing the work of Antonio Genovesi, Milbank and Pabst vehemently deny this charge. They support Genovesi's claim that human beings are naturally political, social, and gift-exchanging beings who by nature need to cultivate the habits of personal and communal living necessary to sustain social life. In the final analysis, the Milbank-Pabst proposal rests upon an account of human nature. For them human cooperation lies deeper than human conflict. Social exchange lies at a deeper level than social conflict. By way of conclusion, they quote Italian philosopher Gaetano Filangieri (with whom Bishop Gore would be in agreement): "A polity cannot be said to be rich and happy save in that single case where every citizen through a definite labor in the course of a reasonable time is able commodiously to supply his own needs and that of his family."[76]

IV. Practical Steps toward a Civil Economy

Milbank and Pabst are fully aware that if their proposal for a postliberal civil economy is to gain public support, they must outline the small steps necessary if economic relations are to be torn away from purely

---

74. Milbank and Pabst, *Politics of Virtue*, 129.
75. Milbank and Pabst, *Politics of Virtue*, 121, 140.
76. Filangieri, *La scienza della legislazione*, cited in Milbank and Pabst, *Politics of Virtue*, 141.

economic exchanges and re-embedded in social networks. In general, this relocation of economic relations within a web of social ones requires three things. One is to show that it is possible to pursue both profit and social benefit. Another is to strike a balance between competition and cooperation. Yet another is to show how business relations can become partnerships between owners, managers, workers, consumers, and suppliers—partnerships with an ethos in which virtues are learned and honored.[77] In short, re-embedding economic relations in social ones requires a renewed business ethos as well as a renewed social vision.[78]

To be sure, a renewed social vision coupled with a renewed business ethos will require significant changes in business practice. These changes will involve, first of all, anti-usury laws combined with the formation of joint enterprises in which both risk and reward are shared by all stakeholders. Further, in a civil economy of this sort, joint enterprises will be required to state clearly the public benefit of their undertaking. Milbank and Pabst believe that a step like this will serve to restore the breach between moral significance and economic undertaking created by late capitalism. The requisite changes from a more competitive to a more cooperative vision and practice will require also a shared scale for the priority of desires—a scale that can be used to establish just wages, just prices, and, most of all, a fair distribution of assets between all stakeholders. Milbank and Pabst state their position on wages, prices and assets in this way: "A post-liberal political economy requires an ethical as well as economic negotiation of wages, prices and profits among owners, workers, shareholders and consumers who would all be given opportunity to acquire real political and economic stakes in every enterprise."[79]

Given the fact that shareholder value now dominates business culture, this proposal may seem to many a bridge too far. It may not be! Interestingly enough, Marc Benioff, a self-described entrepreneur who has become "a very wealthy person" and whose firm has generated billions in profits, in a recent *New York Times* op-ed piece proposed something very much like this as a necessary step if capitalism is to be saved from its own excesses.[80]

---

77. Milbank and Pabst, *Politics of Virtue*, 143.
78. Milbank and Pabst, *Politics of Virtue*, 149.
79. Milbank and Pabst, *Politics of Virtue*, 160.
80. See Benioff, "We Need a New Capitalism."

Like the Christian Socialists before them, Milbank and Pabst champion an alternative social vision, one that focuses on cooperation rather than competition. Toward this end they also, like their predecessors, champion the development of associations that restrict monopolies, encourage new technologies, and provide vocational training. Their contention is that "such institutions can instill an inter-firm ethos based upon the idea that one achieves self-respect and social recognition" by participation in a communal enterprise."[81] Corporations that have moral as well as economic purpose can foster virtue and reward virtuous behavior. They have the potential to produce both profit and pleasure that contribute to a common good. They can be encouraged to take upon themselves more social responsibility, and they might even assume a useful share of political governance.

Associationism seems alive and well in the postliberal proposals of Milbank and Pabst. So also is the Christian Socialist commitment to striking a healthy balance between urban centers of commerce and the surrounding, more agrarian countryside. Associationism encourages multiple centers of economic activity. It also encourages a rational balance between urban and rural forms of life. Such a balance serves to preserve cooperative practices that are friendly to the human enterprise. It also tends to hold up the importance of wise land use. Indeed, a failure to see the importance of land threatens urban life.[82] Yet again a major concern of the Christian Socialists makes its appearance!

The Milbank-Pabst vision for a socially embedded economy depends upon yet another factor—one with multiple aspects. A civil economy, one with economic exchanges embedded in social ones, requires a practice like "primordial gift exchange."[83] An economy understood as a form of gift exchange views debt in relational terms. If viewed in relational terms, incurring debt is an arrangement whereby both profit and risk are shared more equitably among all stakeholders—"stockholders and managers, employers and employees, producers and consumers, as well as suppliers and sellers."[84] Milbank and Pabst make their basic point in this way: "By turning unsecured creditors into shareholders and stakeholders who for a certain period would not receive dividends or the right of share

---

81. Milbank and Pabst, *Politics of Virtue*, 150.
82. Milbank and Pabst, *Politics of Virtue*, 152–53.
83. Milbank and Pabst, *Politics of Virtue*, 157.
84. Milbank and Pabst, *Politics of Virtue*, 157.

repurchases, the conversion of debt into equity would create a more economically and ethically viable model of risk and profit sharing."[85] This change in understanding and practice would, in short, restore the gift-exchange notion of social life because debt would be regarded as a form of gift that promises a complex return.

The account Milbank and Pabst give of a postliberal alternative to capitalism is more extensive than the summary provided above. Their own summary of the postliberal alternative they propose is sufficient, however, to cover the salient points of their position:

> The civil economy model can be summarized as follows. Overwhelmingly, it ties economic profit to ethical and social purpose, and seeks to ethicize exchange. In the same spirit, it replaces the separation of risk from reward with risk- and profit-sharing models. In both respects, it publicly requires an economic pursuit of honorable practice and genuine benefit rather than just abstract wealth and power. It assumes that the seemingly "otherworldly" and soul-regarding pursuit of the truly good is, in fact, in natural alignment with the various goods of concrete human flourishing (work, housing, food, health) and higher fulfillment (work satisfaction, subtle cuisine, beautiful environment, educational development) that human beings everywhere naturally seek. For this reason, it believes that the real economic task is the shared coordination of all these pursuits in terms of a "common good."[86]

V. Assessment of the Postliberal Alternative

Milbank and Pabst insist that the ideas and practical steps they champion are not utopian. Nevertheless, they are aware that their social vision presents formidable challenges. For one thing, the likelihood of the success of a "postmodern alternative" will increase only as the failure of capitalism to produce healthy social results becomes more apparent than it is at present. For another, even under ideal circumstances, a shift in social vision and practice of this magnitude requires both time and education. Education today is utilitarian in nature. It prepares people to be consumers and functionaries but not virtuous citizens in any genuine sense of the term. Indeed, in liberal society education is turned over to the state,

---

85. Milbank and Pabst, *Politics of Virtue*, 160.
86. Milbank and Pabst, *Politics of Virtue*, 171.

and the state in turn uses state-controlled education to buttress its own authority. By way of contrast, classical education, or *paideia*, locates life in a transcendent good, and it seeks to form the soul in relation to that good. From this double perspective, *paideia* promotes the common good by cultivation of the virtues that are necessary for a healthy citizenry. Participation in civic life thus becomes, in turn, a training ground for virtue in the service of a common good.[87] Within a classical form of education, transcendence, the common good, virtue, and civic participation feed each other in a mutually supportive circle of influence. Liberal education, on the other hand, swings back and forth, moving from concerns that have no relation to politics to utilitarian concerns that hand the citizenry over to the forces of the market and the interests of the state.[88]

Clearly, education within liberal society poses a formidable obstacle to any form of education that runs contrary to its basic assumptions. For Milbank and Pabst that contrarian form requires the revival of *paideia*. How is such a change to occur? Their response is scattered and, to the mind of this reader, incomplete and inadequate. They note quite rightly that nothing will change without "a popular inculcation of virtue."[89] In turn, a popular inculcation of virtue will not take place apart from "virtuous elites that lead by example and command popular assent precisely because they uphold and hyperbolically fulfill ideals that are open to all." They go on to say that these elites must be open and "less contemptuous" of folk culture than elites on the left are.[90]

That said, the Milbank-Pabst proposal for a postliberal civil economy takes full account of the fact that moral formation does not take place apart from communities that produce these elites and shape the lives of their members in ways that manifest the goods and virtues the community holds dear. So, as noted previously, they call for society to take upon itself "the mode of Christian *ecclesia*" that defends the "preeminence of the person" within a "fluid sense of the organic whole."[91] The hope for a revival of this sort lies in the fact that there remained, even after the Enlightenment foregrounding of enlightened self-interest and utilitarian ethics, what they call a Christian residuum whereby the church "kept

---

87. Milbank and Pabst, *Politics of Virtue*, 260–62, 275.
88. Milbank and Pabst, *Politics of Virtue*, 283.
89. Milbank and Pabst, *Politics of Virtue*, 267.
90. Milbank and Pabst, *Politics of Virtue*, 267–68.
91. Milbank and Pabst, *Politics of Virtue*, 284.

alive the future of the soul, mutual charity and reconciliation in excess of the legal coercion of the state."[92] We need, they write, "both the mysticism of the individual soul and the spiritual and liturgical community of souls, in whatever sense."[93] In short, the church is necessary because its common life interrupts an overemphasis on the state. As members of Christ's body, adults and children remain before all else citizens of a heavenly city who seek to be formed by the demands of that citizenship.[94] Something in "the mode of the Christian *ecclesia*" is necessary also because the main element of human association is psychic rather than contractual. It has to do with friendship, benevolent sharing, and sharing in a common good more than it does law and the distribution of material goods.[95] In short, politics, in its proper sense, requires a psychic community that has as its foundation a transcendent common good.

It is clearly the hope of Milbank and Pabst that the church will rise to the occasion and, through its structures and common life, bring alive the memory of a lost good and so engender precisely this sort of community. So it is that Milbank and Pabst point in hope to the church and faith-based schools as channels through which we might learn once again to see all realities (both nature and culture) as "symbolizing something higher" and as providing a foundation for a society grounded in reciprocity rather than competition and struggle.[96] It is hard to miss the fact that Milbank and Pabst are here jousting against more than neoliberal valorization of the free market and progressive accounts of the centrality of human freedom. They are also attacking supporters of the sort of Christian realism championed by Reinhold Niebuhr. For Niebuhr, the reality of sin and finitude limits the expression of love in political relations. Because of these facts about human nature, in political relations love must be expressed as justice. Milbank and Pabst object that Niebuhr's elevation of struggle over cooperation leads inevitably not to justice but to violence. They object also that this view of human relations seems to ignore creation, namely, our creation as social beings made for friendship. As

---

92. Milbank and Pabst, *Politics of Virtue*, 286–87.
93. Milbank and Pabst, *Politics of Virtue*, 307.
94. Milbank and Pabst, *Politics of Virtue*, 307.
95. Milbank and Pabst, *Politics of Virtue*, 284.
96. Milbank and Pabst, *Politics of Virtue*, 300–307.

such, sympathy overrides animosity and peace is a more basic drive than self-interest and violence.[97]

It is plain to see that throughout their defense of a "postliberal alternative" Milbank and Pabst rely on a view of human nature that does not share the pessimism they see as lying at the foundation of all forms of liberalism. It also depends upon the relocation of value within a transcendent reality that establishes the nature of the common good of humanity. As best I can determine, Milbank and Pabst believe that the Christian church is the only body by means of which such a reestablishment might take place. Yet the church cannot accomplish this feat by means of its own organization or its own program for social renewal. Rather, the church contributes to this social revolution by being what it is called to be—an organ of transmission—a body that waits upon God and receives the gift of its own constitution from God. This transmission is in turn transmitted to those who are not among its members.

Milbank makes this point in a key article to be found in a collection of his essays.[98] His argument is, to say the least, convoluted, complex, and obscure. To assure adequacy of presentation, I will quote his initial statement in full. Speaking of his earlier work *Theology and Social Theory*, Milbank notes that it was not his purpose to imagine the Church as Utopia. Neither was it his purpose, he continues,

> to discover in its ramified and fissiparous history some single ideal exemplar. For this would have been to envisage the Church in spatial terms—as another place, at which we might arrive, or *as this* identifiable site, which we can still inhabit. How could either characterize the Church, which exists, finitely, not in time, but *as* time, taken in the mode of gift and promise? Not a peace we must slowly construct, piecemeal, imbibing our hard-learned lessons, but as a peace already given, superabundantly, in the breaking of bread by the risen Lord, which assembles the harmony of peoples then and at every subsequent Eucharist. But neither as a peace already realized, which might excuse our labor. For the body and blood of Christ only exist in the mode of gift, and they can *be* gift (like any gift) only as traces of the giver and promise of future provision from the same source. This is not an ideal *presence* real or imagined, but something more like an "ideal transmission" through time, and despite its

---

97. Milbank and Pabst, *Politics of Virtue*, 360.

98. See Milbank, "Enclaves, or Where Is the Church?," in Milbank, *Future of Love*, locs. 2963–3910 of 7928, Kindle.

> ravages. Fortunately the Church is first and foremost neither a program, nor a "real" society, but instead an enacted, *serious fiction* [emphasis added]. Only in its Eucharistic centering is it enabled to sustain a ritual distance from itself, to preserve itself, as the body of Christ under judgment *by* the body of Christ, which after all, it can only receive. In a sense, this ritual distance of the Church from itself defines the Church, or rather deflects it from any definition of what it is. In its truth it *is* not, but has been and will be.[99]

He then goes on to say, in answer to the question of where the church might be, that the short answer is, on the site of the Eucharist. He then qualifies this statement by insisting that the site of the Eucharist is not really a site. It is not a site because "it suspends presence in favor of memory and expectation." Thus the Eucharist "'positions' each and every one of us only as fed—gift from God of ourselves and therefore not to ourselves—and bizarrely assimilates us to the food which we eat, so that we, in turn, must exhaust ourselves as nourishment for others. But the long answer could never be completed, since it would be nothing other than the Church's own act . . . of self-judgment and self-discrimination . . ."[100]

Milbank's prose can be notoriously obscure, and the previous two excerpts are prime examples of that obscurity. However, his meaning seems to be that the church cannot be properly understood or identified by reference to its structure, its order, its forms of worship, the character of its common life, its moral norms or its articles of belief. We cannot find the church by looking at a particular instance of its existence.

As he says, the church is not an ideal *presence* that we can locate. It is rather a gift that comes to us in and through our eucharistic gathering. In this transmission we are called to remember, anticipate, and give ourselves as a gift like the one we have received and continue to receive through remembrance of Christ's sacrificial gift and anticipation of his final presence.

Milbank's presentation of the church as a form of transmission rather than as a definable state is of central importance for his entire case in support of a postliberal form of social life. According to Milbank, society built upon the premise of liberalism will never take on a life-giving

---

99. Milbank, "Enclaves, or Where Is the Church?," in Milbank, *Future of Love*, loc. 2963 of 7928, Kindle.

100. Milbank, "Enclaves, or Where Is the Church?," in Milbank, *Future of Love*, loc. 2976 of 7928, Kindle.

form until it is once more grounded in a transcendent reality—a world of ideas (figures or patterns) that gives form in this world to truth, beauty, and goodness. It is clear that Milbank believes that the Christian church is the only body through which such a regrounding can possibly come about. Nevertheless, given the present state of the church, how is it possible to hope for such a miracle? As Alan Wolfe has observed, "Religion is a powerful force that shapes how people act and what they believe. So is culture. When the two conflict in America, religion yields more to culture than the other way around."[101] The evidence presented not only by Wolfe but also by a host of other knowledgeable observers makes it difficult, if not impossible, to gainsay this observation.

That said, it is entirely appropriate to ask if there is any ground for hope. The clear implication of the Milbank-Pabst account of the nature of the church is that hope will not be found in human struggle. If, however, the church is rightly understood in terms of gift and "transmission" rather than an identifiable state, there is indeed a way forward to a "postmodern alternative" to liberal society. That way, however, does not lie in ecclesial programs that might have a positive impact on social life. Rather, given the profundity of the social crisis now faced by liberal society, the way forward for the church lies not in action but, first, in repentance; second, in a posture of patient waiting upon God; and third, in faithful eucharistic celebration. At present, the proper stance for the churches is not social action but patient waiting and obedient celebration. The true calling of the church in the time of late capitalism is waiting in faith, hope, and love for God to fulfill his promise. That promise is to give the gift of his life to his people and, through that transmission, to the world. Milbank says in a number of ways that the gift necessarily carries traces of its giver. That being the case, one must conclude that love is central to God's transmission of his own nature. Love, it seems, is God's way of rerooting the life of the world in a transcendent reality. By implication, love lies at the foundation of both a culture of honor and a culture built upon the exchange of gifts.

The presence of the church within the passage of time is thus of central importance for the appearance and success of a postliberal alternative to liberal society. In response to Alan Wolfe's doubts about the integrity of the churches in America, Milbank no doubt would reply that the integrity of the common life of the church at any given moment in time does not determine its significance in the grand scheme of things.

---

101. Wolfe, "Whose Christianity? Whose Democracy?," 200.

Rather, its significance is to be found first of all in God's promise to give himself to the church in the body and blood of his Son, and second of all in the long and checkered history of God's transmission of his life to the church. Citing Rowan Williams, Milbank asserts that the long answer to the question of where is the church lies in "the Church's own act . . . of self-judgment and self-discrimination: all the stories of true and failed transmission, of more or less adequate persuasions and receptions."[102] By Rowan Williams's account, this is an ecclesiology that "involves critical narratives of the (endless) genesis of the Church."[103] So, according to both Williams and Milbank, the location of the church is not to be found in a history in which the church measures itself against "the pre-established standard of Christ" (or, for that matter, against any self-defined estimate of the church's ideal state or social importance). Rather, it is to be found in a history that "in detailed judging raises us to a better perception of the pre-given standard—which can only be pre-given in the mode of promise."[104] To put the matter in a different way, the state of the church is not to be measured by self-adopted criteria but by clearer perception of a standard for its life "pre-given" by God in Christ. So Milbank concludes, "To receive Christ . . . is in some minimal way to receive the Church as itself an adequate mode of reception."[105]

It seems that the Milbank-Pabst proposal for a cure of the ills of liberal society requires the rerooting of the common life of that society in a common yet transcendent good. It seems also, on their account, that the church alone, despite its flaws and failures, carries in its common life the possibility of such a rerooting. That possibility is not, however, a natural possession! Rather, it is a gift that comes with a promise, rather than the guarantee of its own continuance. The basic stance of the church within the providence of God is then one of expectant waiting rather than self-assessment or program development. Within the community of faith, an exemplary form of life built on exchange sustained and directed by love, honor, trust, and expectant waiting defines its calling. Love, honor, trust,

---

102. Milbank, "Enclaves, or Where Is the Church?," in Milbank, *Future of Love*, loc. 2976 of 7928, Kindle.

103. Milbank, "Enclaves, or Where Is the Church?," in Milbank, *Future of Love*, loc. 2976 of 7928, Kindle.

104. Milbank, "Enclaves, or Where Is the Church?," in Milbank, *Future of Love*, loc. 2976 of 7928, Kindle.

105. Milbank, "Enclaves, or Where Is the Church?," in Milbank, *Future of Love*, loc. 2976 of 7928, Kindle.

and patience in turn make for just and fair exchanges of all social goods that lead in turn to good order and peace.

The divine gift of life through the blood of Christ awakens love and trust in the human heart and serves to root human life in a common yet transcendent good. That good is social in nature and is pursued through various forms of exchange that are governed by love, honor, and trust. Gift, common good, love, trust, honor, and exchange (rather than competition) are the building blocks of a "politics of virtue." Unless one is prepared to accept the Milbank-Pabst view that no alternative to liberalism will prevail apart from regrounding in a transcendent common good, their views of a postmodern alternative will seem at best far-fetched. If, however, one accepts their premise about the centrality of transcendence, love, trust, honor, and exchange, then another doubt soon makes its appearance. They propose a politics of virtue as an alternative to a politics of competition. Their privileged virtues are love, trust, and honor. But to quote the Beatles, if love indeed is central, then can it be said, "Love is all you need"? If love is not all you need, then Milbank and Pabst have failed to give an adequate account of the virtues that are required for their postliberal alternative. Indeed, despite its importance, they will have left love without a face—without a means of recognition.

The New Testament provides any number of examples of lesser virtues that serve to give love a face. The Letter to the Ephesians provides one of the most extensive accounts of what I will call love's contributing virtues.[106] In Eph 4:1–5, Paul urges his readers to "lead a life worthy of the calling to which you have been called." That calling is to live a life "holy and blameless in love" (Eph 1:4). In Eph 5:1–2 his readers are told to become imitators of God "as beloved children." As such they are "to walk in love, as Christ loved us and gave himself up for us." A worthy (honorable?) life is then a life lived in love, but what does love look like? In 4:1–3, 31–32, Paul gives love a face. It is humble and so open to instruction. It is gentle in its treatment of an erring brother or sister. It is patient with others and so willing to bear with others in love. It is most of all eager to maintain the "unity of the Spirit in the bond of peace." To this end it "puts away" all bitterness, anger, argumentativeness, and malice and in their place puts kindness, tenderheartedness, and forgiveness (4:31–32).

It seems to this reader that the implied centrality of love in a "politics of virtue" requires a more robust characterization of love and its attendant

106. For an extended discussion of the "lesser virtues," see Turner, *Christian Ethics and the Church*, 78–83.

virtues than the Milbank-Pabst proposal provides. It is indeed true that an alternative program cannot adequately address the problems endemic to liberalism. These problems can be addressed successfully only by an alternative form of life—one rooted in transcendence and expressed in exchanges governed by honor, love, and trust; one that has an identity defined by the attributive virtues Paul enumerates. In short, a politics of virtue of the sort championed by Milbank and Pabst, as Bishop Gore saw clearly, requires the contrarian presence of a body in whose various shapes and forms Christ is taking form. As they contend, in the dying days of late capitalism social renewal requires something "in the mode of the Christian *ecclesia*." It is only within smaller associations like those that make up the *ecclesia* that these virtues can be exemplified, learned, and passed on. In short, the credibility of the postliberal alternative they propose requires a more robust account of the church as a school of charity and its contributing virtues.

Had Milbank and Pabst done so they would, at the same time, have given a more nuanced and powerful account of the way in which a virtuous citizenry might serve to restore the present liberal political order to the pattern God originally intended. The pattern originally intended for human rule of humans "always requires a balance of the consent of 'the many' with the advice of 'the few' and the executive decisions of 'the one.'"[107] This arrangement was not intended by God to be a system of checks and balances mitigating the struggle between each of the above but about the mutual contribution of each to a common good.[108] In what might be called "the original situation" representation works all the way up and all the way down, because each makes its particular contribution but also represents those below.[109] These relations are aided and abetted by the fact that the many, the few, and the one share a common good. However, in liberal society people are not held together by attachment to a common good. Rather, it is the case that in a society devoted to liberalism political authority, be it in the hands of the many, the few, or the one, can represent only individuals or artificial aggregates labeled persons.[110] In such a society, central power is necessary to maintain peace and the

---

107. Milbank and Pabst, *Politics of Virtue*, 179.
108. Milbank and Pabst, *Politics of Virtue*, 181.
109. Milbank and Pabst, *Politics of Virtue*, 181.
110. Milbank and Pabst, *Politics of Virtue*, 181.

social contract between conflicting parties.[111] The problem is that "without a shared teleology and virtue" the many, the few, and the one are seen as having different and conflicting interests. As a result, liberal polities live under the threat of a political order dominated by oligarchic rule and class struggle. These alternatives provide the only means available to bring about some peace within the feud.

Milbank and Pabst contend that the only way out of this impasse is restoration of the original threefold order governed by a shared *telos* (the common good) and its requisite virtues. For this sea change to occur society must be reconceived in a corporate way as universal. Within that universality, people live in smaller groups that provide social identity wherein they can be formed as persons who share a common good and the virtues necessary for its pursuit. Milbank and Pabst then go on to say quite directly that in these circumstances "religion can play an important part because it expresses links to a transcendent realm" and at the same time protects "corporate liberties and a wider political participation."[112]

The Milbank-Pabst proposal for a replacement of the liberal political order immediately confronts the reader with a pressing question. Is this presentation of an original political pattern of the many, the few, and the one formed by attachment to a common good and an agreed-upon set of virtues in fact a veiled attempt to defend a hierarchical class system? In view of their conviction that the proposal they champion requires people to focus not on social advancement but upon one's station and its duties, one might reasonably conclude that they join Maurice and Westcott in supporting a rather fixed class system. This conclusion would, however, be false. In championing a given pattern of the many, the few, and the one they do not have in mind any particular institutional form in which this division of labor might be located. They certainly do not have in mind anything like a more or less fixed caste system. They are saying only that the consent of the many, the wisdom of the few, and the executive authority of the one are necessary within any configuration of social, economic, political, and cultural relations if a common good is to be sought and realized. Neither do they believe that there should be no movement between these "stations." They are saying only that within a society that shares a common good, social relations should not be governed by aggressive self-advancement. It should be governed by a desire

---

111. Milbank and Pabst, *Politics of Virtue*, 181.
112. Milbank and Pabst, *Politics of Virtue*, 186.

to contribute to a common good from the place one occupies. It does not mean that one should never seek, as it were, to socially relocate. They are also saying that this pattern of the many, the few, and the one, in a postliberal society, is not a tool for the resolution of conflicting interests, as is the case in liberal society. Rather, these social stations are simply different social locations from which to pursue with others a common good. The place of these stations in the threefold pattern of governance is not intended in a postliberal society as means for competitive advantage (as in liberal society) but as sources of giftedness that in the process of social exchange contribute to a rich and productive common life.

It is in the complex exchanges between the many, the few, and the one that the virtues of love, honor, and trust play their part. I should like to add that it is in these relations also that what I have called the contributing virtues of humility, gentleness, patience, forbearance, eagerness for unity, kindness, tenderheartedness, and forgiveness play a necessary part. These virtues give love a face and provide a check on the drivers of competitive exchange that govern liberal society. It is hard to imagine how a postliberal alternative to liberalism could possibly gain a place in a social imaginary apart from their presence. It is also impossible to imagine their presence apart from communities whose members share an alternative social vision supported by these virtues. In short, it is difficult to imagine their presence apart from the Christian *ecclesia*. So also, apart from their presence, it is difficult to imagine exchanges between the many, the few, and the one not degenerating into exercises in aggressive self-interest. In short, the Milbank-Pabst proposal cries out for a more nuanced ecclesiology than the hint of its necessity they provide.[113] It is a mistake simply to assume, as they seem on occasion to do, that readers in a liberal society will have the slightest idea either of the virtues to which members of the Christian *ecclesia* are called or of the virtues required for the possibility of a postliberal alternative to liberalism.

---

113. In another place I have attempted to provide such a socially contrarian ecclesiology. See Turner, *Christian Ethics and the Church*.

C. Conclusion: Promise

WHAT THEN IS THE promise of Christian Socialism? The original title of this interpretive essay was *Christian Socialism: The Pathos and Promise of an Almost Forgotten Tradition*. However, as interrogation of the tradition progressed, I decided to drop the term "pathos" from the title for the simple reason that the naïveté of its most ardent exponents became quite apparent. The pathos of Christian Socialism is real and it demands notation. It does not, however, require extensive explication. However, things are different when one comes to the question of its promise! By promise I mean, given our present circumstances, in what promising directions does the tradition point? The question of promise is important if for no other reason than it is so easily missed. It is easily drowned out by the failure of Christian Socialists to combine their positive account of human nature and hopes for the future with a realistic account of human finitude and sin. Nevertheless, prescinding from the sometimes utopian views of the tradition's most notable defenders, and taking time for reflection, the promise of Christian Socialism becomes clearer and clearer and, yes, more promising than one might first have thought. Accordingly, this investigation of an almost forgotten tradition concludes with a summary of what careful scrutiny suggests about its promise.

The first thing to say in respect to the promise is that one cannot hope to cure an illness if one does not know what the illness is or what its cure might be. What the Christian Socialists had to say is full of promise because it contains both a diagnosis of and a cure for what they took to be the disease of their society. Following R. H. Tawney, they insisted that the cause of the disease was a rotten foundation. Tawney ascribed the rot to inherent greed. Maurice, Westcott, and Gore, along with Tawney, linked pervasive greed to the valorization of a form of individualism that fostered economic competition but excluded concerns for moral integrity, community health, and social cooperation. They were convinced that the underlying problem of political economy was a faulty view of human nature—one that pictured social life as essentially competitive and self-promoting rather than cooperative and generous. To their minds the way to social health lay in exposing the inadequacy of competitive individualism and replacing this agonistic view of human nature with one based upon the social nature of human beings and the universal love of God. They believed that reclamation of this sort would establish a fundamental human equality and so replace society's competitive character with a cooperative, harmonious form of social life built upon such ideals as equality, fellowship, duty, and service. For many of the early Christian Socialists, the way to social health and tranquility lay in restoring the religious beliefs and ideals that they believed to provide the foundations of "Christendom."

The needed restoration, they held, was above all religious and moral in nature rather than practical and political. Restoration of the religious and moral foundations of English society rather than its institutional and political reform, they argued, comprised the social mission of the Church of England. The promise of Christian Socialism lies first of all in its diagnosis of the sickness of industrial society, its prescription for a cure, and the central role of the Church of England in bringing about change. The diagnosis, the prescription, and the central importance of religious belief and practice, all three, speak as well against the individualism and amorality of the present digital age.

That said, it is still the case that idealism like that of the Christian Socialists faces the dual threat of a lack of realism, on the one hand, and the possibility of fanaticism, on the other. Nevertheless, given its present difficulties, it is hard to imagine a way ahead for any form of liberal (or postliberal) society that does not require of its citizens human sympathy and a focus on the social nature of human life along with the generating, sustaining, and restraining power of community-building ideals. The promise of this form of idealism lies precisely in the central importance it gives to the social rather than the competitive nature of humankind, and to the ideals this social nature serves to generate. Further, the "metacrises" of liberalism, so thoroughly set out by Milbank and Pabst, indicates the immediate relevance of the Christian Socialist tradition. The multiple crises of liberalism serve also to display the promise of an aspect of Christian Socialism that until now has been the subject of severe criticism, namely, the reluctance of many of its most vocal advocates to make institutional reform the focus of their social criticism. To be sure, many of the leaders of the movement did believe institutional reform to be necessary and of immediate concern. Nevertheless, most of them insisted that religious and moral reform rather than institutional reform should be the primary thrust of the social mission of the Church of England. To put the matter in more contemporary terms, they believed that the heart of the social mission of the Church of England was not advocacy for particular political measures intended to reform but repair of the religious and moral foundations of the nation. To their minds, the basic problem of the rotten foundation of their society was not mistaken, inadequate policy but religious defection and moral corruption. Important as indeed they are, political measures are matters requiring practical knowledge and prudential judgment. Thus, social reforms are matters over which reasonable Christian people might disagree. To their minds, the primary job of the church is not to make pronouncements about matters of prudential judgment. It is rather to form a virtuous citizenry capable of considering the issues before the nation in a way shaped not simply by prudence but, more importantly, by ideals capable of providing a firm foundation for a healthy and just society.

This focus on religious and moral formation rather than advocacy is in fact full of promise. As previously noted, in America, since the time of the Vietnam War, the social mission of the churches has been understood in large measure to be social advocacy. However, time and tide have revealed that advocacy for particular measures on the part of the governing bodies of churches rather than their rank and file has produced not a united Christian witness but factionalism within and between the churches. Given the prudential nature of issues concerning public policy and order, such disputes are to be expected. The very divisions produced by institutional advocacy have, however, served to display the Christian Socialist focus on religious and moral foundations as an aspect of the promise of the movement rather as an indication of its inadequacy.

In important respects, the passage of time has revealed promise rather than foolishness in the tradition of the Christian Socialists. Time has made people more aware of the social nature of humankind, and an important debate has arisen about the social mission of the churches. Despite these accomplishments, however, there remains the danger of fanaticism. The present state of political relations in both the United States and the United Kingdom provides ample evidence that fanaticism is a real and present danger for idealists of any stripe. Nevertheless, John

Milbank's proposal of a "politics of virtue" provides a convincing counter to the fanaticism that now corrupts the public square. If virtues like love and honor, in conjunction with those graces listed by Paul, coupled with the classical ones of wisdom, fortitude, temperance and justice, were allowed to encompass and temper these ideals, then they might (as Temple said) set a new tone for public discourse. Indeed, these ideals might well serve as checks on fanaticism and as guides to a healthy, even ideal social life rather than to a series of opinionated and irresolvable social disputes. The presence of these virtues would most certainly allow for the incorporation of the ideals championed by the Christian Socialists into a vision of a just and flourishing common life.

The original diagnoses by the Christian Socialists of the social problems of industrial society and their remedy are full of promise. Rowan Williams and John Milbank have carried this promise forward and in so doing added a depth that renders their predecessors' diagnoses and prescriptions even more relevant now than they were then. Williams's charge is that, because what he terms "programmatic secularism" excludes any transcendent point of reference, social disputes can only be sorted out by establishing the "functionalism" or general utility of any set of proposals. For this reason, programmatic secularism will generate a social practice that is dominated by instrumental or managerial considerations. Any and all other views that might allow one to evaluate outcomes in other terms are deemed merely private opinions that have no place in the public square. In this way, the deepest convictions of most people will simply be excluded from public debate. As Williams has nicely said, if the people who hold these views do go out in public carrying their convictions, they will have to do so wearing borrowed clothes.

Williams clearly implies that secular society does not bring to the world the sort of peaceful order it promises. Far worse, it robs the world of a grasp of human limitation and dependence. Religious belief has the power to hold in check the human temptation to seek limitless economic growth and absolute control over human destiny. Indeed, absent religion, programmatic secularism threatens our very existence. What is more, religious belief along with its practices creates among believers loyalty to a higher power than that of the state. As a result, it provides a point of vantage from which they can assess the actions of the state and the political, economic, and social conditions among which they live.

The clear implication of Williams's diagnosis of the illness of society is that its cure requires the rebirth of Christian faith. He adds that apart from some form of religious revival, society will not have among its residents a particular sort of person apart from whose presence society cannot flourish. He notes that programmatic secularism, because of its functionalism, strips the world of people who believe that there is more to anyone I meet than I can understand. These folk see that people cannot be adequately understood in functional terms of profit and loss. In a real sense people (persons) are a mystery in that they are not just seen by me. In a prior sense, they are seen by and in relation to a reality immeasurably different from my self and all other selves. In traditional religious language, the prior relation of my fellow human beings to their divine source bestows upon them something far more important than freedom, reason, and dignity. That relation renders them holy—touched by God. From this perspective, faith makes it possible to see that the original state of the world is not one of conflict and competition but of giving—of communion and reciprocity between persons. Faith, Williams says, creates space for people who make room for God and their neighbors in situations of hideous extremity. Precisely in such situations, faith renders lives lived on the basis of truth rather than profit and loss. It also renders lives shaped by a sacramental view of the world in which they live. Both the world and the people who live in it are transparent to higher meaning and so are properly to be treated with reverence.

Williams's argument is a bold one. He clearly believes that the tradition of Christian Socialism is full of promise. In the face of programmatic secularism Christian Socialism, because of its religious foundation rather than in spite of it, becomes a tradition filled with promise rather than naïveté. In various ways, it offers an alternative to the functionalism of the age and its instrumental view of human life. It holds in check the exploitive hubris that drives liberal society, and it places a protective penumbra around the world's most vulnerable people—those at the beginning of life, those in the shadows of life, and those at the end of life.[1] Finally, it calls forth people whose lives are founded in the truth rather than estimations of personal gain or loss.

John Milbank disagrees neither with Williams's diagnosis of our illness nor with his prescription for its cure. He adds, however, a diagnosis of his own—one drawn in the first instance from social analysis. In

---

1. I owe this phrase to the late Hubert Humphrey Jr., who said that "the ultimate moral test of any government" is the way it treats "those in the dawn of life" (children), "those in the shadows of life" (the poor, the sick, the disabled), and "those in the twilight of life" (the elderly).

making this move he expands, even deepens, the promise of the tradition of Christian Socialism. By Milbank's account, it is apparent that social life is not first a matter of reconciling or controlling competing wills. Rather, it is rooted in and built upon friendship and exchange. Simply put, we are social beings. As social beings we are dependent upon one another as we, each in our own way, pursue a common good. When it comes right down to it, we seek community and cooperation before we seek competitive advantage. In short, friendship is more basic to our nature and our common life than competition. Both Williams and Milbank trace the basic fact of friendship to an original giftedness—giftedness established by God in creation and completed by God's love given in Christ. We are by nature and by gift in essence social, cooperative beings who, because of our created nature, are in search of a common good. Sociality and cooperation come to us from God and consequently, in a number of ways, are more fundamental to our being than individual identity, competitive advantage, or strife.

It is this assessment of human nature and destiny that opens the way for Milbank and Pabst to make proposals about the replacement of both neoliberalism and progressive liberalism by a series of postliberal alternatives. These proposals demand scrutiny in respect to wisdom, adequacy, and cost, but they nonetheless point in directions that accord with the Milbank-Pabst account of a postliberal alternative. Indeed, they point in directions that expose the inadequacy of present arrangements and turn many of them upside down. They certainly expose the fact that liberalism has failed in its attempts to manage competitive aggression and conflict. The "metacrises" of liberal society are in fact turning the attention of many away from the nostrums of the various forms of liberalism and once again toward a more cooperative vision of social order. To an increasing number of people, liberalism looks more and more like a god that has failed, and this failure has prompted a search for an alternative—one built upon the cooperative rather than the competitive nature of human life. Christian Socialism has carried this promise through time, and now Williams and Milbank believe the time is right for a cooperative alternative to the neoliberal and progressive gods that are failing. The promise of the tradition of Christian Socialism, despite the naïveté of many of its adherents, is the possibility of a new world order based in cooperation rather than a fragile truce between competing wills. The disintegrating state of the world has brought forth a serious question once expressed in Psalm 11:3: "If the foundations are destroyed, what can the

C. CONCLUSION: PROMISE

righteous do?" The answer to this question given by the prophet Isaiah is "Look to the rock from which you were hewn" (Isa 51:1). The answer of the Christian Socialists is similar: "Dig down to the foundations upon which your civilization was originally built." There you will find a solid floor upon which to stand and rebuild.

Christian Socialists, throughout their history, believed that regeneration of the religious and moral foundations of society is linked to regeneration of the Church of England. They also realized that the renewal of British society along with its established church presents daunting challenges—challenges to which there has yet to appear an adequate response. Nonetheless, the Christian Socialists did map out several ways to approach the problem. Taken together, their proposals are not without promise. Leading Christian Socialists turned first to attempts to educate members of the working class in ways that would both improve their standard of living and awaken in the general populace moral ideals the educated elite believed lay dormant but still alive as a sort of Platonic memory of a lost good. Their efforts did have modest results, but their very modesty testifies to the fact that social renewal does not live by education alone. Realizing the need for other initiatives, they deployed the primary means of communication of their day—the spoken and printed word. They gave lectures and preached sermons. They published newspapers and journals. They even wrote whole books, some of which were successful novels. These literary efforts, in fact, did attract public attention. Leaders of the movement also started voluntary societies like the Guild of St. Matthew and the Christian Social Union in an effort to gain public support for their concerns and proposals. Again, these efforts proved useful, though not overwhelmingly so. They also began social experiments they called "associations" in order to provide living examples of ways to further profit sharing and mutual benefit for producers and consumers alike. These efforts had many problems and were not long-lived. Nevertheless, the Christian Socialists never relied upon one response. Fully aware of the importance of living examples, some of their number began a religious order (the Community of the Resurrection) whose common life they hoped would provide a concrete example of holy lives lived in a community built upon worship, love, cooperation, mutual help, and outreach to the poor. Finally, some of their more adventuresome followers, shaped by the Oxford Movement and under the influence of Maurice and Ludlow, took parishes in poor areas, hoping to provide worshipers a sense of the sacramental character of life and so also a reverence for God's world and the people who inhabit it.

This list of initiatives is impressive and expansive. Further, it was not without positive results. Their efforts clearly stand as a part of the promise carried in the tradition of Christian Socialism. It is difficult to imagine major social change apart from a complex effort of this sort. The list does, however, lack one thing—a focus on the importance of the common life of the parish church as a pervasive source of renewal. This is an odd omission given the central importance they attached to religious belief and practice. Yet, despite the urgings of F. D. Maurice, John Ludlow, and A. G. Hebert, attention to the parish church as the primary locus for the social mission of the church never became a movement with sufficient strength to galvanize the church as a whole. As previously noted, recent attempts to defend the established character of the Church of England have noted that through the parish system, the Church of England is a "presence" in all parts of the United Kingdom. So far as I can tell, however, the potential of a pervasive presence as a source of renewal has as yet not become a focus of attention. As a result, the common life of the local congregation has yet to become the epicenter of reforms that define and empower the social mission of the Church of England. This "aporia" in efforts by the Christian Socialists to renew the life of the Church of England and the life of English society is, in an odd way, a part of the promise of their tradition. It sits there like an empty chair at a dinner party, waiting to be filled.

There is, however, a notable exception to this failure to explore the potential of the parish church as a center for social renewal and church reform. This initiative has links to the Christian Socialist movement. As previously noted, a significant number of Anglican clergy took parishes in working-class areas, believing in the power of sacramental worship to mediate the transcendent glory of God and so draw into the church disaffected workers and their families. Stewart Headlam was one such priest. Later, this belief in the power of liturgy to mediate transcendence and revive the church found expression in the work of one of the most important leaders of liturgical renewal—A. G. Hebert. In his seminal work *Liturgy and Society*, Hebert shows himself to be an advocate of "the Parish Eucharist."[2] Participants in the Liturgical Movement pressed for making the celebration of the Eucharist the principal form of Sunday

---

2. Hebert, *Liturgy and Society*, 207–14.

worship in the Church of England. As Hebert wrote, "The Holy Eucharist is not one service among many, but the center of all. The Church of God assembles to celebrate the One Sacrifice upon which the whole life of salvation depends."[3] He goes on to say, "As therefore the parish is the local unit of the Church of God, the Parish Eucharist is of necessity the central act of its life."[4]

In a very real sense, as the church gathers for eucharistic worship, it becomes, in Milbank's words, an organ of "ideal transmission" between God, his people, and the world. As such, in Williams's terms, it becomes a point of contact between the transcendence of God and the whole of creation. Thus, for Williams and Milbank, God's people gathered for eucharistic worship constitute the parish as the central location for the formation of a people whose common life provides an alternative to the secular hyper-individualism and competitive struggles of liberal society. The worship of God's people in a way provides the one great hope of the world. It opens the way for humankind once more to view the good, the beautiful, and the true as aspects of God's world and not just stuff we make up and paste on its surface.

The sacramental/eucharistic focus of many Christian Socialists certainly comprises a significant aspect of the promise of their tradition. Nevertheless, its promise will never come to fruition apart from greater attention to the process of moral formation it most certainly implies. As Paul urges the worshipers in Ephesus, they are to be "imitators of God, as beloved children"; this means that they are to "walk in love, as Christ loved us and gave himself up for us, a fragrant offering and sacrifice to God" (Eph 5:1–2). In other parts of this letter, Paul makes it clear that the sacrificial offering of the people requires them to learn to walk in a different way—not as foolish but as wise (Eph 5:15). Wise walking means giving up one form of life shaped by "deceitful desires" and putting on another "created after the likeness of God." This new form of life requires walking not in deceitful desires but in love—love like that which marks Christ's sacrifice. This sort of love must be learned. It is like learning to walk. Among other things, one must learn humility, gentleness, and patience. One must acquire an eagerness for unity and peace. One must learn also to speak the truth and in so doing "put away" bitterness, anger, contentious argument, and slander. For these combative habits of being

---

3. Hebert, *Liturgy and Society*, 207.
4. Hebert, *Liturgy and Society*, 209.

one must substitute kindness, tenderheartedness, and forgiveness (Eph 4:1–3, 25, 31). This way of walking, Paul insists, is the natural expression of the fact that the Christians in Ephesus are urged to think of themselves not as competitors but as members of one body.

A moment's thought will make clear that the way in which Paul urges the Ephesians to walk is in direct contradiction to the moral instruction that marks the way in which competitive individuals are formed within liberal society. In short, the Christian Socialist tradition is on solid ground when it insists that closing off contact with the transcendent reality of God leads to the destruction of the bonds that make social life rewarding and fulfilling. Williams and Milbank also are on solid ground when they note the central importance of the worshiping community. Apart from such a body transcendence is lost. Where they fall short is in insisting that openness to transcendence requires an adequate moral as well as religious response. That is, the presence of the transcendent reality of God in the Eucharist requires that the community gathered to worship become a community that forms its members in a way of walking that is very different from the way in which the members of liberal society walk. This is a challenge the churches busily avoid by placing their hope in schemes for church growth. The result is that they fail to become communities in which Christ is taking form and so also they fail to be communities whose members are formed with the virtues so essential to responsible citizenship.

It seems to be the case that the promise of parish life, though noted, remains like an empty chair at a great feast. That said, despite this failure, it is fair to say that the Christian Socialists were and are right to point first to the religious and moral rather than the policy issues that define the "metacrises" of liberal society. The promise of the tradition points also to the divisive and sometimes destructive character of the vocabulary with which the inhabitants of liberal society are prone to address social conflict. The Christian Socialists saw that political discourse was being carried on first of all in the language of rights rather than the language of duty. They saw also that to begin with individuals claiming rights rather than citizens seeking to do their duty in pursuit of a common good produces ongoing conflict and social division rather than cooperation and domestic tranquility, though they failed to see clearly that if there is no sense of duty, then an appeal to rights may well be the only recourse one has to have just claims honored. On the other hand, they did see that if society lacks a sense of duty that exists prior to justifiable claims upon it, then citizens will have little reason to act in ways that make demands on personal resources and so require sacrifice. Given the economic, political, and social crises now plaguing liberal society, it is difficult to avoid the fact that if the crises are to be adequately addressed, then great sacrifices will be required on the part of all members of society. Absent religion and its attendant duties, it is hard to imagine widespread willingness to make those sacrifices. For this reason, Williams concludes that programmatic secularism threatens our very existence. It certainly is the case that the issues we face will not be resolved by parties to the conflicts asserting their dignity and claiming their just rights. If, however, in the process of social reconstruction, all members of society were to begin with our social nature, our mutual indebtedness, and our attachment to a common good, they would ask first not what is my right as an individual but what is my duty as a citizen with other citizens in service to a good we share. A major aspect of the promise of Christian Socialism is that it calls citizens, rather than autonomous individuals, to assume their duties as fellow human beings, as members of a commonwealth, who, as such, are bound by duty, even if not by charity, to seek assurance that their fellow citizens be given their rights and so be justly and fairly treated.

The priority of duty in relation to rights is no small issue, but the Christian Socialists have, nonetheless, offered a profound defense of rights—one that is not based on freedom, reason, autonomy, and dignity. Current debates about the morality of genetic modification and assisted suicide, for example, have shown that appeals to freedom, reason, and dignity do not go as far as one might like in defending the rights of the innocent and vulnerable. The Christian Socialist tradition, however, does not begin with some capacity or social state (like dignity) that might well be questioned as relevant in any number of cases. Rather, it begins with status conferred by God's creation of humankind in his image and his bestowal of holiness through the love he has shown for all people. Claims to self-possession of a property or capacity by individuals simply do not offer the same protection to the vulnerable as does a status conferred by God and as such inalienable and permanent.

The priority of duty and the derivative status of rights are not small issues. Neither is the nature and extent of state authority—a subject closely tied to matters of duties and rights. One aspect of the promise of Christian Socialism is its understanding of the proper role and function of government in relation to both of these things. In this respect, looking back over the history of the Christian Socialist movement, one does not see a static position but one that develops and shifts over time. F. D. Maurice, for example, had a very conservative view of the nature and extent of state authority. The state exists to insure and defend public order. Bishop Westcott added to this mandate another—to see that the order of society was built upon Christian ideals. By the time of William Temple, the state was not only to support moral ideals; it was also to foster conditions that support human flourishing and the life of "persons" with fully developed "personalities."

Stated baldly, some of the Christian Socialists over time seem to have supported a state with terrifying powers—powers that on the surface allow government, in the name of human flourishing, to intrude in the most intimate aspects of life. This reading of their view of the authority of government, however, does not do justice to the subtlety of their position. Government may well have wide-ranging responsibilities for the wellbeing of its citizens. Indeed, it is plain to see that free and open markets along with personal responsibility cannot, apart from occasional actions on the part of government, address all the needs of the citizenry. Neither can private philanthropy and local institutions. The wellbeing of a citizenry cannot be adequately defended apart from the role of government. Many of the Christian Socialists recognized this fact from the beginning and consequently saw the need for government intervention and support if healthy social conditions were to be sustained. Many also recognized the importance of limiting the reach of government while strengthening local initiatives and institutions. In order to limit the role of state authority while enhancing the role of local efforts and institutions, they supported two checks on the overextension of state authority. The first was the purpose of government itself. Its final purpose, they held, is the flourishing of persons. Such flourishing cannot occur if the welfare of persons is subordinated to the interests of the state. In short, the authority of government is limited by its very purpose. The centrality of persons and personality is thus the first check on the overextension of state authority. The second check, the principle of subsidiarity, flows from the first. Responsibility for the flourishing of the citizenry is not to be assigned to a larger group or institution if it can be accomplished by a smaller one. This second principle in support of limited government does not rob central authority of its social responsibilities, but it does push responsibility away from the center and outward toward local actors.

As previously noted, this aspect of the Christian Socialist tradition makes way for important links with Roman Catholic social teaching and carries promise both for ecumenical relations and for political initiatives that address the very real problems that have emerged in the midst of the metacrises so well described by Milbank and Pabst. Finally, the Christian Socialist tradition has ecumenical promise in that it calls the churches to return to an aspect of Christian tradition that dates back to the letters of Paul and the writings of the church fathers. That is, the chief social duty of the church is to be a community in which Christ is taking form. In fulfilling this calling the churches also form citizens who are capable of living in a way that honors God, political authority, and the common good of the people. The practical implications of this calling are matters over which Christians will most certainly disagree, but insofar as their lives reflect the form of Christ, their disagreements will lead them to a deeper search for a common good in a spirit that makes them eager to "maintain the unity of the Spirit in the bond of peace" (Eph 4:3). Not only among themselves, but also in their struggles and conflicts with their fellow citizens, they will conduct themselves in a worthy manner—"with all humility and gentleness, with patience, bearing with one another in love" (Eph 4:2). Apart from such a citizenry can the earthly city long endure? The Christian Socialists thought not and so insisted on this point above all others. That insistence gathers all the promises of their tradition in one place.

Bibliography

Appelbaum, Binyamin. *The Economists' Hour: False Prophets, Free Markets, and the Fracture of Society.* New York: Little, Brown, 2019.
Auden, W. H. *Collected Poems.* Edited by Edward Mendelson. New York: Modern Library, 2007.
Avis, Paul. "Anglican Social Thought Encounters Modernity: Brooke Foss Westcott, Henry Scott Holland and Charles Gore." Chap. 4 in *Theology Reforming Society: Revisiting Anglican Social Theology*, edited by Stephen Spencer. London: SCM, 2017. Kindle.
Benioff, Marc. "We Need a New Capitalism." *New York Times*, October 14, 2019. https://www.nytimes.com/2019/10/14/opinion/benioff-salesforce-capitalism.html.
Brown, Malcolm, ed. *Anglican Social Theology Today.* London: Church House Publishing, 2014.
Carpenter, James. *Gore: A Study in Liberal Catholic Thought.* London: Faith Press, 1960.
Chadwick, Owen. *The Victorian Church: Part One, 1829–1859.* London: SCM, 1987.
Christensen, Torben. *Origin and History of Christian Socialism, 1848–54.* Aarhus: Universitetsforlaget, 1962.
Collier, Paul. "Greed Is Dead." *The Times Literary Supplement*, December 6, 2019.
Diniejko, Andrzej. "Christian Socialism in Victorian England." *The Victorian Web* (website), last modified February 24, 2014.
Douglas-Fairhurst, Robert. Introduction to *London Labour and the London Poor: A Selected Edition*, by Henry Mayhew. Oxford: Oxford University Press, 2010.
Fassin, Didier. *Humanitarian Reason: A Moral History of the Present.* Translated by Rachel Gomme. Berkeley: University of California Press, 2012. Kindle.
Figgis, John Neville. *Churches in the Modern State.* London: Longmans, Green, 1918.
Goldman, Lawrence. *The Life of R. H. Tawney: Socialism and History.* London: Bloomsbury Academic, 2013. Kindle.
Gore, C., ed. *Property: Its Duties and Rights; Historically, Philosophically and Religiously Regarded.* New ed. New York: Macmillan, 1922.
Grimley, Matthew. *Citizenship, Community, and the Church of England: Liberal Anglican Theories of the State between the Wars.* Oxford: Clarendon, 2004.
A Group of Churchmen. *The Return of Christendom.* New York: Macmillan, 1922.
Headlam, Stewart, et al. *Socialism and Religion.* Fabian Socialist Series 1. London: A. C. Fifield, 1908.
Hebert, A. G. *Liturgy and Society: The Function of the Church in the Modern World.* London: Faber and Faber, 1961.

Heclo, Hugh. *Christianity and American Democracy.* Cambridge: Harvard University Press, 2007.

Himmelfarb, Gertrude. *The Idea of Poverty: England in the Early Industrial Age.* New York: Knopf, 1983.

———. *Poverty and Compassion: The Moral Imagination of the Late Victorians.* New York: Knopf, 1991.

———. *The Roads to Modernity: The British, French, and American Enlightenments.* New York: Knopf, 2004.

Hobhouse, L. T. "The Historical Evolution of Property, in Fact and in Idea." In *Property: Its Duties and Rights; Historically, Philosophically and Religiously Regarded,* edited by C. Gore, 1–33. New ed. New York: Macmillan, 1922.

Hunt, Lynn. *Inventing Human Rights: A History.* New York: Norton, 2007.

Kaus, Mickey. *The End of Equality.* New York: Basic Books, 1992.

Kidd, Colin. "Moral Sentiments: Connecting Misreadings of an Influential Philosopher." *The Times Literary Supplement,* January 18, 2019.

Lovibond, Sabina. *Ethical Formation.* Cambridge: Harvard University Press, 2002.

Lucas, Susan. "The Temple Legacy Today: Beyond Neoliberalism." Chap. 6 in *Theology Reforming Society: Revisiting Anglican Social Theology,* edited by Stephen Spencer. London: SCM, 2017. Kindle.

MacIntyre, Alasdair. *After Virtue: A Study in Moral Theory.* Notre Dame: University of Notre Dame Press, 1981.

MacKinnon, Donald M. "Revelation and Social Justice." In *Malvern, 1941: The Life of the Church and the Order of Society; Being the Proceedings of the Archbishop of York's Conference,* edited by William Ebor [William Temple], 81–116. London: Longmans, Green, 1941.

MacLeod, George. *Only One Way Left: Church Prospect.* 3rd ed. Glasgow: Iona Community, 1961.

Maurice, Frederick Denison. *The Kingdom of Christ.* 1838. Reprint, Nashotah, WI: Nashotah House, 2013.

———. *Reconstructing Christian Ethics: Selected Writings.* Edited by Ellen K. Wondra. Louisville: Westminster John Knox, 1995.

Mauss, Marcel. *The Gift: Forms and Functions of Exchange in Archaic Societies.* Translated by Ian Cunnison. New York: Norton, 1967.

Mayhew, Henry. *London Labour and the London Poor: A Selected Edition.* Edited by Robert Douglas-Fairhurst. Oxford: Oxford University Press, 2010.

Milbank, Allison. "Maurice as a Resource for the Church Today." Chap. 2 in *Theology Reforming Society: Revisiting Anglican Social Theology,* edited by Stephen Spencer. London: SCM, 2017. Kindle.

Milbank, John. *The Future of Love: Essay in Political Theology.* London: SCM, 2009. Kindle.

Milbank, John, and Adrian Pabst. *The Politics of Virtue: Post-Liberalism and the Human Future.* Lanham, MD: Rowman & Littlefield, 2016.

Mill, John Stuart. "Of Individuality, as One of the Elements of Well-Being." Chap. 6 in *Individualism: A Reader,* edited by George H. Smith and Marilyn Moore. Washington, DC: Cato Institute, 2015. Kindle.

Morris, Jeremy. "F. D. Maurice and the Myth of Christian Socialist Origins." Chap. 1 in *Theology Reforming Society: Revisiting Anglican Social Theology,* edited by Stephen Spencer. London: SCM, 2017. Kindle.

Moyn, Samuel. *Christian Human Rights*. Philadelphia: University of Pennsylvania Press, 2015.
———. *The Last Utopia: Human Rights in History*. Cambridge: Belknap Press of Harvard University Press, 2010.
Murray, A. D., ed., *John Ludlow: The Autobiography of a Christian Socialist*. London: Frank Cass, 1981.
Niebuhr, H. Richard. *Christ and Culture*. New York: Harper & Row, 1951.
Norman, Edward. *The Victorian Christian Socialists*. Cambridge: Cambridge University Press, 2002.
O'Donovan, Oliver. *The Desire of the Nations: Rediscovering the Roots of Political Theology*. Cambridge: Cambridge University Press, 1996,
———. "The Practice of Being Old." In *Church, Society, and the Christian Common Good: Essays in Conversation with Philip Turner*, edited by Ephraim Radner, 203–18. Eugene, OR: Cascade, 2017.
———. *Self, World, and Time*. Ethics as Theology 1. Grand Rapids: Eerdmans, 2013.
O'Donovan, Oliver, and Joan Lockwood O'Donovan, eds. *From Irenaeus to Grotius: A Sourcebook in Christian Political Thought, 100–1625*. Grand Rapids: Eerdmans, 1999.
Pelikan, Jaroslav. *The Vindication of Tradition*. New Haven: Yale University Press, 1984.
Preston, Ronald. *Church and Society in the Late Twentieth Century: The Economic and Political Task*. London: SCM, 1983.
Rad, Gerhard von. *Old Testament Theology*. Vol. 1, *The Theology of Israel's Historical Traditions*. New York: Harper, 1962.
Radner, Ephraim, ed. *Church, Society, and the Christian Common Good: Essays in Conversation with Philip Turner*. Eugene, OR: Cascade, 2017.
Ramsey, Paul. *Who Speaks for the Church? A Critique of the 1966 Geneva Conference on Church and Society*. Nashville: Abingdon, 1967.
Rashdall, Hastings. "The Philosophical Theory of Property." In *Property: Its Duties and Rights; Historically, Philosophically and Religiously Regarded*, edited by C. Gore, 35–64. New ed. New York: Macmillan, 1922.
Reckitt, Maurice. *Maurice to Temple: A Century of the Social Movement in the Church of England*. Scott Holland Memorial Lectures, 1946. London: Faber & Faber, 1946.
———. "The Moralization of Property." In A Group of Churchmen, *The Return of Christendom*, 147–82. New York: Macmillan, 1922.
Redgrave, Vanessa. "It Might Be Us." *Times Literary Supplement*, December 21 & 28, 2018.
Rosen, Michael. *Dignity: Its History and Meaning*. Cambridge: Harvard University Press, 2012.
Rowlands, Anna. "Fraternal Traditions: Anglican Social Theology and Catholic Social Teaching in a British Context." In *Anglican Social Theology Today*, edited by Malcolm Brown, 133–74. London: Church House Publishing, 2014.
Ruskin, John. *Unto This Last and Other Writings*. Edited by Clive Wilmer. New York: Penguin, 2005. Kindle.
Ruston, Roger. *Human Rights and the Image of God*. London: SCM, 2004.
Smith, George H., and Marilyn Moore, eds. *Individualism: A Reader*. Washington, DC: Cato Institute, 2015. Kindle.
Spencer, Stephen, ed. *Theology Reforming Society: Revisiting Anglican Social Theology*. London: SCM, 2017. Kindle.

Suggate, Alan M. *William Temple and Christian Social Ethics Today*. Edinburgh: T&T Clark, 1987.
Tawney, R. H. *The Acquisitive Society*. New York: Harcourt, Brace, 1928.
———. *Religion and the Rise of Capitalism: A Historical Study*. London: J. Murray, 1926. Kindle.
Temple, William. *Christianity and Social Order*. London: Shepherd-Walwyn, 1987.
———. *Christianity and the State*. London: Macmillan, 1928.
———. *Religious Experience and Other Essays and Addresses*. Edited by A. E. Baker. London: James Clarke, 1958.
———. *Studies in the Spirit and Truth of Christianity*. London: Longmans, Green, 1926.
Terrill, Ross. *R. H. Tawney and His Times: Socialism as Fellowship*. Cambridge: Harvard University Press, 1972.
Turnbull, Colin M. *The Mountain People*. New York: Simon & Schuster, 1972.
Turner, Philip. *Christian Ethics and the Church: Ecclesial Foundations for Moral Thought and Practice*. Grand Rapids: Baker Academic, 2015.
———. "How the Church Might Teach." In *The Crisis in Moral Teaching in the Episcopal Church*, edited by Timothy F. Sedgwick and Philip Turner, 137–59. Harrisburg, PA: Morehouse, 1992.
———. "Tradition in the Church." In *The Oxford Handbook of Theological Ethics*, edited by Gilbert Meilaender and William Werpehowski, 130–47. Oxford: Oxford University Press, 2005.
Vidler, Alec R. *F. D. Maurice and Company: Nineteenth Century Studies*. London: SCM, 1966.
Visser 't Hooft, Willem, and J. H. Oldham. *The Church and Its Function in Society*. London: Allen & Unwin, 1937.
Walzer, Michael. *Spheres of Justice: A Defense of Pluralism and Equality*. New York: Basic Books, 1983.
Weil, Simone. *Waiting for God*. Translated by Emma Craufurd. New York: Putnam's, 1951.
Westcott, Arthur. *Life and Letters of Brooke Foss Westcott, D.D., D.C.L.* Vol. 2. London: Macmillan, 1903.
Westcott, Brooke Foss. *Christus Consummator: Some Aspects of the Work and Person of Christ in Relation to Modern Thought*. 4th ed. London: Macmillan, 1906.
———. *The Incarnation and Common Life*. London: Macmillan, 1893. Kindle.
Wilkinson, Alan. *Christian Socialism: Scott Holland to Tony Blair*. London: SCM, 1998.
Williams, Rowan. *Faith in the Public Square*. London: Bloomsbury, 2012.
Williams, Thomas D., and Jan Olof Bengtsson. "Personalism." In *Stanford Encyclopedia of Philosophy*, edited by Edward N. Zalta. https://plato.stanford.edu/entries/personalism/.
Wolfe, Alan. "Whose Christianity? Whose Democracy?" In Hugh Heclo, *Christianity and American Democracy*, 185–208. Cambridge: Harvard University Press, 2007.
Wondra, Ellen K. "Introduction." In *Reconstructing Christian Ethics: Selected Writings*, by F. D. Maurice, ix–xxxii. Louisville: Westminster John Knox, 1995.
Wood, H. G. *Frederick Denison Maurice*. Cambridge: University Press, 1950.

Index

abyss, 49, 112
accomplishments, 49, 148
"the acquisitive society"
    class system of, 124
    "competitive individualism" characteristic of, 72
    manifest "sickness" of, 6
    neoliberalism compared to, 16–17
    promoting acquisition of wealth, 15–16
    theological warrant as an alternative to, 19
The Acquisitive Society (Tawney), 15, 92
After Virtue (MacIntyre), 118
agrarian form of life, obsession with, 91
all people, as equal in worth, 121
"the ambiguities of Christendom," 79
American culture, 59, 61
Anglican clergy, parishes in working-class areas, 182
Anglican Social Theology (Brown), 118
anticlericalism, among the working classes, 11
anti-usury laws, 162
applicability, problem of, 73
Aristotle, on property, 128
Arnold, Thomas, 26
assertion of rights, 132
associationism, 163
associations
    championing the development of, 163
    changing public opinion, 62
    furthering profit sharing and mutual benefit, 181
    London Working Men's Associations, 64
    protecting against atomism, 150
    struggled and never proved to be very successful, 63
atomism, 135, 150
atonement, doctrine of, 20, 33
Auden, W. H., 50, 112
authoritarianism, rise of, 144
authority of government, 186
autonomy
    of individuals, 78, 131, 136, 142, 144
    of others, 146–47
    referring to freedom and reason, 123
Avis, Paul, 42

banking system, reform of England's, 58
Baptism, 21–22
Barth, Karl, 44, 49
behavior, 30, 144
St. Benedict, provided an exemplary form of life, 59
benevolence, 17, 42
Benioff, Marc, 162
biblical witness, on the course of human history, 47
Borges, Jorge Luis, 134

British Empire, to endure
    indefinitely, 42
Brown, Malcolm, 54, 118

capitalism
    basis of, 81
    becoming a criminal oligarchy,
        147
    centralization of power in,
        159–60
    challenging the global
        hegemony of, 155
    changes brought about by, 121
    church disciplining the powers
        of, 53
    class struggle in, 159
    in free fall, 157
    laissez-faire, 71
    metacrisis of, 158
    natural law and, 44–45
capitalist society, social atomism
    of, 135
Carpenter, James, 32n31, 33
Carter, Jimmy, 131–32
Catholic Christianity in Europe,
    seeking a new moral
    foundation for society, 135
central power, necessary in a liberal
    society, 172–73
Chadwick, Owen, 10, 11
character, 88, 89, 93, 125
Charity Organization Society, 8
Chemin Neuf, 62, 62n20
children of God, 85, 90, 100
cholera epidemic, in 1849 in
    London, 9
Christ
    all people under the dominion
        of, 21
    bringing reconciliation, 43
    death on behalf of all people, 40
    encompassing all humankind
        united with God, 30
    established his kingdom
        including all people, 74
    as example, 34, 112
    fulfilled the law of life, 127
    gathered fragments of
        humankind into unity, 76
    God in, 20, 117
    as the highest instance of
        personhood, 88
    incarnation of, 22, 28, 29
    liberated humankind from the
        power of sin, 111
    life of, 33, 35
    the Logos, 74–75
    person of, 33
    presence of, 35
    redemptive work of, 34
    showing us the abyss, 49
    transforming lives and social
        relations, 24
    the Word, 41
Christ of Culture (Niebuhr), 23
Christendom, 18, 73, 79, 80, 81
Christendom Group, 80–81
Christian America, churches
    longing for, 79
Christian civilization, dream of, 80
Christian Democracy, 136
Christian Fellowship League,
    formation of, 64
Christian missions, establishing in
    poor areas, 64
Christian personalism, 88, 135
Christian perspective, socialism
    viewed from, 5
Christian residuum, after the
    Elightenment, 165–66
Christian social ethic, foundation
    of, 51
Christian Social Union (CSU), 47,
    63–64, 181
Christian Socialism
    as an alternative to
        functionalism, 179
    Charles Gore on, 32
    on duties, 82
    Jeremy Morris on, 20
    John Milbank on, 137
    making a socially conscious
        faith available to the Church
        of England, 20

offering a path forward for
  Western society, 142–43
as an organized movement in
  England, 3
promise of, 175–87
Rowan Williams on, 137, 138,
  142, 179
Stewart Headlam on, 63
tension regarding principles and
  policies, 28
*The Christian Socialist: A Journal of
  Association*, 64
The Christian Socialist journal, 64
Christian Socialists
  believing that the church ought
    never to support state
    socialism, 36
  calling England back to an ideal,
    52
  on the Church of England's
    inadequate response to
    changing social conditions,
    11
  on community life shaping
    individuals, 77
  counternarrative of, 118
  on crediting a competitive
    economic system with any
    form of social betterment,
    121
  developed a Christian
    conscience, 56
  digging down to the
    foundations, 181
  on each person fulfilling duties,
    130
  on economic relations excluding
    moral considerations, 8, 17
  expressions of the movement in
    its English guise, 28
  faced a daunting challenge, 62
  failed to recognize the dark side
    of cooperation, 120
  on the flourishing of individuals,
    77
  focused in England on the
    British populace, 55
  focused on the teaching
    ministry of the church, 58
  on fulfilling their social role, 80
  Gore on the views of, 5–6
  list of initiatives of, 182
  looked to the Middle Ages, 18
  moral vision of, 19–20
  as not original thinkers, 88
  position against individualism,
    119
  on the positive implications of
    the incarnation, 46
  on the problematic nature of
    rights claims, 123
  promoting ideals, 22
  public witness to a Christian
    Sociology, 65
  on the relation of ideals and
    political measures, 96
  reluctance to use institutions of
    the church as instruments of
    policy advocacy, 67
  reluctant to enter the fray of
    public policy, 13
  on the role of the Church of
    England, 13, 66
  sacramental/eucharistic focus
    of, 183
  sought fully developed persons,
    77–78
  sought no social or political
    revolution, 6
  on the state of the poor, 10, 12
  tradition of, 185
  troubled by the first
    understanding of rights, 132
  view of social conditions, 4–5
Christian Sociology
  as Christian ideals, 31–32
  depending upon duties and
    rights, 129
  educating the public conscience
    through, 4
  foundation for, 74
  healthy society requiring, 155
  incarnation as a charter for, 29
  public witness to, 65
  searching for, 17–18

196 INDEX

Christian witness within society, aim of, 5
Christianity and American Democracy (Heclo), 67
Christianity and Social Order (Temple), 85, 90, 99, 107
Christianity and the State (Temple), 57
Christians
  belief and practice, 141
  concerned with all aspects of human life, 35
  in Europe provided a foundation for a conservative view of liberal democracy, 135
  judging the "best" interests of their country, 99–100
  as members of one body, 184
  picturing as "resident aliens," 79
Christology, aspects of a complete, 51
church. *See also* churches
  cultivating social ideals, 97–98
  educating and inspiring society, 53
  as an enacted, serious fiction, 168
  gathering for eucharistic worship, 168, 183
  linking to common human enterprise, 25
  location of found in detailed judging, 170
  necessary to interrupt an overemphasis on the state, 166
  role in society, 52–68
  role of for Milbank and Pabst, 154–55, 166, 167
  stance of expectant waiting, 170
  supplying principles for citizens to judge policy, 99–100
  as a universal society for Maurice, 21
  way forward for, 169
"The Church and its Function in Society," conference on, 105
Church of England
  addressing the misery of the poor prior to the Industrial Revolution, 12
  becoming an exemplary community, 34
  called to develop moral rectitude, 23
  called to take the lead in a national moral revival, 26
  calling posing a question to the Protestant churches of America, 5
  declining position in the life of English people, 54
  diminished social position and growing incapacity of, 10
  Evangelicals dominating, 19
  failing to address social issues, 32
  foundation of voluntary societies within, 63
  inability to fulfill social ideals, 10
  ineffective because of anticlericalism, 11
  influencing highly placed people within, 63
  Milbank and Pabst not speaking for, 157
  mission to provide a religious and moral base, 52
  moral wisdom of, 111
  ordained to shoulder "the white man's burden," 42
  as a presence coextensive with the boundaries of the nation, 66, 182
  regeneration of the religious and moral foundations of society linked to, 181
  reluctance of Christian Socialists to speak for, 99
  responsibility to address moral challenges, 8
  social mission to restore moral foundations, 176
  on the state of the poor, 12

Temple's attempt to provide the
   guidance of, 104–5
churches. *See also* church
   in America suffering from a lack
      of integrity, 60
   called upon to teach and bear
      witness to ideals, 68
   calling to return to Christian
      tradition, 187
   changed social location of, 54
   on firmer ground denouncing
      evil, 67
   focus of America's, 5
   nationalist flavor of, 55
   not grasping the passing of
      Christendom, 79
   placing hope in church growth,
      184
   taking a step back from the
      world, 59, 61
Churches in the Modern State
   (Figgis), 139
"churchlike" society, of Milbank and
   Pabst, 154
citizens
   church supplying principles for,
      99–100
   faith-based schools provided by
      the church to nurture, 156
   government responsibilities for,
      186
   having rights, 131
   injuring by ignoring family, 105
   state existing for, 90, 139
   state recognizing as superior to
      itself, 139
   virtuous, 60, 172, 177
citizenship, for Christians, 79
civil economy, practical steps
   toward, 161–64
"civil society," composition of, 151
class structure, 86, 124
class struggle, 159
class system, 120
classes, 84, 160
classical education, 165
commercial forces, destroying
   communal solidarities, 81

"commodification," of all aspects of
   life, 145
common good
   belonging to ordered
      communities, 118
   Christian Socialists looked
      to the Middle Ages for a
      society organized around, 18
   contributing to from the place
      one occupies, 174
   difficulty of determining, 94
   disagreements of Christians
      leading to a deeper search
      for, 187
   duty doing in pursuit of, 184
   embedded in practices of honor
      and reciprocity, 147
   honor given to those promoting,
      149
   human flourishing needing
      sharing of, 160–61
   ideals in the name of, 65
   importance of service for, 125
   late capitalist economies not
      pursuing, 158
   meaning of changed for
      neoliberals, 16
   mutual contribution to, 172
   promoting a search for shared
      ends, 147
   promoting by cultivation of
      paideia, 165
   pursuing as social beings, 180
   rights language not generating,
      85
   search of, 180
   shared coordination in terms
      of, 164
common ideals, as necessary, 71
common life
   exemplary character of, 61
   forming exemplary, 59
   friendship basic to, 180
   making property possible, 128
   rerooting in a common yet
      transcendent good, 170
   righteousness manifest in, 34

common life (*continued*)
  as yet to become the epicenter of reforms, 182
common origin, of all people sharing one Father, 30
communal character of Christian life, 62
communal claims, priority of over individual ones, 36
communal foundation, of ideals, 74
communal identity, of humankind, 41
communal setting, locating individuals, 136
communal ties, 130
communal views, 76, 131
communal vision, linking with flourishing, 87
communication efforts, of Christian Socialists, 181
communitarian ideals, of Christian Socialists, 74
community
  as the chief social duty of the church, 187
  providing society with a virtuous citizenry, 61
  realizing ourselves in, 128
  requiring some degree of cooperation, 120
  small intentional holding exemplary promise, 62
Community of Character (Hauerwas), 59
Community of St. Anselm, 62, 62n20
Community of the Resurrection religious order, 58–59, 61–62, 181
community witness, importance of, 59
competition
  exchange as an alternative to, 148
  friendship more basic to our nature than, 180
  individualism fostered, 175
  politics of virtue as an alternative to, 171
  positive social effects of, 72, 121
  reciprocity as an alternative to, 166
  striking a balance with cooperation, 162
  as the watchword of an antisocial person, 20
competitive egoism, 86
competitive individualism
  as characteristic of "the acquisitive society," 72
  in contrast to commonality of English society, 6
  exposing the inadequacy of, 176
  moral ideals as an alternative to, 71
  social ideal offered in opposition to, 78
condescending manner, of Christian Socialists to the disadvantaged, 121
constitutionalism, protecting corporate bodies, 150
consumption, as the purpose of production, 158–59
convictions of people, excluding from public debate, 178
cooperation
  as an alternative to liberalism, 180
  as deeper than human conflict, 161
  focusing on, 163
  linking with the ideal of service, 120
  social life impossible without, 119
  striking a balance with competition, 162
  valorization of, 121
cooperative activities, learning virtues within, 118
corporations, having moral purpose, 163
cosmos, sharing in a transcendent principle, 152

covetous machine, human being as
    merely, 7
craft associations, 150
"creation of credit," supporting
    consumption, 159
cult of progress, opposed by Gore,
    36
culture
    American, 59, 61
    business, 162
    debased by liberal education,
        154
    honor, 148
    human achievement as, 23
    liberal, 156
    religion and, 60, 169
    self-created, 49

Darwin, Charles, 14
debt, 163, 164
Declaration of Independence
    (America's), on self-evident
    truths, 133
democracy, 24, 35, 103
Democracy in America
    (Tocqueville), 67
democratic citizen, religion no
    longer producing, 60
denatured human beings, 48, 112
depravity, of the human spirit, 102
derivative principles, 100, 102,
    103–4, 106
"deserving and undeserving" poor,
    12
desires, 162
dialectical reasoning, 107
a "digger," Maurice as, 75
digital economy, arrival of, 6
digital revolution, social changes
    presented by, 4
dignity, 40, 100, 122, 123
disease of society, diagnosis of and
    cure for, 175
distinctions between men, as the
    base of capitalism, 81
divine gift of life, 171
divine love, 33, 130

divine provisions, family, nation,
    and church as, 75
doctrine of the incarnation. *See*
    incarnation
"dogmatic foundation," healthy
    society requiring, 155
due procedure, 145
duty (duties)
    doing in pursuit of common
        good, 184
    holding together social ideals,
        130
    of humans toward one another,
        74
    as a language, 82
    as necessary, 87
    primacy of over rights, 82, 86,
        103, 129, 130, 185
    property coming with, 92
    social relations resting upon, 98
    understanding in many ways,
        130

ecclesiastical authority, political
    judgment and, 98
ecclesiology, 20, 170, 174
economic activity, multiple centers
    of, 163
economic and political power,
    centralization of, 159–60
economic growth, 140, 158
economic relations
    having no place for moral
        concerns or guidance, 15
    re-embedding of, 161
    relocation of within a web of
        social ones, 162
    stripped of human meaning, 158
    subordinating everything to the
        accumulation of abstract
        wealth, 160
economic self-interest, 15
economic strength, crisis of
    declining, 159
economic system, not meant to
    serve itself alone, 45

economic-political liberalism
    (neoliberalism), of the right,
    144
economy, re-embedding in social
    relations, 160
ecumenical promise, of the
    Christian Socialist tradition,
    187
education
    development of personality
        requiring, 105
    as key for Christian Socialists,
        46
    measuring equality by access
        to, 126
    offered by a well-educated elite,
        57
    producing consumers and
        functionaries, 154, 164–65
educational institutions. *See
    also* institutions; social
    institutions
    founded by Christian Socialists,
        65
egoism, 121
elites, required for inculcation of
    virtue, 165
enemies, loving, 22
England, government funds
    available for poor relief, 13
English Land Restoration League,
    resolution of, 91
Enlightenment, focus on self-
    interest and utilitarian
    morality, 154
environmental challenges, religious
    belief and, 140
Epistle to Diognetus, 79
equality
    of all people, 33, 50, 74
    fundamental, 40, 125, 126
    before God, 82, 123, 132
    holding in check imbalances of
        wealth and rank, 121
    human, 40, 124, 176
    inclusive notion of, 126
    leading to greater freedom, 89
    Maurice's understanding of, 81
    proposed by the Christian
        Socialists, 122
    qualified ideal of, 127
    recognized and sustained by
        social ideals, 118
    rooted in the universality of
        God's love, 35
equitable sharing, requiring a valid
    hierarchy, 149
an era, Christendom as, 79
Ethical Formation (Lovibond), 119
Ethics as Theology (O'Donovan), 106
Eucharist, suspending presence, 168
Evangelicals, 19, 20, 30, 48
evil, recognition of, 58
example, Christ as, 34
exchanges, levels of, 148–49
"extension of the Incarnation," the
    church as, 34–35

Fabian Socialists, 25
Fabians, 63
fact and value, dialectic between,
    108
factionalism, produced by churches
    in America, 177
failure, of liberalism, 180
fair distribution, 126
fair wages, 91
fairness, sense of, 147
faith, 20, 141, 178–79
Faith in the Public Square
    (Williams), 141
faith-based schools, 155, 156, 166
false gods, failure of, 157
family, 75, 101, 105
fanaticism, 73, 153, 176, 177, 178
Fassin, Didier, 86, 120
Feinberg, Joel, 122
fellowship
    defending as a social ideal, 50
    with God, 41
    as God's aim, 102
    of love for each person, 76
    producing community, 129
    requiring some degree of
        cooperation, 120

INDEX

Fellowship of Persons, as a true principle, 87
fiction of control, letting go of, 141
Figgis, John Neville, 87, 139
Filangieri, Gaetano, 161
final destiny, that God has assigned us, 43
"financialization," supporting consumption, 159
fixed class system, 173
Forbes, Charles, 26
freedom
    anchoring in tradition, 147
    as a derivative principle, 102–3
    ideal of, 127
    linked to fulfillment, 82
    requiring training, 90
    within the populace, 89
French Socialists, 25, 26
Friedman, Milton, 16, 89
friendship, as more basic than competition, 180
functionalism, 138, 139, 144, 179
The Future of Love: Essays in Political Theology (Milbank), 155

Gandhi, 98
gap, between ideal and particular judgment, 96
Genovesi, Antonio, 161
giftedness, established by God in creation, 180
gifts
    carrying traces of the giver, 169
    universal practice of exchanging, 148, 163, 164
God
    in Christ, 20, 117
    equality of status before, 81, 123
    established families and nations, 21
    love for humankind, 45, 130
    universal rule over the human community, 40
goods and services, exchange of, 148
Gore, Charles
    on Christian Socialism as a church tradition, 32
    on the Church of England failing to address social issues, 32–33
    on the difference between "Christian Socialists" and "Socialists," 5
    on examples of individuals and intentional communities, 58
    failed to understand difficulties applying moral principles, 72
    formed Christian Social Union (CSU), 63
    on the incarnation, 28–29, 32
    on the proper use of property, 129
    on providing principles, 127
    seeing God at work in the process of history, 35
    on the success of civilization, 128
    on the tenure of property, 128
government
    calling of distinguished from that of the church, 52
    curbing unrestricted individualism and rampant greed, 93
    obligation to bring about beneficial social change, 35
    ordering life so that self-interest prompts what justice demands, 102
    purpose of, 160, 186
    responsibilities for the wellbeing of its citizens, 186
    role and function of, 185
    serving only as a referee between rival forces, 139
grace, over the abyss, 112
The Great World of London (Mayhew), 9
Guild of St. Matthew (GSM), 63, 64, 181

happiness, as individual, 15
Hauerwas, Stanley, 59
Hayek, F. A., 89
Headlam, Stewart, 25, 63, 91, 98–99, 182
Hebert, A. G., 182, 183
Heclo, Hugh, 59, 67
Himmelfarb, Gertrude, 7, 11, 17
"The Historical Evolution of Property, in Fact and in Idea" (Hobhouse), 93, 126
historical progress, naïve and overly optimistic view of, 42
history
    God at work in, 35
    kingdom of God and, 46, 100
    knowledge of the goal and limits of, 100
    as a struggle, 47
Hobhouse, L. T., 93–94, 126
holiness, 123, 140, 179, 185
Holland, Henry Scott, 24–25, 36, 63
holy lives, examples of, 181
homes, visiting poor people in, 8–9
honor, 147, 148, 149, 152
hope
    not found in human struggle, 169
    placing in church growth, 184
    in restored Christendom, 73, 79
    that God is present, 100
"human achievement," culture as, 23
human association, as psychic, 166
human behavior, under liberalism, 144
human beings
    bound together, 78
    "broken up into innumerable fragments," 29
    defined as a form of capital, 16
    dismal philosophy dehumanizing, 7
    divine source bestowing holiness, 179
    eclipse of the social nature of, 145–46
    existing within the love of God and the governance of Christ, 41
    not existing apart from fellowship and community, 119
    rebellion against God, 50
    setting in conflict one with another, 144
    as social beings created in the image of God, 78
human capacity, human worth not rooted in, 101
human difference, understanding, 151
human flourishing, 76–77, 142, 160–61, 186
human nature
    communal understanding of, 134
    faulty view of underlying political economy, 76, 176
    liberal picture of, 142
    Milbank and Pabst's view of, 161, 167
human relations, reducing to profit and loss, 141
human rule, pattern originally intended for, 172
human temptation, to seek economic growth and control, 178
human worth, bestowed by God in creation, 101
Humanitarian Reason: A Moral History of the Present (Fassin), 86
Humphrey, Hubert, Jr., 179n1
Hunt, Lynn, 81–82, 133
Huxley, Thomas Henry, 65

"The Idea of Christendom in Relation to Modern Society" (Reckitt), 78
ideal premise, leaving open the possibility of fanaticism, 73

INDEX   203

ideal society, described by Christian Socialists, 87
"ideal transmission," 167, 183
idealism, 46, 176, 177
idealist school of philosophy, Personalism as, 88
ideals. *See also* common ideals; moral ideals; social ideals
    applicability to problems of limited resources and limited altruism, 73
    as aspects of a way of life, 110–11
    binding a populace together, 65
    as checks on fanaticism, 178
    of Christendom, 81
    contributing to a healthy social life, 97, 175
    defining characteristics of a view of the world, 110
    doing little work on their own, 133
    of equality before God, 132
    as a firm foundation for a just society, 177
    as guiding principles dependent upon a sense of duty, 129
    guiding the populace to practical measures, 98
    having motive as well as cognitive power, 110
    having power to establish duties, 134
    at the heart of the social mission of the church, 71
    helping believers "walk as wise rather than foolish," 111
    incarnation drawing all people in the kingdom of God to, 47
    leaping from a particular moral or practical judgment, 73
    as necessary and effective action guides, 109
    not acting like theorems, axioms, or postulates, 110
    not charting the way to utopia, 111
    notion of rejected by the Milbank-Pabst proposal, 152
    power of community-building, 176
    quest for, 6
    regulating the "temper" of social relations, 83
    relation of in English tradition to politics, 96
    relevance within an economic and political order, 5
    resonating with non-Christian people, 117
    self-enclosed leading to closed-mindedness and fanaticism, 153
    shaping from below the social life of a nation, 31
    unmeasured by additional moral reasoning and sentiment, 124
    as values invented and pasted on to a morally neutral world, 153
    world devoid of, 109
ideas, 153
Ik East African tribe, 119–20
image of God, created in, 78, 100, 117
imperialism, 42
incarnation
    allowing no separation between theology and ethics, 35
    as the central fact of the life of the world, 29
    Christian Socialists' blanket use of, 50
    as a firm foundation, 39
    as a foundation for social ethics and ecclesiology, 19–36
    as a general assumption, 41
    religious interpretation of, 111
    setting aside individualistic account of life, 74
    as a starting point for a Christian social ethic, 67
    as the theological charter for Christian Socialists, 28

incarnation (continued)
  as a theological foundation for Christian Sociology, 22
  undergirding the primacy of duties over rights, 84
  Westcott's account leaving out a lot, 43
The Incarnation and Common Life (Westcott), 29
indebtedness, 129, 130
indigent poor, oligarchs coming to despise, 159
individual striving, useful social purposes of, 72
individualism, 22, 76, 83, 119, 175
individuals, born out of social relations, 118
individuation, distinguishing from individualism, 89
"indolent" class, 12
inductive learning from below, conscience based on, 56
Industrial and Provident Societies Act, 63
Industrial Revolution, 4, 71, 124
industrial society, sickness of, 176
inequality, 4, 81, 124, 159
innovation, 121
innumerable fragments, gathered into Christ, 29–30, 76
insight and application, problem of, 109
institutional advocacy, divisions produced by, 177
institutions, 45, 66. *See also* educational institutions; social institutions
integrity, 60, 67
intellectual climate, excluding the introduction of moral considerations, 13–17
internal ethos, proposed, 147
intervention, of government, 102
Inventing Human Rights: A History (Hunt), 132–33
invisible hand, 14, 160

Jesus Christ. *See* Christ
joint enterprises, stating the public benefit of, 162
justice
  government ordering life so that self-interest prompts, 102
  love expressed as in political relations, 166
  as no longer a matter of judgment, 145
  as the primary form of love in social organization, 104
  provision of for one's neighbor, 72–73
  reduced to procedural rules, 145
  sin rendering as distorted, 46
  spheres of, 95, 124

Kant, Immanuel, 100, 122, 131
Kaus, Mickey, 126
The Kingdom of Christ (Maurice), 21, 74, 83, 84
kingdom of God, 46, 47, 100

La Fraternité Chrétienne, 27
laissez-faire capitalism, 71
laity, exercising practical wisdom, 57
land, 6, 91
language (meaning), exchange of, 148
liberal assumptions, Williams's critique of, 143
liberal culture, postliberal alternative to, 156
liberal education, church providing a way around the obstacle of, 155
liberal ideology, failing, 157
liberal polities, threat of oligarchic rule and class struggle, 173
liberal society
  economic, political, and social crises plaguing, 185
  ever-hastening collapse of, 137
  given up on moral formation as a social goal, 153

holding in check the exploitive
hubris driving, 179
people not held together by
common good, 172
replacing the "rotten
foundation" of, 155
unable to provide resolution to
endemic disputes, 145
liberalism
failed to manage competitive
aggression and conflict, 180
metacrisis of, 142, 143–46
problems endemic to, 172
ridding society of an exemplary
elite, 154
liberals, priority to political and
economic solutions to social
conflicts, 145
liberty, 92–93, 144
life. *See also* common life; social life
of Christ, 33, 35
lived in love as worthy, 171
not lending itself to deduction,
110
social and divinely based
account of, 74
value of for Christian Socialists,
123
Liturgical Movement, 182–83
liturgical renewal, leaders of, 182
Liturgy and Society (Hebert), 182
local congregation, 62, 182
London Working Men's
Associations, 64
love
for all people, 74
central to God's transmission of
his own nature, 169
centrality of in a "politics of
virtue," 171–72
expressed as justice in political
relations, 166
of God, 40
as the governing principle of
political and social life, 26
mutual mirroring the unity
binding the Trinity, 75

overemphasis on the power of,
44
Paul's description of, 171
as "the predominant Christian
impulse," 104
restorative power of, 42
trust and, 156n59
walking in, 183
love, honor, and trust, between the
many, the few, and the one,
174
Lovibond, Sabina, 119
Ludlow, John
account of a dying woman living
in a closet, 133
against defenders of political
economy, 27–28
favoring particular policy
solutions, 98–99
on founding associations in
England, 62
founding journals and writing
articles, 64
on having Duties, 83
helping pass the Industrial and
Provident Societies Act, 63
as a man of action, 27
resistance to Maurice's social
conservatism, 25
as a supporter of democracy, 27
visiting poor people in their
homes, 8–9

MacIntyre, Alasdair, 32
MacKinnon, Donald, 48, 106,
111–12
Macklin, Ruth, 122
Malthus, on population growth, 14
Mandeville, Bernard, 14
the many, the few, and the one, 173,
174
Maritain, Jacques, 131
marital partners, between social
groups, 148–49
market, 16, 109, 125, 160
marketplace, devoid of moral
guidance, 14

materialism, resulting in inequality, 31
Maurice, F. D.
  belief in the love of God for all people, 74
  discussion of Methodism, 118
  on equality not applying to the hierarchical structure of English society, 123–24
  focus on incarnation rather than atonement, 20
  on God providing societies with social and political order, 97
  on the ideal of service, 84
  on individual acts depending upon social relations, 119
  influence on the more liberal expressions of Anglicanism, 42
  on the job of the church to cultivate a moral climate, 56
  on liberty, fraternity, and equality, 64
  on the nature and extent of state authority, 186
  on political economy, 146
  on responsibility for a moral foundation for society, 62
  on structures of society as the work of divine providence, 24
  sympathy for humanity, 8
Mauss, Marcel, 120, 148
Mayhew, Henry, 9, 12, 133
measurement, of equality, 126
media, raising public conscience, 62
meeting of human needs, importance of, 104
metacrisis
  of capitalism, 158
  of liberalism, 142, 143–46, 176, 180
"middle axioms," between basic principles and specific policy proposals, 105
Milbank, Alison, 20, 85, 143
Milbank, John
  adding a diagnosis, 179–80
  body of work as examined here, 143n19
  full-blown retrieval of the Christian Socialist tradition in the work of, 142–74
  on the notion of individual or subjective rights, 131
  on providing a religious and moral compass, 137
  on social cooperation, 120
Milbank and Pabst, 143, 146–57, 162, 164, 180
Mill, John Stuart, 14, 77
millennial generation, forming small communities, 61
mission of the church, 31–32, 67–68
mode of Christian *ecclesia*, 165
monasticism, 58–59
monetary reward, distributing, 125
money, circulating in its own world, 158
moral agents, embedded in a shared way of life, 146
moral aspects of Christianity, primacy of, 33
moral concern, of Christian Socialists, 8
moral corruption, rotting the foundation of society, 177
moral deliberation, 73
moral earnestness, 35
moral education, 57
moral ends, 15
moral formation, 90, 153, 156, 165
moral foundations, for a healthy society, 149
moral grounds, condemning an economic system on, 45
moral ideals, 33, 71, 143, 147, 181
moral insights, ideals as, 110
moral instruction, church providing, 59
moral judgments, 97, 98
moral knowledge of God, guiding our behavior, 30
moral lives, changing, 22–23
moral perspectives, socially passed on, 153

moral philosophy, 17
moral principles, 56
moral reasoning, 56, 98, 107, 108, 109
moral reflection, 97
moral reformation, 64
moral state, poverty as a possible indicator of, 12
moral substructure, digging down to find, 57
moral vacuum, leaving only utilitarian bargaining, 144
moral vision
    acknowledgment of sin as, 31
    of the Christian Socialists as broad, 87
    Christian Socialists sought, 19–20
    church as duty bound to provide, 56
    social institutions brought into, 24
    stressing the importance of a renewed, 18
moral vocabulary, developing, 5
moralistic interpretations, not inspiring novel social aims, 48
morality, emerging spontaneously from nature, 153
Morris, Jeremy, 20
Moyn, Samuel, 134, 135
mystery, programmatic secularism stripping the world of, 140

national identities, of many Protestant churches, 55
nationalization, 92
nations, 55, 75, 101, 103
natural law, 44, 45, 55, 104
natural progression, Christ not arising from, 33
natural state, as "denatured," 111–12
neoliberal and progressive liberal thought, basic assumptions on assuming rights, 130
neoliberalism, 16–17, 71, 144

"Neoliberalism and Its Prospects" (Friedman), 16
new life, 34, 35
Niebuhr, H. Richard, 23
Niebuhr, Reinhold, 44, 45, 46, 99, 166
Norman, Edward, 8

obedience, requiring sacrifice, 34
obscurity, of Milbank's prose, 168
O'Donovan, Oliver, 79, 106
"Of Individuality, as One of the Elements of Well-Bing" (Mill), 77
The Old Regime and the French Revolution (Tocqueville), 76
oligarchs, 159, 160
the one, the few, and the many, restoring to political relations, 160
orders of human society, Maurice on, 75
organ of transmission, church as, 167
"organic pluralism," 150
"original situation" representation, 172
Our Neighbours (Holland), 24
outlooks and onlooks, interplay of, 108

Pabst, Adrian, 120, 131, 143
paideia, promoting the common good, 165
parish, 183
parish church, 182
Parish Eucharist, 182, 183
parish life, promise of, 184
partnerships, business relations becoming, 162
pathos, of Christian Socialism as real, 175
Paul, 171, 183–84
peace, 167
Pelikan, Jaroslav, 32
perfect social order, 106

person of Christ, kenotic doctrine of, 33
personal commitments, of Christian Socialists to policy solutions, 99
personal freedom, link with property, 93
personal transformations, effects of, 24
Personalism, 77, 88
personality, 77, 87, 88–89, 125, 151
"personhood," as the primary goal of social living, 151
Pius XII, on dignity, rights, and human persons, 135
Platonic ideas, beckoning to a transcendent world, 153
pluralism, as characteristic of all cultures, 23
plutocracy, 80, 92–93
policy advocacy, 66, 67, 157
policy initiatives, by Temple as an individual, 105
political action, 97
political activism, divisions resulting from, 66
political and economic processes, not providing resolution to endemic disputes, 145
political economy
  assertion of individual rights as inevitable, 132
  as the economic system of the Industrial Revolution, 71
  F. D. Maurice on, 146
  of Himmelfarb and Ruskin, 7
  John Ludlow against defenders of, 27–28
  not producing the best results for society, 109
  operating by the law of self-interest, 14
  replaced by neoliberalism, 16
  supporters on "acquiring, retaining, and perpetuating property," 128
  thought to operate on the basis of internal laws, 14
  underlying problem of, 176
  view of human nature, 76, 78
political exchanges, 134
political institutions, not sacrosanct for Ludlow, 27
political judgments, fallibility of, 98
political opinions, compromising the integrity of religious belief, 67
political processes, not remedying the effects of inequalities, 159
political system, locating rights within, 131
political utopias, rights as a moral alternative to, 135
"politicization," of public speech and action by the church, 67
politics, 102, 166
Politics for the People penny journal, 64
Politics of Jesus (Yoder), 59
politics of virtue, 157, 171, 172, 178
The Politics of Virtue (Milbank and Pabst), 143
"the poor," 9, 11, 12
poor relief, 12–13, 19
popular inculcation of virtue, 165
postliberal alternative, 146–57, 164–74, 180
postliberal society, honoring moral excellence, 148
postliberalism, 146, 150, 152
"postmodern alternative," 164
poverty, 11–12, 13
power, 93, 125, 127, 186
practical affairs, Christians guided by "primary" and "derivative" principles of the church, 100
practical reason, 106–7
presence of Christ, in the life of the church, 35
preservation, Maurice's focus was on, 26
Preston, Ronald, 109
primary principle, of the church, 100

"primordial gift exchange," civil economy requiring, 163
principles
    arranged by Temple from primary to derivative, 106
    Christian, as Temple's new reference point, 45
    Christian not charting the way to utopia, 100
    as the concern of the church instead of policy, 99
    derivative, 100, 102, 103–4, 106
    giving up for ideals, ideas, and habits of mind and behavior providing "outlooks," 108
    moral, 56
    teaching to toleration of differences of judgment and policy, 58
    Temple speaking of rather than natural law, 56
"principles of society," quest for, 6
printed word, as a prong of attack, 64
private prosperity, various sorts of, 92
privilege, 81, 124, 125
procedural secularism, as not antireligious, 138
producers, of products for social wellbeing, 45
producers and consumers, duties and rights of, 45
production and consumption, forming an autonomous system, 71
profit and social benefit, possible to pursue both, 162
profit or loss, all relations measured by, 16
profits, increased pressure to maximize, 158
programmatic secularism, 138, 140, 178, 179, 185
proletariat, 10
promise, of Christian Socialism, 175–87

property
    "duties and rights" of ownership, 127
    functions of, 94
    necessity for, 92–93, 127, 128
    supporting the exercise of freedom, 129
"property for power," retaining for the democratic state, 95
Property: Its Duties and Rights, 92
property rights, in private hands, 93
Protestant churches, in North America, 66
Protestant social teaching, giving prominence to the nation-state, 54
proverbs, ideals serving as, 110
psychic body, proposal for the revival of, 155–56
psychic community, politics requiring, 154, 166
public opinion, changing through "association," 62
public political discourse, 138

Queen's College, London, F. D. Maurice began, 65

Rad, Gerhard von, 110
Rand, Ayn, 71, 89
Rashdall, Hastings, 93
realism, of Christians, 100
reason, 104. *See also* moral reasoning; practical reason
reciprocity, 147, 161, 166
Reckitt, Maurice B., 4, 78, 80, 92–93
"Reconnecting Human Rights and Religious Faith" (Williams), 142
redemption, 34, 74
Reformation, 55
religion
    adopting in America the trappings of modern democratic cultural life, 59–60
    culture and, 60, 169

expressing links to a
  transcendent realm, 173
  with political power as prone
  not really to be religion, 67
Religion and the Rise of Capitalism
  (Tawney), 16
religious and moral reform,
  preferred by Christian
  Socialists, 177
religious belief, 138, 140, 176, 178
religious defection, rotting society,
  177
religious foundation, 130, 141
religious interpretation, of the
  incarnation of Christ, 48
relocalizing, the economy, 161
respect, for each person as a child of
  God, 90
responsibility, taking for the other,
  141
restoration, as religious and moral
  in nature, 176
restored Christendom, ideal of as a
  vain hope, 79
"return of Christendom"
  call for, 121
  education as the way to bring
    about, 57
  as the encompassing goal of
    Christian Socialists, 78
  as ideal for Reckitt, 92–93
  sought by Christian Socialists in
    England, 6
  Temple continued to believe in
    and work toward, 46
The Return of Christendom (Gore),
  5, 18
The Return of Christendom (Reckitt),
  92
revolution, asking for a peaceful and
  gradual, 6
Ricardo, David, 14
righteousness, manifest in common
  life, 34
rights
  assertion of individual, 132
  beginning with individuals in
    conflict, 129–30
  claiming, 184
  as compatible with conservative
    forms of moral government,
    136
  derivative status of, 185
  existing prior to duties, 130
  fluid notion of the nature and
    function of, 131
  lacking power to become
    imbedded in political
    discourse and action, 134
  as necessary, 86, 87
  present notion of as a
    construction, 135
  producing social conflict, 134
  prominence of dignity in
    discussions of, 122
  social relations pitting one
    person against another, 82
  understandings of, 131, 142
rights claims, 83, 98, 123, 144
rights language, 83, 85, 135, 136
"the rights of man," meaning of,
  135–36
risk- and profit-sharing models, 164
ritual distance, of the Church from
  itself, 168
Roman Catholic social teaching, 54,
  151, 186–87
Roman Catholic thought, using
  dignity to justify a fixed
  hierarchy, 122
Rosen, Michael, 122
Rossetti, Dante Gabriel, 65
Rowlands, Anna, 53–54
Ruskin, John, 7–8, 65

sacramental nature, of incarnation
  for Maurice, 75
"sacramental" understanding, loss
  of, 140
sacramental view of creation, 30
sacramental worship, power of, 182
sacrifice, 34
sacrificial offering, of God's people,
  183
salvation, 48

"the sanctity of personality," 87
saving action of Christ, 49
scarcity, limiting circumstances of, 86
schools, for the education of working class, 62
secular society, 139–40, 178
secular tradition, locating dignity in human reason, 100
secularism, 136, 138. *See also* procedural secularism; programmatic secularism
self-created culture, 49
self-development, 82, 94
self-emptying, of Christ, 33
self-evidence, claims of for rights, 133
self-fulfillment, 82, 89
self-interest, 14, 102
selfishness, 72
self-judgment and self-discrimination, of the Church, 170
self-made platform, standing over the abyss, 112
self-realization, 128
self-restraint, honor serving as, 148
self-salvation, attempt at, 112
self-worth, coming from social recognition, 148
service, 82, 84, 103–4, 125
Service to Humanity (Headlam), 25
shared aims, roles required for the mutual achievement of, 146
shareholder value, dominating business culture, 162
shareholders, turning unsecured creditors into, 163–64
sin
    acknowledgment of as a moral vision, 31
    Christian Socialists underestimating, 46
    Christ's victory over the power of, 34
    finitude and, 166
    Gore not denying the intractable, pervasive nature of, 33
    as a religious condition, 111
    rendering love and justice as partial and often distorted, 46
    as a theological notion, 48
"Sinless Head" of "the human race," Christ as, 30
skill, as a means of overcoming an opponent, 31
slavery, 132
slums of London, human waste characteristic of, 9
small groups, 103, 161, 173
Smith, Adam, 14, 71
social advance, 46, 111
social advocacy, as the social mission of the churches in America, 177
social asset, Christian Socialists saw land as, 91
social awareness, bringing ideals into view once again, 133
social beings, humans as, 21, 74, 101, 117, 180
social bonds, 120, 149
social calling, understanding as moral exhortation, 111
social change
    bringing social and political conflicts, 4
    focused on the moral lives of the citizenry, 22
    forced large numbers of people off the land, 6
    government's obligation to bring about, 35
    as not completely bad, 121
    postliberals supporting but pointing to the past, 150
social character, of human nature and destiny, 76
social conflict, 98, 134, 145, 161
social dislocation, 6
social duties, 28

social enterprise, moral formation as, 90
social ethics, 19–36, 39–51, 106
social exchange, 120, 148, 156n59, 161
social fellowship, as a derivative principle, 103
social focus, shift from communal identity to the autonomy of individuals, 136
social goods, ideals forming a coherent set of interlocking, 117
social health, 148, 176
social hierarchies, 120
social ideals
  of the Christian Socialists, 71
  church cultivating, 97–98
  Church of England's inability to fulfill, 10
  duty (duties) holding together, 130
  equality recognized and sustained by, 118
  William Temple's vision of, 99
social institutions. *See also* educational institutions; institutions
  brought into moral vision by the incarnation, 24
  Christian Socialists's views on, 28
  as the expression of a scale of moral values, 15
  Ludlow seeing a need for the reform of, 25–26
  Maurice on the reform of, 22
  modification as properly a matter of prudence, 56
  testing to see if they fulfill God's will on earth, 27
social interaction, 84
social issues, 32–33, 90–91
social life
  built upon friendship and exchange, 180
  changing from the bottom up, 23
  Christian Socialists failed to understand complexity of, 72
  existing to further freedom and maintain fellowship, 85
  impossible without some degree of cooperation, 119
  original situation of as one of war and struggle, 160
  purpose of as an ideal, 125
  restoring the gift-exchange notion of, 164
  supporting the development of each member of society as a personality, 77
  viewing as a sort of peace within a feud presided over by government, 139
social mission, 33, 60, 61, 177
social nature of humankind, assumption of, 147
social order, 61, 149
social reform, 26, 31, 177
social relations
  Christ transforming, 24
  desire to manage from the top down, 121
  dismal science demoralizing, 7
  economy re-embedding in, 160
  fostering the growth of personality, 151
  God's concern for, 40
  ideals regulating the "temper" of, 83
  individual acts depending upon, 119
  individuals born out of, 118
  as a jumble of individual rights claims and conflicting private interests, 15
  re-embedding economic relations in, 162
  resting on duty (duties), 98
  rights and, 82
  rights language speaking about, 85

should not be governed by aggressive self-advancement, 173
Wittgenstein on, 119
social renewal, not living by education alone, 181
social responsibility, Christian Socialists on the church's, 56
social revolution, church contributing to, 167
social space, society honoring the differentiated character of preserving diversity, 149
social stations, as simply different social locations, 174
social structures, 25, 27, 149
social theology, of Maurice, 20
social tumult, eroding social solidarity, 119–20
social virtues, 72
social vision, 20, 73, 117, 162, 163
social welfare, first principle of, 101
social-cultural liberalism, of the left, 143–44
socialism, 5, 20, 137. *See also* Christian Socialism; state socialism
socially productive wealth, increasing inability to generate, 158
society. *See also* "the acquisitive society"; liberal society
  bound together by mutual generosity and honor, 149
  existence of implied by the existence of individuals, 74
  moulding the State, 53
  not looking to the churches to serve as moral tutor, 54
  power of education to shape, 57
  principles of, 6
  reconceived in a corporate way as universal, 173
  role of the church in, 52–68
  secular, 139–40, 178
Society for Promoting Working Men's Associations, Christian Socialists formed, 63
Son, becoming the servant of humankind, 33
soul
  of life, 31
  of a nation, 66
space, faith creating, 179
spatial terms, envisaging the Church in, 167
speculative economy, producing vast inequalities, 159
"spheres of justice," of Walzer, 95
"spiritual power," the church as, 53
stability, requiring tradition, 149
stakeholders, turning unsecured creditors into, 163–64
state
  church interrupting an overemphasis on, 155
  duty to deal with human beings in their freedom, 139
  existing for its citizens, 90, 128
  overseeing religious communities under procedural secularism, 138
  as "temporal power" having a moral end, 52–53
  using state-controlled education, 165
state authority, 185, 186
state of the church, measuring, 170
state socialism, not supported by Christian Socialists, 36
stock, in limited liability companies, 91
Structural Anthropology (Levi-Strauss), 148
Studies in the Spirit and Truth of Christianity (Temple), 108
subsidiarity, principle of, 103, 151, 186
Suggate, Alan, 118
super-rich, power of, 159
sympathy, 8, 82, 133, 167
"synthesis," of human knowledge and practice, 48

Tawney, R. H.
    on the disease of society as inherent greed, 175
    on England as an "acquisitive society," 15–16
    favoring particular policy solutions, 98–99
    on the ideals of Christendom, 81
    on the incarnation as a divine act, 39–40
    on individual differences, 89
    on the inequalities of the class system, 124
    on the world ceasing to believe in God, 81
Temple, William
    on the Church never committing to any kind of political programme, 57
    declared England to be a secular society, 79
    favored particular policy solutions, 98–99
    on his vision of social ideals, 99
    hoped for general acceptance of social vision, 73
    on the incarnation and its import, 28–29
    on the linked ideas of equality, duty, and service, 85
    middle axioms of, 105
    moved away from natural law, 45
    moved toward the theological center, 42
    on natural law, 44, 55
    predicted a post-Christian era, 54
    on provision of justice for one's neighbor, 72–73
    reluctant to give the church a warrant to support particular measures, 56
    on respect for every person, 90
    on rights and duties, 82–83
    on the state fostering human flourishing, 186
    on "true principles," 87
    unwilling to allow markets simply to self-adjust, 102
    warning against church teaching espousing particular policies, 58
Terrill, Ross, 89
theological charter, for social concerns, 39
theological warrant, for an alternative to the acquisitive society, 19
theology, 43, 44
thinking, Temple on, 108
Thornton, L. S., 80
time, presence of the church within, 169–70
Titanism, 49, 50
Titans, becoming, 112
Tocqueville, on "individualism," 76
Toynbee Hall, 64
Tract on Christian Socialism (Maurice), 20
Tractarians, 34
Tracts on Christian Socialism, 64
tradition, 149, 177
transactional relations, 144
transcendence, 152, 155, 184
transcendent good, rooting human life in, 171
transcendent reality, 153, 169, 184
transcendent values, 139
"transformer of culture," Christ as, 23
transmission, the church as a form of, 168
trust, 161
trust-based exchange, system of, 148
Turnbull, Colin, 119–20
tyranny, 81

unity
    of people in a community, 75
    of the Spirit, 187
Universal Declaration of Human Rights, 131–32
universal dispensation, Christ came to establish, 21

universal love expressed in service, 33
universal society of the church, 75
Unto This Last (Ruskin), 7
urban and rural forms of life, balance between, 163
urban dwellers, depressed condition of displaced, 6
utilitarian calculations, 144
Utopia, Milbank not imagining the Church as, 167–68
utopian proposals, 157, 161
utopianism, Christian Socialists justifiably accused of, 134

valorization, of cooperation, service, and sacrifice, 121
value of a life, 123
virtues
  allowing to encompass and temper ideals, 178
  central importance of within a political system, 152
  as the foundation of the postliberal alternative, 148
  giving love a face, 171, 174
  learned in part by example, 155
  list of, 156
virtuous citizenry, 172, 177
virtuous society, 155
vision, 57, 157–61. *See also* communal vision; moral vision; social vision
vocabulary of liberal society, 184
voluntary organizations, for clergy and laypeople, 62
voluntary societies, started by Christian Socialists, 181
von Humboldt, on human flourishing, 76–77
the vulnerable, providing protection to, 185

wages, prices and assets, Milbank and Pabst position on, 162
Walzer, Michael, 95, 124
war and struggle, as endemic to liberalism, 160
wars, exposed the sickness of European society, 65
wealth
  concentrations of, 6, 127
  inequalities of, 16, 158
  redistribution of, 94
  as the standard of success, 31
wealth and power, 124, 144
Weil, Simone, 100
welfare, promoted by honor, 148
welfare state, existing for the sake of its citizens, 139
Westcott, Brooke Foss
  on Christ as the representative of all people, 41
  on Christian teachers, 46–47
  on the doctrine of the incarnation, 28–29, 32, 76
  on fulfilling duties rather than maintaining rights, 83–84
  on the merits of self-discipline and sacrifice, 42
  on the mission of the church, 53
  optimism of, 47
  on the order of society built upon Christian ideals, 186
  on the power of love to change the world, 31
  on the role of government, 52
  on the role of the clergy, 57
Wilkinson, Alan, 54
will, leading in turn to the disruption of mobs, 83
Williams, Rowan
  on ecclesiology, 170
  on programmatic secularism, 185
  providing a religious and moral compass, 137
  on secular society, 138, 178
  on the tradition of Christian Socialism, 179
wise walking, 183
Wittgenstein, 119
Wolfe, Alan, 59, 60, 169

Word of God, all people created by, 41
working class, 64, 65, 181
Working Men's College (WMC), 65
working people, 57, 59, 63
Working Tailors' Association, 63
world
- as a divine gift that is to be treasured, 140
- as morally neutral, 144
- of rights, 142
- secular society not bringing peaceful order to, 178
- serving as an attestation to divine mysteries, 30

worldly realities, 152
worshipping communities, 62, 184

Yoder, John Howard, 59

www.ingramcontent.com/pod-product-compliance
Lightning Source LLC
Chambersburg PA
CBHW020408230426
43664CB00009B/1234